Unlocking
the Book of Hebrews

Unlocking the Book of Hebrews

A Spatial Analysis of the Epistle to the Hebrews

ANNANG ASUMANG

WIPF & STOCK · Eugene, Oregon

UNLOCKING THE BOOK OF HEBREWS
A Spatial Analysis of the Epistle to the Hebrews

Copyright © 2008 Annang Asumang. All rights reserved. Except for brief quotations in critical publications or reviews, no part of this book may be reproduced in any manner without prior written permission from the publisher. Write: Permissions, Wipf and Stock, 199 W. 8th Ave., Suite 3, Eugene, OR 97401.

ISBN 13: 978-1-55635-306-2

Unless otherwise stated, scripture quotations are from the New International Version of the Bible, made available by the International Bible Society. Copyright © 1973, 1978, 1984 and accessed online at http://www.ibs.org/niv/index.php. All rights reserved throughout the world. Used by permission of International Bible Society.

Manufactured in the U.S.A.

To Edna, my beloved wife and Christine, John, and Paul, our children, for all the blessings we continue to share together in our migration into the city of God.

Contents

Abbreviations ix

Preface xi

List of Illustrations xv

List of Tables xvii

1. Introduction 1
2. What is the Problem with Hebrews 11
3. Spatial Analysis of a Biblical Text 39
4. The Camp of God's People Around the Tabernacle: Spatial Analysis of the Expositions of Hebrews 80
5. The Migration of God's People to the Promise: Spatial Analysis of the Exhortations of the Hebrews 119
6. Hebrews, the Metaphor of Migration, and Discipleship 166

Bibliography 189

Abbreviations

ABC	Anchor Bible Commentary
Bib	*Biblica*
BibSac	*Bibliotheca Sacra*
BTB	*Biblical Theological Bulletin*
CBQ	*Catholic Biblical Quarterly*
EvQ	*Evangelical Quarterly*
Int	*Interpretation*
JAAR	*Journal of the American Academy of Religion*
JBL	*Journal of Biblical Literature*
JETS	*Journal of the Evangelical Theological Society*
JSNT	*Journal for the Study of the New Testament*
JSOT	*Journal for the Study of the Old Testament*
JTS	*Journal of Theological Studies*
NICNT	New International Commentary on the New Testament
NIGNT	New International Greek New Testament
NICOT	New International Commentary on the Old Testament
NovT	*Novum Testamentum*

Abbreviations

RevExp	*Review and Expositor*
SBLDS	Society of Biblical Literature Dissertation Series
SJT	*Scottish Journal of Theology*
SNTSMS	Society for New Testament Studies Monograph Series
TDNT	*Theological Dictionary of the New Testament*
TrinJ	*Trinity Journal*
TynBul	*Tyndale Bulletin*
WBC	Word Biblical Commentary
WTJ	*Westminster Theological Journal*

Preface

LIKE MANY other believers, my more than three decades of Christian experience in reading the epistle to the Hebrews was, until recent years, similar to reading some of the Old Testament Psalms. The powerful language of the epistle stimulated, challenged, encouraged, frightened, comforted, and animated my Christian life in equal measures, yet unlike the other New Testament books, I struggled to understand and explain the whole book in such a way that its lessons fit together to be applicable for teaching, exhortation, and practical relevance in my own Christian discipleship. Most commentaries and study notes on Hebrews only seemed to aggravate this sense of lack of lucidity due to their divergent and often disconnected approach to the exegesis of Hebrews.

The more serious study that started my journey leading to the present conclusions began while in my final year of my BA (biblical studies) with the Trinity College of the Bible, Indiana. At the time, I elected to write a mini-thesis on the use of typology by the author of Hebrews for expository preaching. The results of that investigation stimulated further inquiry on the theology of the epistle during my MTh research with the South African Theological Seminary under the supervision of Dr. Bill Domeris. Starting from the basic observation that each block of exposition of the epistle is confined to an individual space and the exhortations are dominated by the metaphor of movement, I employed sociological models in the interdisciplinary paradigm of spatiality to investigate the epistle. The outcome has been very instructive and resulted in the present work, in which my thesis has been substantially revised and expanded.

To my knowledge, only one other attempt in the English-speaking scholarly literature to analyze Hebrews from the singular point of view of its spatiality has been made in recent years. Marie E Isaacs's *Sacred Space: An Approach to the Theology of the Epistle to the Hebrews*[1] a decade and a half ago significantly moved the understanding of the spatial aspects of the epistle's theology forward, yet, as we shall later discuss in more detail, the investigative theories of the phenomenology of space and the assumptions that she employed are largely disputed among social scientists today.

1. Isaacs, *Sacred Space*, 1992.

Preface

In addition, though Isaacs's hypothesis that the purpose of Hebrews was closely related to the destruction of the temple of Jerusalem in AD 70 is plausible, her proposal does not adequately explain the severe anxiety in the author's tone. It also does not sufficiently clarify why the author should rather depend on the theology of the wilderness tabernacle to address such a supposedly temple-related problem.

By employing a more up-to-date and nuanced interdisciplinary social science method of spatial analysis and relating it to the Old Testament theology of the tabernacle, our study will address these gaps in Isaacs's thesis. It will also account for the severe nature of the author's tone and how he aimed to address the pastoral difficulties for which his homily was designed. Moreover, unlike Isaacs's hypothesis, our proposal explains the unique literary and rhetorical style of Hebrews.

This book has been written with "the average Christian in the pew" in mind—the believer who is interested in understanding and applying the lessons of the epistle in a consistently holistic manner for practical discipleship and teaching in a small group or church setting. In my view, such a goal can only be realized through an investigative methodology that is imaginative yet easily accessible to the non-professional Bible student. I have therefore attempted to strike a balance between an academic discussion that interacts with several different scholars and commentaries and a popular approach so that the conclusions will be more easily available and applicable. I trust that this balance has been achieved. Needless to say, the book does not attempt to answer all the major questions that are related to interpreting Hebrews. However, by providing this consistent understanding of the overall theme of the epistle, the hope is that the various issues related to the interpretation of the epistle will now fit together.

Since the methodology with which the investigation is conducted is not that commonly known, I have attempted a detailed explanation with several examples of its use in other areas of biblical studies. Though this may give some sections of the study an academic flavor, it is hoped that the emphases in these parts will nevertheless enhance rather than hinder the "average" Christian's understanding of the method of spatial analysis of biblical texts and in particular of the epistle. The final chapter indeed provides some suggestions on a number of application, preaching, and discussion topics so that Hebrews may accordingly be employed with excellent results.

A final "disclaimer" is in order. I share the view of many scholars that the author of Hebrews remains unidentified. Paul is certainly not the writer, even though I agree that the author is male and may well have been in Pauline circles. However, to reduce the jarring outcome that results from having to refer to him all the time as "the author or writer of Hebrews," I have opted, in certain places, to call both the author and the book he has written simply as "Hebrews" and to occasionally refer to his congregation who received the epistle as "the Hebrews." It is hoped that this non-conventional way of referring to an author, his first readers, and his book will not detract readers.

It remains for me at this stage to express my heartfelt gratitude and appreciation to all those who have been instrumental in producing this book. First and foremost is Dr. Bill Domeris, whose encouragement, intellectual stimulation, and careful supervision guided me through my investigation of the epistle. Dr. Anthony Akobeng and Dinah Baah-Odoom were extremely helpful in proofreading some chapters. Thanks to my former pastor and mentor, Rev. Dr. T. B. Dankwa, for his inspiration and also thanks to all my dear brothers and sisters of Accra Chapel, Ghana, whose encouragement continues to strengthen and support me in my ongoing migration toward heaven. Last but not the least are Edna, my dear wife, and Christine, John, and Paul, our children, who have patiently endured my "absentmindedness" as I have over the last few years continued to reflect on the epistle to the Hebrews. To all these, the Lord richly bless them—and you also for reading. And unto Him be the glory.

List of Illustrations

Fig. 2.1: The Concentric Ring Structure of Hebrews
(Albert Vanhoye) · 23

Fig. 2.2: Concentric Ring Structure of Hebrews
Based on Spatial References · 25

Fig. 4.1: The Sacrificial Spaces Influencing the Spatiality of Hebrews · 94

Fig. 4.2: The Tabernacle According to Hebrews · 106

Fig. 5.1: The Concentric Arrangement of the Camp of Israel
in the Wilderness (Numbers 1–10) · 161

Fig. 5.2: The Chiastic Structure of the Book of Numbers
(Adapted from Douglas) · 162

Fig. 6.1: The Wilderness Camp Scheme
and Doctrine of Sin in Hebrews · 179

Fig. 6.2: The Migrant Camp of the People of God:
A Summary Diagram · 188

List of Tables

Table 3.1: Examples of Spatial Symbols and Metaphors in the Bible · 69

Table 3.2: Summary of Spatial Theories of Relevance to Biblical Studies · 71

Table 3.3: Spatial References in Numbers 13 · 73

Table 4.1: Contrasting Features of the Two Spaces of Hebrews 5–10 · 108

Table 4.2: Comparison of the Functions of the Levitical with Christ's Priesthood · 113

Table 5.1: The Five Elements of the Exhortations of Hebrews · 124

Table 5.2: The Migration Scheme in the Exhortations of Hebrews · 156

Table 5.3: The Similarities Between the Books of Numbers and Hebrews · 164

Table 6.1: The Multiple Interpretations of the Tabernacle in Hebrews · 169

Table 6.2: Common Theological Themes of Hebrews · 172

Table 6.3: Five Categories of Sermons from Hebrews · 187

1
Introduction

Since the end of the apostolic age, the epistle to the Hebrews has in one way or another, seriously challenged every generation of Christians. In some past generations, Hebrews was at the center of invigorating Christian worship, energizing spiritual growth, and warning Christians against spiritual laxity and backsliding. In other generations, the book was the source of controversies about the doctrine of Christ, the nature of church discipline, and the results of apostasy. Some generations accepted the challenge offered by this precious book of the Bible and devoured its teachings that powerfully enrich our spirituality and spur us on to perseverance in the faith. Other generations avoided and excused themselves by claiming that it is too strange a book, with a meaning too difficult to grasp and a message much too mysterious to apply.

Our generation, it appears to me, is in the latter category. J. H. Davies accurately echoed how the present generation of believers regarded the letter to the Hebrews when he likened the epistle to a "work of art from another time and place—a medieval stained glass window, for example, whose general meaning and beauty are clear enough, but whose style and details are strange and puzzling."[1] Similarly, Ellingworth hilariously assessed the difficulty of the modern interpreter of Hebrews as comparable to "a journey through patchy fog. In places, the path is obscure . . . From time to time, the sun shines through . . ."[2]

There is something profoundly special about Hebrews that makes it popular for personal devotions and driving Christians on to deeper and richer things in Christ. Yet, at the same time, it has the reputation of being difficult to study or exegete from our pulpits. Preachers love to quote from it to support their arguments, all right, whether on the divinity of Christ, the purpose of his death, the definition of faith, the nature of New Testament worship, the nature of the new covenant, or Christian discipline. When it comes to systematic exposition or even selecting a portion of this epistle

---

1. Davies, *Hebrews*, 1.
2. Ellingworth, *Hebrews*, 70.

to explain so that its full message may be grasped and applied for practical daily living, however, many of our present-day pulpits avoid Hebrews. The same may be said of several Sunday school lessons or group-based Bible studies. It is fair to say that apart from the book of Revelation, Hebrews is perhaps the book of the New Testament most avoided by Christians today. Yet this epistle is one of the most important of the sixty-six books of the Bible and very much so in these postmodern days.

The Postmodern Relevance of Hebrews

Hebrews is one of the most important biblical documents to our Christian faith, so much so that our avoidance of its serious study results in our own spiritual impoverishment. Without it, our Bible would have been poor indeed and any generation that has shunned Hebrews has lacked something of the deeper sense of spiritual vitality that the epistle instills.

There are several reasons for the epistle's indispensability. First, it is the one book of the Bible that presents us with a full and balanced Christology. The doctrine of Christ, about his person and his work, is always a complex subject to teach and understand. Concerning the person of Christ, for instance, his full divinity needs always to be balanced together with his full humanity. Every book of the New Testament presents certain aspects of this doctrine, but it is in Hebrews (and also perhaps the epistles of John), however, that these two facets of his person are presented in such a fashion that we are able to hold them together in their glorious tension. Hebrews portrays our Lord as the eternal Creator of all things, who is worshipped by the angels in heaven (Hebrews 1), and who became a little lower than the same angels to redeem fallen humanity (Hebrews 2). As a human being, Jesus is "of the same family" (Heb 2:11) as us, shared the same "flesh and blood" (Heb 2:14), and is "like his brothers" (Heb 2:17) in every way, "yet without sin" (Heb 4:15). Like us, "he learned obedience" (Heb 5:8) and was made "perfect through suffering" (Heb 2:10) and so sets for us the example that we should "consider" (Heb 12:2). If we need a thorough understanding of the person of Christ, it is to Hebrews that we should turn.

In addition, Hebrews is the one book that describes the full spectrum of the work of Christ. It is from this epistle that we can understand the past, present, and future work of Christ in one fell swoop through the doctrine of the high priesthood of Jesus. Oscar Cullmann correctly made this observation by stating, "Hebrews' development of the high priest concept offers a full Christology in every respect. It includes all the three fundamental aspects of Jesus' work: his once-for-all earthly work . . . his present work as the exalted Lord . . . and his future work as the one coming again . . . 'Yesterday, today and for ever' (13:8)."[3] In these times, when there is theological confusion and fogginess of thought regarding the person and mission of the "historical Jesus," a study of Hebrews will make plain to our postmodern world the real identity of the Jesus of pre-history, history, and "post-history."

Hebrews is also important for today's Christian because of its philosophical approach to the religion of Judaism. The epistle's attitude to Christianity's parent religion was not fully appreciated by a segment of previous generations of Christians, who rather perceived it as being anti-Judaist or, more seriously, as anti-Semitic. It is when we have fully appreciated the intricate and nuanced philosophical approach that Hebrews adopts toward Judaism, however, that we realize how wrong such conclusions were. On the contrary, when the author's philosophical approach to Judaism is fully grasped, it will provide a critical window to teaching the postmodern Christian how to relate to other religions, especially with regard to evangelism.

The epistle to the Hebrews delicately sets out how the old Jewish religion foreshadowed the final one, which is in Christ. It accepts the validity of the faith of Judaism in so far as it was a prefigurement of the Christian faith and hence continued into and at the same time discontinued when Christ fulfilled it. Hence, the faith of the people of the Old Testament, to the author of Hebrews, was the same as that of the people of the New only when Christ was the interpretive key. Abraham's faith, for example, is therefore interpreted as if it were a Christian faith that believed in the resurrection (Heb 11:19), and Moses, according to the author, persevered in faith because he "regarded disgrace for the sake of Christ as of greater value . . . he persevered because he saw him who is invisible" (Heb 11:26–27). Moses, according to Hebrews, "fixed his eyes" on Christ to enable him to persevere. To the author of Hebrews, therefore, the people of God, from Abraham, Moses, and David, to Isaiah and Jeremiah, and in our time, you and I, have always remained the same, for it was the same Christ that we have experienced that the people of Israel also experienced through the sacrifices and rituals in the Old Testament. Now that the full person of Christ has been revealed, the religion of Judaism has been fulfilled and completed in him "once for all" (Heb 10:10). This theological analysis by the author of Hebrews is a remarkable interpretation of the Old Testament.

3. Cullmann, *Christology*, 103–4.

The significance of the magnificent philosophical approach that the author of Hebrews adopts toward Judaism, compared to our contemporary attitude to other religions, is immense. It immediately condemns the anti-Judaism that characterized some earlier generations of Christians and is in danger of resurfacing in our time. It also transforms the way we approach other religions, such as Islam, with regard to missions and evangelism. An example of this is illustrated by comparing the nature of pilgrimage theology in the New Testament to that in Islam. One of the major themes of Hebrews, as we shall later discover in this study, is the theology of pilgrimage to heaven. Though this has been noted for several centuries, the idea of pilgrimage itself was not sufficiently understood by western Christian readers until relatively recently. Partin's[4] study of the components of the Muslim pilgrimage has enabled a number of authors[5] to analyze and define more fully the whole concept and its relationship to the theology of Hebrews for our better understanding.

The presence of aspects of this theology in Hebrews, and the way the author fashions it for his purposes, provides us the opportunity to witness to and critique the Muslim pilgrimage by teaching that the real goal of pilgrimage is to the heavenly sanctuary where Christ, our eternal high priest, sits at God's right hand. Osborne has, for example, noted how the pilgrimage theology of Hebrews is so potent when pitted against the teachings of Islam. He observes, "The emphasis on the new direct access to a personal God on the basis of Christ's heavenly ministry will be quite appealing to Muslims. Muhammad's trip to heaven from the spot in Jerusalem, on which the Mosque of Omar sits, pales into insignificance compared to the heavenly ministry of Christ."[6] Plainly, if we were able to understand and apply this epistle by adopting its author's superb philosophical approach to Judaism, we will make much more headway in our evangelistic efforts toward not only Islam but also all the other religions that have pilgrimage as their central theology. A study of Hebrews calls on us to preach Christ, without antagonism, as the end of all religions. What boldness and yet what sensitive humility this knowledge adds to our witness to people of other religions.

Another reason why we neglect this epistle to our peril is the lessons it teaches on how to study the Bible. Hebrews is essentially a sermon that uses a number of Old Testament passages that the writer has selected to

---

4. Partin, *The Muslim Pilgrimage*, 1967.

5. See, for example, Johnsson, "The Pilgrimage Motif," 239–51.

6. Osborne, "The Christ of Hebrews," 249–67.

make his pastoral "word of exhortation" (Heb 13:22). From this epistle, we see how the early church handled the Old Testament in all its theological fullness. By using the life, ministry, death, resurrection, ascension, and exaltation of Christ as the lens to examine the Old Testament and unearth its lessons to address the pastoral problems of his congregation, Hebrews teaches us how we may also study God's word in order to discern spiritual principles for victorious living.

The author's mixture of a keen Jewish theological style of interpretation with typology, allegory, and other interpretive methods that our generation has discarded as "unscientific" makes the Old Testament "come alive" to any who would listen. It has been fashionable for some scholars to note the strangeness and primitiveness of the interpretive style of Hebrews, but we have missed the whole point of biblical interpretation with this stance. Though we may not exactly copy its style of biblical interpretation, Hebrews should be a rebuke to our barren hermeneutics, which depend entirely on humanly constructed history and the grammar of the dictionary and so have lacked theological conviction and spiritual power. Postmodernity, despite all its faults, has rightly questioned the false certainties of historical inquiry and though it has brought difficult challenges to evangelical hermeneutics, we are beginning to realize that the classical historical-grammatical study of the Bible should only be a beginning and not the end of biblical interpretation. A thorough study of Hebrews will teach us how to fully read and apply God's word.

Hebrews is also important for today's church because it warns against a compromised Christianity, and how much we need that kind of message today. Its exhortations against laxity and backsliding, or warnings against not moving on to perfection, and against the danger of not entering into God's rest are designed to instill godly fear in the reader. Though its admonishment to "be careful that none of you be found to have fallen short if it" (Heb 4:1), with the grave threats about the God who is a "consuming fire" (Heb 12:29) and who does not have pleasure in those who "shrink back" (Heb 10:39), may sound rather harsh to some ears, that is fortunately the kind of message that we surely need in these compromise-prone postmodern times.

On the other hand, Hebrews' fervent pastoral encouragement, even to the weary and battered believer, to persevere, to "pay more careful attention" (Heb 2:1), to "hold firmly to the faith we profess" (Heb 4:14), and even "approach the throne of grace with confidence, so that we may receive mercy and find grace to help us in our time of need" (Heb 4:16) is both heartening and invigorating for all of us. The cure for the spiritual exhaustion that has overtaken some of our Christian fellowships and brothers and sisters, who in years past were zealous for the Lord but appear lately to be drained of spiritual energy and commitment, is here in the book of Hebrews. This epistle, without doubt, is very contemporary for every one of the challenges we face today, and understanding it holds an important key to a revitalized Christian life and witness. If I may be permitted to borrow and paraphrase from the author of Hebrews, "How shall we escape if we neglect so great an epistle"!

It is with this highest degree of appreciation of the incalculable value of Hebrews that we approach our study. Our singular aim is essentially to establish a consistently applicable overall theme and message of Hebrews that will then be the key to unlocking the rich blessings of its various parts. When that is achieved, the epistle will prove itself to be truly practical and priceless for spiritual formation and discipleship. Because the whole epistle was a homily or a "word of exhortation," we must begin with the basic assumption that the author had a uniting theme or master idea in mind that fit all its various parts into one whole. Though some scholars[7] have rejected this assumption and have instead insisted on a piecemeal approach to interpreting the epistle, the results of such approaches have in many ways contributed to the lack of understanding and applicability of Hebrews. In addition, it is difficult to imagine that such an effective sermon would not have had a running uniting theme shaping the various ideas and concepts that the author brings together to bear on the spiritual difficulties of his congregation.

Despite the challenging complexities, ours is not to give in but to pursue and find this uniting theme. The basic assumption that there is one such theme that the author utilizes to frame his homily therefore seems to be in order. Such a theme must no doubt fit in with the author's pastoral purpose as well as the socio-historical context, as much as that may be adequately ascertained. It must also explain the unique features of the epistle, particularly its literary and rhetorical structure. Of necessity, therefore, our investigation must interact with other attempts at locating a uniting theme. The point here, however, is to build on the great foundations that others have laid rather than erecting a new one.

The interpretation of Hebrews that follows is surely not the final word on it. This epistle's deep treasures will not be fully mined by any one generation, let alone one person. The proposal set out here has merely been drawn from the nature of the questions that I have asked of the epistle.

---

7. See, for example, Lindars, *Theology*, 26, who regards such an assumption as "a mistake."

Other types of questions would perhaps generate different sets of answers and so will come different sets of lessons. There may therefore be better explanations and approaches to Hebrews than what is being proposed. Nevertheless, I am of the view that the proposal may hold vital answers to producing a holistic understanding of such an important book of the Bible and so unlock its blessings.

An Overview of the Study

This study proposes that the author of the epistle to the Hebrews was significantly influenced by the theology and literary style of the book of Numbers. That Old Testament book depicts the migrating camp of the Israelites in the wilderness, organized and arranged into concentric rings around the tabernacle and with the Ark of the Covenant at its center. This concentric arrangement was a picture of spiritual order and loving devotion to Jehovah who reigned in the midst of his migrant people as they journeyed toward the promised land. The tabernacle itself served as the religious and social center of their wilderness migration. Together with the leadership of Moses and Aaron, the guiding angel of the Lord, and the pillars of fire by night and cloud by day, the people of God were to charge triumphantly toward God's promise ahead of them. However, when the people failed to appropriate the spiritual benefits that this encampment around the tabernacle of God brought them, and instead shrunk back into unbelief, persistent grumbling, and rebellion against God and His servant Moses, Israel forfeited the "rest" that God had prepared for them. Their refusal to persevere in faith during their migration to God's promise resulted in apostasy and a life of wandering in the desert for forty years, ending in the destruction of the Exodus generation.

It is this simple message of the book of Numbers, interpreted through the lens of the death, resurrection, and exaltation of Christ, which directed the author of Hebrews to construct his sermon, which was aimed at addressing the very severe pastoral crisis in his congregation. He perceived that typologically, his congregation shared similar spiritual and social characteristics to the Exodus generation in the wilderness and hence the message of the book of Numbers would also be applicable when Christ was used as the interpretive key.

Consequently, in his sermon Hebrews employed his Jewish style of exegesis that combined elements of typology and allegory in the limited sense to interpret the *spaces* of the concentric arrangement of the migrating camp of Israel surrounding the tabernacle in Numbers. He then utilized this interpretation to exhort the congregation to *re-orient* themselves in the direction of travel and with Jesus their "Moses and Aaron" leading them, to *move* toward the promise for which they were *migrating*. The four concepts of *spaces, orientation, movement,* and *migration* hence provide the interpretive link between Numbers and Hebrews, and the uniting theme of Hebrews is, accordingly, woven around them. This is the theory that this study proposes, explains, and defends as an approach to understanding the epistle to the Hebrews.

In the next chapter, I shall present a concise summary of the major issues that together have contributed to making the epistle to the Hebrews a challenge to many Christians. It is fair to say that this epistle has received a reasonable degree of welcome theological and academic attention in the last fifteen years or so and that is indeed encouraging. Questions about its historical, cultural, and contextual background, the author's philosophical pattern of thought, the book's theology, and its use of the Old Testament have all been debated. The epistle is unique in the New Testament and does not provide us with that many clues to help answer several contextual questions that we normally take for granted with some of the other books of the New Testament.

Therefore, in discussing the issues, we shall also broadly summarize some of the various viewpoints and contributions to shed more light on the various aspects of Hebrews. There are many interesting suggestions and conclusions that have been made, some of which, unfortunately, depend on assumptions and speculations. These assumptions need to be stated and considered in any examination of the theology of Hebrews. Knowledge of the different perspectives is useful because they help us to appreciate the various aspects of the epistle.

Chapter three presents the theoretical basis of the methodology of our study. Through the simple observation that each block of the expositions of Hebrews is circumscribed within a particular *space* and the exhortations by metaphors of *movement*, I will set out in chapter three how the interdisciplinary paradigm of spatiality may be used to study a Bible passage. Though spatiality has been recognized for centuries as fundamental to the human thought process, it has not received sufficient attention. Certainly it has not received as much attention as temporality (i.e., what is normally called "history"). One of the benefits of the "literary turn" in biblical studies is that it has also assimilated many other investigative methodologies of the social sciences that may be used to help solve old unresolved questions. Spatiality is one of the buzzwords of postmodernity in the social sciences and I propose to use its theories to analyze Hebrews in order to identify its uniting theme.

Though we commonly establish the truthfulness of an event by trying to detail its chronological sequence, we all know that real events are never that simple in terms of chronological sequence, and that for some events, using geographical locations or spaces (whether rooms, various fields, regions, or countries) to organize their narration makes the description more understandable and meaningful. This way of portraying events or making an argument has always been fundamental to the human thought process, but we have tended not to take it as seriously as we do with chronological sequence of organizing our thoughts.

The Bible does, however, take spatiality seriously. So, for example, the story of the fall of Adam and Eve in Genesis 3 is described in terms of spatiality rather than temporality. That story is set in a garden that God selected and circumscribed for the first humans. Within it, in its very "middle" (Gen 3:3), was the tree of the knowledge of good and evil, from which God instructed the first humans not to eat. If we consider the spatial aspects of the Garden of Eden narrative, it comes as no surprise to read that the devil exploited the human desire for power through knowledge to tempt our first parents. As we shall see in this study, space, hierarchical relationships, and contests for power and knowledge are intricately linked and spatiality holds an important interpretive key to the story of Adam and Eve. After they sinned, Adam and Eve heard the sound of God "walking in the garden" (Gen 3:8), from whom they attempt to "hide." God inquired, "Where are you?" (Gen 3:9) but Adam excused himself by pointing to the woman God "put here" (Gen 3:12) with him. God consequently punished the first humans by "banish[ing] him from the Garden of Eden to work the ground from which he had been taken" (Gen 3:23). All these have vital spatial connotations. We miss the point of this story if we lose sight of its spatial elements.

This is why chapter three will explain a method by which we can study the spatiality of a Bible passage so as to draw out principles and lessons for application. The chapter may appear to be a rather long detour or digression from Hebrews, but that is deliberate. The use of social science models in spatiality to biblical studies is new and not that common. Hence, a deliberate explanation and wider deployment of the concepts are necessary if we are to grasp their application in Hebrews.

Chapter four uses the method of spatial analysis to examine the expositions of the epistle to the Hebrews. The aims of this chapter are threefold. First, it demonstrates how spatiality as a Bible study method works. Second, it will highlight the big influence of spatiality on the whole organization of the argument of Hebrews. This will also underscore that the expositions of Hebrews have been organized by the author into a deliberate spatial arrangement in order to communicate his messages. The third aim is to discuss some of the proposed explanations for this spatial arrangement and recommend that the migrant camp of Israel around the tabernacle as depicted in the book of Numbers best represents this purposeful organization of the expositions of Hebrews.

Chapter five examines the exhortations of Hebrews to show how the author presents the migration of the camp of God's people toward the promise. It will demonstrate that each of the four blocks of the exhortations contains similar concepts that are best analyzed by employing the sociological model of migration. This is because the background narrative that influenced the author's teaching is the migration of Israel from Egypt to the promised land. Following that, the parallels between the epistle to the Hebrews and the book of Numbers will be explored and we shall suggest that the fourth book of the Old Testament may have had a major influence on the author of Hebrews. The theology of the camp and tabernacle, as portrayed in both Numbers and the epistle to the Hebrews, will also be examined, not only to show the parallels, but also to provide some interpretive principles to aid in understanding Hebrews.

The final chapter explains how the whole book of Hebrews can therefore be understood when the background picture of the migrating camp of the people of God around the tabernacle is employed. It will provide examples of how this will serve as a principle for the interpretation of Hebrews. I trust that we will indeed find this study an "eye-opener" containing keys to unlocking the blessings in this glorious epistle.

2
What Is the Problem with Hebrews?

THE ACCOLADES that many have heaped on Hebrews reveal the extent of the difficulties that scholars have experienced with regard to this epistle. E. F. Scott noted, "The Epistle to the Hebrews is in many respects the riddle of the New Testament . . . Almost from the beginning the church was aware of something strange and perplexing about this Epistle."[1] Gager described Hebrews as "an enigma"[2] and Matera thought the book was "as strange as the figure of Melchizedek, whom it describes as being 'without father, without mother, without genealogy, having neither the beginning of days nor end of life.'"[3] Lane points out that Hebrews has "a reputation for being formidable and remote from the world in which we live"[4] and more recently Wright has noted that the theology of Hebrews is "bracing and challenging."[5] What makes the epistle to the Hebrews deserve such negative reviews?

Hebrews in a Gist

On the surface, the message and style of Hebrews appears to be packed with confusing twists and turns. The author, without any self-introduction, plunges immediately into a magnificent language of praise that also compares Jesus, the Son of God, with the angels. He emphasizes in different ways that Jesus "became as much superior to the angels as the name he has inherited is superior to theirs" (Heb 1:4), while at the same time stressing that Jesus is divine: he is "the radiance of God's glory and the exact representation of his being" (Heb 1:3). One is immediately tempted

---

1. Scott, *Hebrews: Doctrine and Significance*, 1.
2. Gager, *The Origins of Anti-Semitism*, 180.
3. Matera, *New Testament Christology*, 185.
4. Lane, *Hebrews 1–8*, xii.
5. Wright, *Hebrews for Everyone*, x.

to ask: since Jesus is divine, why does the writer elaborately compare him to his own ministering angels?

In the middle of these comparisons, the author seems to deviate from the lofty exposition in order to exhort, admonish, and challenge his readers in Heb 2:1–4. He warns them to be careful not to drift away in their faith and that there will be no escape if they were to ignore the salvation that Jesus, being greater than the angels, has announced. The average reader is right to ask again: Is there a particular problem with the Hebrews congregation that the author is using the comparison with the angels to address? And if so, what is the nature of the problem? Does it have to do with doctrinal understanding of the functions of angels or rather a practical issue of not paying enough attention to the salvation that Jesus had inaugurated?

Our author does not directly answer these questions but returns to the comparisons of Jesus with the angels in Heb 2:5–18, this time involving all creation, humanity, and the devil in the discussion. He declares that Jesus became human and shared in our "flesh and blood" (Heb 2:14) in order to defeat the devil, who held humanity in bondage to the fear of death. This feat by Christ again makes him better than the angels, but more than that, it also makes him "a merciful and faithful high priest" (Heb 2:17). This is strong stuff indeed but something that we recognize as also described elsewhere in the New Testament with different style of words.

Just when we are settling down to what appears to have been a sermon on "Why God Became Human," our author switches to another comparison in Hebrews 3, this time of Jesus with Moses. Does the congregation have an exaggerated view of Moses? If so, what is the nature of such views: was it doctrinal or rather a problem of a practical nature? Hebrews praises Moses, no doubt, asserting, "Moses was faithful in all God's house" (Heb 3:2), but he also emphasizes that Jesus is more worthy of honor than Moses (Heb 3:3). Jesus is Son over the house but Moses is servant in the house. In that case, why does Hebrews compare them?

Next, Hebrews uses the brief discussion on Moses to encourage the readers. He interprets the Old Testament story of the failure of Moses and the majority of the Israelites to enter into the promised land as a warning against the consequences of unbelief. Beyond this moral interpretation of the story of the failure of the Israelites that is narrated in the book of Numbers, Hebrews also perceives a deeper eschatological message. The author therefore affirms, "There remains, then, a Sabbath-rest for the people of God" (Heb 4:9). The destination, which represented the promised land to biblical Israel, is being typologically interpreted by Hebrews as "Sabbath-rest" for Christians. This author's style of biblical interpretation, through which he makes double or even triple interpretations of some parts of the Old Testament, is clearly a major factor that must be reckoned with if one is to understand what he is saying.

Many readers would have found the epistle to the Hebrews easier to understand if the writer had finished with Heb 4:14, 16: "Therefore, since we have a great high priest who has gone through the heavens, Jesus the Son of God, let us hold firmly to the faith we profess . . . Let us then approach the throne of grace with confidence, so that we may receive mercy and find grace to help us in our time of need." This glorious passage is not the end of it, however, for the author returns to his comparisons in Hebrews 5, this time comparing and contrasting Jesus' qualifications to be our high priest with those of Aaron. After hinting about the high priesthood of Christ earlier on in Heb 1:3, 2:17–18, 3:1, 4:14–16, Hebrews is now ready to discuss it in full. Before he could do that, however, he interrupts himself again to give more exhortations and warnings. This is because he felt that what he was about to discuss was so critical and needed their mature attention; it was "solid food" (Heb 5:12) and required spiritual maturity to grasp. To Hebrews, any Christian who does not continue to grow to maturity retrogresses. He reckoned, therefore, that some of the members of his congregation who were not maturing were at least in danger of "falling away" and this was the opportunity to warn them not "to become lazy" (Heb 6:12) but to progress and move on to perfection. A sense of movement by faith to something ahead evidently colors the exhortations, but what was going on with this congregation?

The long and detailed discussion in Hebrews 7–10 constitutes the portion of Hebrews whose import and relevance to the author's pastoral purposes is least understood. Here, the author continues his comparisons of Jesus with Aaron but this is a more thorough comparison and deals initially with the different natures of their high priestly offices (Hebrews 7) and then of their functions (Hebrews 8–10). Regarding Jesus' high priestly office, Hebrews explains that according to Ps 110, Jesus is high priest in the order of Melchizedek. Hebrews 7 is a clarification of this order of priesthood. It is in a sense a higher order of priesthood, a divinely ordained priestly-king office and an eternal position that is much superior to the Aaronic high priesthood.

Regarding the framework of Jesus' functions as high priest, Hebrews explains that he performs these functions in the heavenly Holy of Holies, in comparison to Aaron's ministry that was in the wilderness tabernacle.

Using his typological style of biblical interpretation, the author teaches his congregation that the wilderness tabernacle was "a copy and shadow of what is in heaven" (Heb 8:5), which therefore makes Jesus' ministry superior and more enduring than Aaron's. This is perhaps what he has been driving at all along with the contrasts and comparisons. Clearly, we will best understand Hebrews if we can comprehend the author's typological style of interpreting the migrant camp of Israel surrounding the wilderness tabernacle as is depicted in the Old Testament.

After his typological interpretation of the tabernacle (Hebrews 8), explaining the significance of the *space* where Christ ministers as high priest the characteristics of that ministry (Hebrews 9) there, and therefore the features of the new covenant that he has inaugurated in this heavenly Holy of Holies (Hebrews 10), Hebrews returns to his exhortations in the rest of the book. Characteristic of many other New Testament exhortations, the author focuses on the three Christian virtues of faith (Hebrews 11), hope (Hebrews 12), and love (Hebrews 13). In Hebrews 11, he defines faith as faithful perseverance toward what is hoped for and provides examples of how some of God's people in the past have lived their lives in faithfulness as part of a spiritual camp of migrating believers who are heading toward the heavenly "city" (Heb 11:16) and the "kingdom" (Heb 12:28) that God is preparing for them.

In Hebrews 12, the author encourages the congregation to bear with their suffering in perseverance, fixing their hopes on Jesus, who, after his suffering "sat down at the right hand of the throne of God" (Heb 12:2). They should eschew the bitterness that could result from suffering and instead remember that they are part of a group of traveling worshippers who have arrived at "Mount Zion, to the heavenly Jerusalem." This knowledge of the congregation's identity as a worshipping migrant community of believers who are heading to God's promise ahead should instill in them the hope that enables them to "worship God acceptably with reverence and awe" (Heb 12:28). In his concluding chapter, the author focuses on love within the Christian fellowship and deals with the various problems that could hinder fellowship among believers. He also exhorts them to cooperate with the leaders of the fellowship.

To what do all these twists and turns of a sermon amount? What were the reasons for the comparisons of Jesus with the angels, Moses, and Aaron? What really was at stake in the very serious warnings that the author gives in parts of the exhortations? What problems and challenges in the congregation was our author trying to address in such a manner that now appears to be "convoluted"? And how may we transform the lessons of this epistle into principles that we can practically apply to the postmodern Christian? These are the challenging questions that we face in studying Hebrews today. For though the epistle seems to have been clear enough to the earliest believers who first read and heard it, coherent enough for them to have preserved it, we must admit that despite its captivating intensity, it does not seem that clear to many who read it today.

The Problem with Hebrews

The task of any Bible interpreter is not only to try and explain what a Bible verse means, but more importantly to formulate principles by which one can apply the passage to our present-day circumstances. To be able to do that, the interpreter must have an overall understanding of the message of the book, which then guides him or her to interpret its parts. It is not enough to know what a verse or passage of Hebrews says. Instead, we need a mechanism by which we can understand its whole message so that it guides us to interpret its various verses. When the parts are interpreted in the light of the whole, then the parts become meaningful enough to enable us to apply them in situations that are removed by thousands of miles and years from the original setting. The problem with Hebrews is that many do not understand its whole message sufficiently enough to use it to interpret its parts.

Thankfully, a problem that is understood is half solved. If we can appreciate the nature of the difficulties with interpreting Hebrews, we will be in a better position to seek their solutions. We will therefore examine the contours of the various issues that present themselves as challenges in Hebrews. For the sake of convenience, I will group the various problems into four categories: contextual issues, Hebrews' interpretive approach to the Old Testament, the warning passages, and the uniting theme of Hebrews.

The Problems with the Context of Hebrews

The basic axiom of any effective Bible study remains true: interpreting a text without considering its context is a pretext. Unfortunately, when it comes to Hebrews, the context is not fully available to us, and that constitutes a major hurdle to be cleared in attempts to understand the epistle. Different opinions have been expressed regarding the author, his philosophical background, the date of writing, the recipients, the literary genre, and the structure of Hebrews.

The Authorship of Hebrews

No one knows the identity of the author of Hebrews. Paul evidently did not write the epistle, since the author was not an apostle (Heb 2:3–4), even though he may well have been a member of Paul's team, since he was acquainted with Timothy (Heb 13:23). The use of the masculine Greek word for "tell," (or literally, "narrating") in Heb 11:32 suggests that the author was male, contrary to a suggestion that it could have been written by Priscilla. He was separated from the recipients at the time (Heb 13:19), perhaps was still in prison (Heb 10:34), hoping to be restored to them shortly (Heb 13:19). That is all the information about the author of which we can be sure. The guesswork[6] that has accompanied attempts at identifying the writer of this epistle has only served to put many people off studying Hebrews. Thankfully, authorship is not a major interpreting requirement and it is best to accept that we do not know who wrote the epistle.

The Author's Philosophical Background

If the philosophical background of an author is known, it goes a long way to aid interpretation of his or her writing. Knowledge, for example, of Paul's Jewish and Pharisaic background enables identification of some of his train of thought and style of biblical interpretation. Due to its unique features, however, the tendency has been to seek to identify Hebrews' background on the peripheries of first-century Hellenistic Jewish religious circles.

Parallels with Philo's brand of Platonism, such as the tendency to allegorize the Pentateuch, references to Melchizedek, and to the logos and wisdom theology have been made. But the differences between Hebrews' philosophy and Philonism are so immense that there certainly is no dependence of the writer on Philo. Spicq's observation is astute, that if even our author "borrowed from (Philo) this or that biblical theme or hermeneutical process, he has determinedly repudiated his allegorical, subjective and superficial method, so as to achieve a reading which was profoundly religious and singularly more penetrating than all those that had hitherto been proposed."[7] Hebrews' allegorization is controlled and subject to his Christological reading of the Old Testament. The references to Melchizedek are equally restrained and typological. The Logos and Wisdom theology

---

6. Barnabas, Luke, Clement, Silas, Apollos, Phillip, Priscilla, and Epaphras have all been at one stage or another suggested as the author.

7. Spicq, *Hébreux*, 63–64.

in Hebrews is never pushed as much as Philo's, and as for Platonism in Hebrews, this again is not substantiated. In Williamson's words:

> Plato's Ideal world is not a heaven that could be entered even by Jesus; it can be penetrated only by intellect. And there is no room among the Ideas for one who was prepared to humble himself and become flesh in the world of men and phenomena; and the crucial point which the Author of Hebrews wishes to stress is that Jesus who at a particular time in history became a real man and lived a full and authentic human life, entered into the "true tent" at the completion of his work on earth, the climax of which was the consummation on the Cross of his perfect obedience, holiness and love (a strongly un- Platonic note in the contrast).[8]

Parallels with Alexandrian Hellenism have also been made. Hebrews' use of the Greek translation of the Old Testament (also called the LXX), the references to the tabernacle, the role of the angels in the giving of the Law, the focus on the Pentateuch, and the polished eloquence of the writing itself parallels parts of Stephen's speech in Acts 7. There are significant differences from Stephen's emphasis, however, since Stephen's focus was on the positive significance of the wilderness tabernacle, whereas our author's approach was less upbeat and rather emphasizes the typological meaning of the tabernacle. The author of Hebrews is no doubt a Jew who has received a Hellenistic education but that is as far as one can state in this respect. Linkage to some of the priestly community or the Qumran Essenes has been made but remains unproven.

Despite its apparent uniqueness, the similarity of Hebrews with the primitive Christian faith of the apostles should direct us to the author's background. Hebrews is the one epistle that, on a number of occasions, refers or alludes to events in Jesus' earthly life: his temptation (Heb 2:18), his "loud cries and tears" in Gethsemane (Heb 5:7), his shameful crucifixion (Heb 12:2–3), his death outside the city gate of Jerusalem (Heb 13:12), and the tearing of the veil of the temple (Heb 10:20). Indeed, despite the verbal differences between Paul and this author, the theological ideas are similar. Montefoire has, for example, identified as many as thirteen points of contact between Hebrews and 1 Cor 1–4 and the theology of Heb 2:5–18 is so similar to Rom 3–8 that it even appears to be its summary.[9] Ultimately, when correctly distilled, the philosophical theology of Hebrews is situated in the primitive apostolic preaching (i.e.,

---

8. Williamson, "Platonism and Hebrews," 419.
9. Montefoire, *Hebrews*, 9–11.

the kerygma of the earliest Christians). As demonstrated by Bruce,[10] the writer shared the common ground with the gospel that was preached by the apostles and that is where we should seek to understand his philosophical background.

The Date of Writing

Similar to authorship, the date when Hebrews was written is also unknown. That Clement of Rome cited Hebrews in AD 96 means the epistle was perhaps well known in Rome by then. The date of Timothy's death is unfortunately unknown, but if Paul was dead at the time that Hebrews was written, then it was written after AD 64. Some attach relevance to the date of the fall of Jerusalem in AD 70, believing that Hebrews may have been written while the temple and its sacrifices were still in place. Though references to the Levitical system are made in the present tense (Heb 5:1–4; 7:20, 23, 27, 28; 8:3, 4, 13; 9:6, 13; 10:2–3, 11) this is no proof that the sacrifices were still occurring. The author likes using present tenses when referring to the scriptures, which to him are "living and active" (Heb 4:12). He does not direct his address to the temple but rather the wilderness tabernacle and its sacrifices.

On the other hand, other interpreters[11] have suggested that Hebrews was written in response to the fall of the Jerusalem temple in AD 70. We cannot be sure of this theory, though it is possible. What we may be sure of is that these Christians, like our author, were second-generation believers. Thus the circumstance would have been at least thirty to forty years after the death and resurrection of Christ. Knowing the date when Hebrews was written, like knowing who wrote it, is fortunately not so critical to interpreting Hebrews. It does appear to me that if we interpret the epistle after we have chosen a particular date, it overly restricts our understanding. I will rather own up to not knowing when Hebrews was written.

The Ethnicity of the Congregation

One does understand why the early church quickly concluded that this epistle was written to Jewish Christians. It focuses on Jewish rituals, appeals widely to the Old Testament, and does not seem to address many of

10. Bruce, "Kerygma of Hebrews," 3–19.

11. For example, Isaacs (*Reading Hebrews*, 8–14) suggests that the theology of Hebrews is meant to help the Jewish Christians stop grieving about the loss of the Jerusalem temple and rather refocus their attention on the ministry of Christ in the heavenly tabernacle.

the concerns that the other epistles to the mainly Gentile congregations did. Some scholars[12] have even suggested that the writer, together with the recipients, may have been converted Jewish priests.

Not all scholars agree that the members of the congregation were Jewish, however. The detailed explanations that the writer gives concerning the sacrifices, it has been noted, could suggest that "the Hebrews" were not all that familiar with the Jewish rituals as we might conclude. In addition, the language of the epistle is thoroughly Greek. The author uses the LXX for all his quotations and many of the applications he refers to, such as the argument about the relationship between the ratification of a covenant or will and death of the testator in Heb 9:16–17 and on education of children in Heb 12: 9–11, are based more on Greco-Roman customs than Jewish practices. The congregation at least knew another group of believers somewhere in Italy (Heb 13:24) and may well have been based within that area.

I think, considering the author's style of exegesis and the issues that dominate his homily, it is unlikely that the letter would have been aimed at a purely Gentile congregation. Accordingly, the recipients of this epistle may have been Hellenized Jews, such as one of the large number of Jewish communities in Diaspora who were living in other parts of the Roman Empire outside Palestine, perhaps somewhere in Asia Minor.

Unlike the situation regarding the authorship and date, one's view on the ethnicity of the recipients makes a difference to how one interprets the parts of the epistle. If one believes that the recipients' ethnic background was largely Gentile, one may locate the explanation of many of the teachings of this epistle based on Greco-Roman and non-Jewish conventions. For example, some scholars have sought to explain the author's teaching on Melchizedek in Hebrews 7 using non-Jewish themes and motifs.[13] This approach, though, seems to be far-fetched. By far many of the interpretations of the epistle to the Hebrews that heavily rely on a non-Jewish backdrop appear rather implausible and hence the Jewishness of Hebrews is far stronger than its Gentile inclinations.

---

12. For example, Bruce, *Hebrews*, 7, notes how scholars such as Karl Bornhauser and C. Spicq suggest that the recipients may have been some of the "great number of priests" (Acts 6:7) converted in the early stages of Christianity.

13. Neyrey, "Without Beginning," 440, has, for example, suggested that the description of Melchizedek in Heb 7:3 represents "topoi from Hellenistic philosophy on what constitutes a true god," though Hebrews directs this ascription not to Melchizedek but to Christ.

The History of the Congregation

Several references to the past historical experiences of the congregation within the epistle enable us to piece together what appears to have been the social history of this church.[14] The group was started through the proclamation of the gospel "by those who heard" the Lord Jesus (Heb 2:3) (i.e., the apostles). This beginning was accompanied by "signs, wonders and various miracles, and gifts of the Holy Spirit distributed according to his will" (Heb 2:4). The impressive beginning was soon followed by a major persecution (Heb 10:32–34).

The church responded positively to this persecution by enduring (Heb 10:32), joyfully persevering with confidence, and "became companions" of those who were beaten and imprisoned. When the persecution lolled down, however, the church entered a third stage characterized by low-grade external verbal harassment (Heb 13:13), a highly unstable internal demoralization (Heb 12:12), and spiritual malaise (Heb 3:12, 10:26–28). The believers now turned on each other, thus causing internal friction in the fellowship (Heb 10:25) and their spiritual growth therefore became stunted (Heb 5:12–14) and their witness stale (Heb 6:6–8). Some began to "shrink back" (Heb 10:39) and started to "give up meeting together" (Heb 10:25), not willing any more to bear the shame of the cross (Heb 12:2). At the time of writing, it appeared the group was even separated from its leaders (Heb 13:17, 24). The situation was so serious that the writer of this epistle feared that some could "fall away" from the faith, hence the urgency in the tone of the sermon (Heb 6:1–12, 26–27).

Knowledge of this social history contributes tremendously to understanding the epistle. We will later demonstrate in this study that the author of Hebrews perceived this social history as typologically corresponding to the history of the people of Israel during their wilderness migration from Egypt to Canaan. Perceiving that the precarious pastoral situation of his people paralleled in similar severity to the Exodus generation who failed to enter God's promise, our author employed his Christology as an interpretive key to transform the theology of the migration of Israel. By identifying his people with this wilderness congregation, Hebrews also couched his homily to parallel the theology of the book of Numbers, thereby providing an answer to the pastoral difficulties.

---

14. This has been very well documented in Koester, *Hebrews*, 64–72.

The Literary Genre of Hebrews

It is now almost unanimously agreed among scholars that Hebrews is primarily a written sermon that was sent out as a letter. The author calls it a "word of exhortation" (Heb 13:22) and many of his statements (Heb 2:5, 5:11, 6:9, 8:1, 9:5) suggest that he was intending to speak or had perhaps already spoken some of the words he has written. He also uses the phrase, "if I may say so" (Heb 7:9), and in Heb 11:32 says, "What more shall I say?" Furthermore, he indicates that his speech was time limited (Heb 11:32) and there are strong oratorical features in the epistle. Even though the book itself begins like an essay and continues as a sermon, the author concludes it with a classical epistolary greeting (Heb 13:22).

Identifying the genre of Hebrews as a sermon is vital, for not only does it mean that the purpose of Hebrews was to stir and spur rather than to give theological information, it also implies that we should interpret the words in terms of how a sermon "works" on its hearers or readers. As a result of this emphasis in the last few decades, rhetorical study of Hebrews has yielded much fruit. As a sermon, Hebrews is clearly made up of two sub-genres: expositions and exhortations. These are interwoven in an interesting literary structure so that the expositions alternate with the exhortations.

The Literary Structure of Hebrews

The literary structure of a piece of writing defines the way its author has organized the thought units into a coherent whole and helps us identify the intentions of the author and how he or she went about achieving them. An examination of the literary structure shows that its author has deliberately organized it to achieve his pastoral purpose. We shall find that this strongly hints at the relationship between the epistle and Numbers.

Like other New Testament epistles, the present divisions of Hebrews into chapters and verses are artificial and do not identify the thought units of the author. Unlike the other epistles, however, its expositions and exhortations are arranged in an alternating fashion that has made the literary structure of Hebrews appear rather disorganized and difficult to define. David Black's humorous statement about the literary structure of Hebrews that it is "like those mysterious species of fish which live on the ocean floor As soon as they are brought to the surface to be examined, the change in pressure is too great for them, and they explode, leaving their investigators in a state of frustration and bewilderment,"[15] is rather true of this epistle.

15. Black, "Literary Structure of Hebrews," 163–77.

Generally, there are two main groups of proposals for the literary structure. The first group envisages a linear flow to the argument. Typically the expositions are separated from the exhortations into two parallel linear arguments which together move forward to end in the epistolary greetings of Heb 13:18-25. The most recent comprehensive work that makes this proposal is by George Guthrie, who combines the strengths of the linguistic, literary, thematic, and rhetorical-critical approaches to identify Heb 1:1-4, 1:5-14, 2:5-18, 3:1-6, 4:14-16, 5:1-10, 7:1—10:18 as the expositions and Heb 2:1-4, 3:1—4:13, 4:14-16, 5:11—6:20, and 10:19—13:17 as the exhortations.[16] Heb 3:1-6 straddles both.

The difficulty with this approach is that it has not been easy to link the expositions with the exhortations and some have therefore tended to privilege one sub-genre in favor of the other. Synge, for example, suggested that the expositions and exhortations were from two independent sources that were merged together by the author.[17] Very few scholars today will agree with this view. As DeSilva notes, the author of Hebrews had the "ability to weave his material together so artfully that no scheme will be able to separate perfectly what he has so closely joined together."[18]

On the other hand, not taking the alternation of the expositions with the exhortation seriously may result in losing grasp of the author's theme, flow of thought, and message. It is clearly possible to discern breaks between the doctrinal expositions and the practical exhortations through a cursory reading of the epistle, even though the exact verse where one stops and the next begins may be disputed. We can surmise, therefore, that though Hebrews fits the alternating expositions and exhortations together very well, they are in such a way that the exhortations are obvious enough to appear as if they are, in Koester's words, "digressions."[19] As we shall later see, the exhortations are not mere "digressions" but form an integral part of the author's argument.

It is also important to notice that whereas the flow of the argument in the exposition is linear, that of the exhortations, especially in Heb 2:1-4, 3:7—4:11, and 5:12—6:20 are cyclical and repeat the same or similar concepts of paying attention to God's word, of being careful not to fall back into old habits and beliefs but entering by faith, approaching the throne of grace for help, mercy and strength, and persevering to the promise.

---

16. Guthrie, *The Structure of Hebrews*, 1998.
17. Synge, *Hebrews and the Scriptures*, 43–52.
18. DeSilva, *Perseverance in Gratitude*, 71.
19. Koester, *Hebrews*, 84.

What Is the Problem with Hebrews?

A second group of proposals envisages a chiastic or circular structure to the epistle and is exemplified by the groundbreaking work by Albert Vanhoye.[20] Using five literary devices[21] as criteria, Vanhoye not only identified the expository and exhortational sections of Hebrews, but also made a very important observation—that the thought units of Hebrews are arranged in a chiastic fashion around the central exposition in Hebrews 5–10. He argued that Heb1:5—2:18 and 12:14—13:18 majored on eschatology, Heb 3:1—5:10 and 11:1—12:13 majored on ecclesiology, and the central portion, Heb 5:11—10:39, majors on sacrifice (Fig 2.1). The name *Christos* (Christ) in Heb 9:11 lies at the very center of this chiastic ring structure. Each ring contains its own exposition and exhortation in accordance with Guthrie's proposal, but there is an overall configuration of Hebrews that is architectural. The arguments are therefore not linear but deliberately constructed to produce these concentric rings with corresponding matching sections around the central portion.

A number of criticisms have been leveled against this chiastic arrangement of the structure of Hebrews. Thornton, for example, protests against its complexity and claims that the proposed structure is too elaborate,

Fig 2.1: The Concentric Ring Structure of Hebrews (Albert Vanhoye)

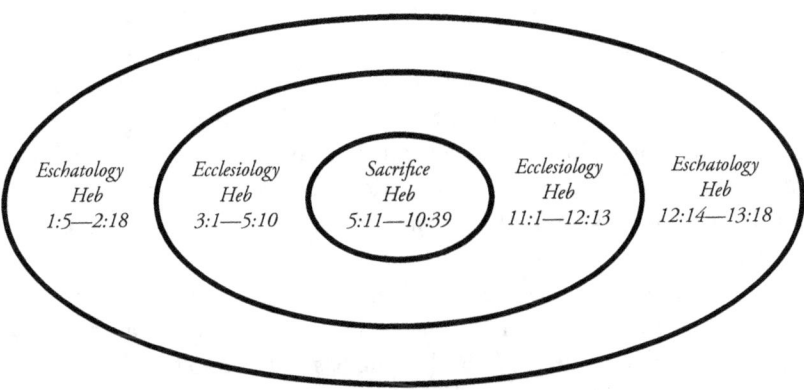

20. Vanhoye, *La structure*, 1963. For a detailed analysis of this see Ellingworth, *Hebrews*, 50–58.

21. These devices are (i) announcement of subject, (ii) inclusios, (iii) hook words, (iv) characteristic terms, and (v) alternation of genres.

saying, "None of the first readers would be able to appreciate the elaborate symmetrical patterns."[22] Similarly, Kummel branded such a structure "contrived,"[23] claiming that it may only be a reflection of Vanhoye's creativity rather than that of Hebrews.

Such doubts about the probability and capability of the author of Hebrews to deliberately construct such a complicated chiastic arrangement perhaps betray a rather condescending attitude by some modern exegetes on an ancient author and his congregation. Since equally sophisticated chiastic arrangement of literary works characterized ancient Sumero-Akkadian and Ugaritic texts from as early as the third millennium BC and was also common in ancient Jewish literature and the Bible,[24] it should not be impossible for the learned and clearly artistic author of Hebrews to produce such a well-balanced chiastic literary work.

Also, the other argument, that for an orally delivered homily, such a complicated and highly visual literary arrangement of Hebrews would have defeated its rhetorical purposes, is not persuasive. Since there were several other ancient writings with similar rhetorical purposes as Hebrews and even more complex chiastic and architectural structures, this objection does not negate Vanhoye's proposal. Ancient ears, perhaps unlike our modern ones, were trained to listen to literary works such as Hebrews with imaginative and architectural chiastic structures in mind. The literary structures in many cases acted as mnemonics that enabled the text to be understood and recalled. They therefore served not only as means of making memorization easier, but also indicated the central issues being addressed to its readers. As noted by Stock, "Chiasmus afforded a seriously needed element of internal organization in ancient writings, which did not make use of paragraphs, punctuation, capitalization, and other such synthetic devices to communicate the conclusion of one idea and the commencement of the next."[25]

In addition, some ancient writings employed architectural patterns to build the literary structure in such a way that they were easily recognizable by their first readers. Michael Payne has, for example, noted that the chiastic structure of the book of Revelation resembles "the structure of the menorah [the Jewish seven branched lamp stand], linking the first branch with the seventh, the second with the sixth, the third with the fifth, leaving

---

22. Thornton, "Reviews," 139–40.
23. Kummel, *Introduction*, 390.
24. See Avishur, *Studies in Biblical Narrative*, 1999.
25. Stock, "Chiastic Awareness and Education in Antiquity," 24–25.

What Is the Problem with Hebrews?

a central unpaired fourth branch."[26] The author of Hebrews may therefore have indeed employed a chiastic structure to give a form to his sermon.

Another criticism of Vanhoye's proposal was that the titles he gave to the various sections did not fit all the contents of those sections. Hebrews 11, for example, is not only focused on ecclesiology (the people of God) but also depicts the eternal hope of the people of God for the "heavenly city" (eschatology). That section therefore contains as much ecclesiology as eschatology. It is better, therefore, to exclude the titles that Vanhoye gave to each section and rather analyze their contents.

When the contents of the various sections in Vanhoye's proposal are structurally analyzed, it becomes clear that each ring is circumscribed by specific spatial and movement references. The outermost ring is bounded within the *space* of the "inhabited world" and is later in Hebrews 13 referred to as "the camp." The next ring is within the *space* of the "house of God" and has later connotations of "the migrant believers" in Hebrews 11–12, and the central core is within the space of the "Holy of Holies" where the throne of grace is (Fig 2.2).

Fig 2.2: Concentric Ring Structure of Hebrews Based on Spatial References[27]

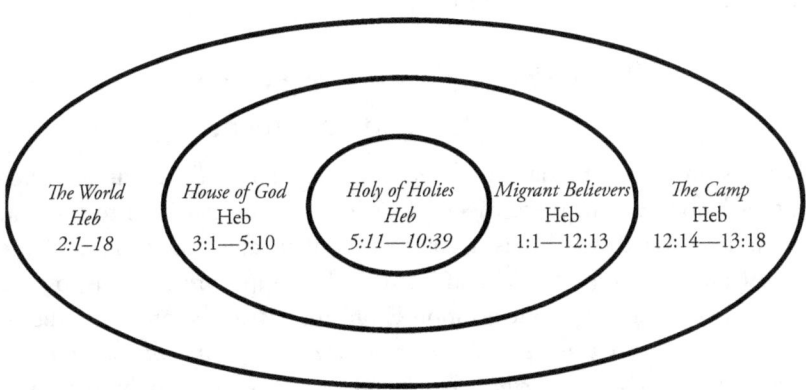

Typical of chiasmic arrangements, the two sides of the structure are not exactly the same but are mirror images of each other. The temporal sense in the first sections (the world and the house), for example, is rather

---

26. Payne, "Voice, Metaphor and Narrative," 369.
27. Hebrews 1 is an extended introduction and Heb 13:19-25 is the epilogue.

static, whereas that of its mirror image on the other side involves movement (migrants who are *moving* toward the heavenly city and believers being exhorted to *go* outside the camp). Similarly, whereas the example of the members in the "house of God" cited in Hebrews 3–4 died in unbelief without reaching the promised land (Heb 3:19), the migrants moving toward the heavenly city in Hebrews 11 died in faith, also not "receiving the promise" (Heb 11:13). The opposites are consistent with chiastic arrangement. Consequently, by analyzing the spatial references in the passages in each concentric ring, it will be possible to demonstrate the scheme that the author has deliberately used for his sermon.

Identification of Chiasmus plays an essential role in biblical interpretation,[27] and we shall demonstrate in chapter five that the writer of the epistle to the Hebrews has consciously structured his sermon in this chiastic ring to resemble the book of Numbers's migrant camp of Israel surrounding the tabernacle, so that the outermost ring typologically represented the camp itself, the next ring represented the priestly courtyard and the Holy Place of the tabernacle, and the central core corresponds to the space of the Holy of Holies. This literary structure served as a mnemonic that enabled Hebrews and his first readers to piece the message of the sermon together in their minds. We will equally find Hebrews easier to interpret by adopting this approach.

How Did the Author of Hebrews Interpret the Old Testament?

Perhaps one of the fundamental determinants of an accurate understanding of Hebrews is to piece the author's interpretive approach to the Old Testament together. This is a complex and debated question, but one whose answer is very crucial and it is therefore appropriate for us to state in the beginning what our position is on this matter before clarifying it. Hebrews uses *a Christological reading of the Old Testament that involves typology, limited allegory, citations, allusions, and echoes* to apply to the unstable pastoral circumstances of his congregation.

---

27. For a review on Chiasmus in the New Testament, see Lund, *Chiasmus in the New Testament*, 1992.

Christ as the Key to Interpreting the Old Testament

With the opening statement, "In the past God spoke to our forefathers through the prophets at many times and in various ways, but in these last days he has spoken to us by his Son," our author declares his intention to interpret every bit of the Old Testament through a Christ-tinted lens. Christ to him is the fulfillment of the scriptures and it is only through the lens of his life, ministry, death, resurrection, ascension, and exaltation at God's right hand that we may understand what is written in the Old Testament.

In this respect, the author understood the new covenant to be in continuity with what had pertained in the old, and yet at the same time, it has abrogated the old covenant by the fact that Christ has fulfilled it. Ellingworth's statement about this Christological approach is hence correct. "The author's approach to the OT may be summarized as follows: Christ by whom God has now spoken in His final word (1:1f.) was alive and active in creation (1:2) and throughout Israel's history. Any part of the OT may thus in principle be understood as speaking about Christ or as spoken to or by him."[28] In other words, in Hebrews, the Old Testament is interpreted as if the Lord Jesus was physically present in its story. This is why the author places Jesus in each of the concentric spaces around the tabernacle that governs the literary structure of his sermon.

Citations, Allusions, and Echoes of the Old Testament in Hebrews

It is obvious by the sheer number of citations in this epistle that the author is steeped in the Old Testament. He makes forty-one citations from the Old Testament. Fourteen are from the law (Genesis six times, Exodus twice, and Deuteronomy six times), one is from the historical books (1 Samuel or 1 Chronicles), and seven are from the prophets (Isaiah thrice, Jeremiah twice, Habakkuk once, and Haggai once), and nineteen are from the writings (Psalms eighteen times and Proverbs once). The epistle also contains the longest Old Testament citation in the New Testament (Jer 31:31–34 is quoted in Heb 10:16–17) and also the longest chain of biblical citations (also called catena—Heb 1:5–13). Moreover, each section of the epistle appears to be influenced by particular Old Testament citations: Heb 1:1—2:4 by Ps 2 and 110 (and perhaps 2 Sam 7), Heb 2:5–18 by Ps 8:4–6, Heb 3:1—4:13 by Ps 95:7–11, Heb 4:14—7:28 by Ps 110:4,

---

28. Ellingworth, *Hebrews*, 41–42.

Heb 8:1—9:28 by Jer 31:31–34, Heb 10:1–18 by Ps 40:6–8, and Heb 10:19—13:25 by Ps 95:7–11 and perhaps Heb 2:3–4.

The key to the author's use of the Old Testament, however, is not as much in the citations as it is in the allusions and echoes, the biblical assumptions that governed his references to the Old Testament. Allusions[29] are forms of intertextual cross-referencing whereby subtle references are made to information that exists in another text. They are usually summarative statements, sometimes a peculiar word or phrase that transports us back into another text and all the semantic connotations that come with it and so illuminates both the old and the new text for our understanding. The author may so incorporate the allusive reference into the new environment that on some occasions it is not completely certain whether an allusion was being made at all. This is often because, to the community who first received and read the original document, the allusion would have become so much embedded in their everyday language that no direct references were necessary. Whereas it may have been easier for his primary readers, identifying allusions may sometimes be difficult for us reading his work two thousand years later. Echoes are even fainter indirect references to a concept or idea in the Old Testament.

Much of the theology of Hebrews is expressed through allusions and echoes, more than the direct quotations, and this is one of the main reasons why the theology of Hebrews is sometimes difficult to understand. Longenecker has, for example, identified as many as fifty-five allusions to the Old Testament in the epistle.[30] If we do not take serious account of how allusions and echoes affect the theology of Hebrews, we will fail to appreciate what the author is saying. It is debatable, for example, if Numbers is ever quoted in Hebrews, but as we shall demonstrate later, allusions to and echoes of this Old Testament book's narratives, rituals, and literary style occur throughout the epistle.[31]

---

29. For more detailed review of allusions and echoes in the New Testament, see Moyise, "Intertextuality and Biblical Studies," 418–31 and Hays, *Echoes of Scripture*, 1989.

30. Longenecker, *Biblical Exegesis in the Apostolic Period*, 1975.

31. There are word similarities in Heb 3:5 (cf. Num 12:7), Heb 3:17 (cf. Num 14:29), Heb 8:5, Heb 9:4 (cf. Num 17:8–10), Heb 9:19, and Heb 10:26–29 (cf. Num 15:22–31) but it is uncertain if these are citations.

Hebrews' Typological and Allegorical Interpretation of the Old Testament

Typology is a method of biblical interpretation whereby a person, an object, an event, or an institution (the type) in an earlier phase of biblical history is shown to correspond by analogy to another person, object, event, or institution (the antitype) in a latter phase of history. The Exodus of Israel from Egypt is, for instance, portrayed in the Old Testament as new creation and in the New Testament as typological of redemption or liberation from slavery under the power of sin into liberty and new life in Christ. It is evident throughout Hebrews that the author understood the Old Testament as full of types that are fulfilled in Christ. To him, God's word was not a fixed historical relic but full of dynamic living messages for his generation (Heb 4:12).

An example of the author's style is the way he expounds the connection between Jesus and Melchizedek in Hebrews 7. He begins by what we might call a simple "word study" of Melchizedek, bringing together the two Bible passages which make references to Melchizedek (Ps 110 and Gen 14) to "canonically" fit them together. He then uses the etymology of names to make a symbolic interpretation of the person of Melchizedek (priest and king of Salem) and then applies a Jewish style of exegesis to demonstrate the superiority of Melchizedek over "even the patriarch Abraham" (Heb 7:4). He next uses typology to demonstrate that Melchizedek was in some way typological of Christ. Jesus is "another priest like Melchizedek" (Heb 7:15), who in turn "resembled the Son of God" (Heb 7:3). By appreciating this author's typological style of interpretation, we will be able to understand his argument better.

The author's use of terms and phrases such as "testifying" (Heb 3:5), "copy and shadow," "pattern" (Heb 8:5), "illustration" (Heb 9:9), or "figure" (Heb 9:24; Heb 11:16) are all expressions of this typological interpretation rather than Platonic thought pattern. In Hebrews, Moses (Heb 3), Aaron (Hebrews 5), Melchizedek (Hebrews 7), the Red Heifer (Hebrews 9), Abel (Hebrews 11), and the veil of the tabernacle (Heb 10:20) are all interpreted in some way as types of Jesus. Similarly, the people of Israel are typological of the Church and the promised land is typological of a complex of concepts including salvation (Heb 2:1–4), divine rest (Hebrews 3–4), perfection (Hebrews 5–6), and "the promise" (Hebrews 10–13). "The promise" itself is a multifaceted complex made up of the heavenly city, the kingdom that cannot be shaken, and eternal life in the everlasting presence of God and others.

All these analogies and types are submerged within an overall typological interpretation of the camp of Israel as depicted in the book of Numbers so that the camp represented the world where Christ comes to identify with his brothers and sisters, suffer, and be sacrificed for their redemption (Heb 2:5–8); the priestly courtyard of the tabernacle together with the Holy Place, which was accessible only to the Levitical priests, was representative of the "house of God" where the priestly people of God are; and the inner core, the Holy of Holies, represented the presence of God where Christ is seated at God's right hand and into which we are beckoned to approach to receive grace and mercy for the migration into the promise (Heb 4:14–16). Clearly multiple interpretations of the Old Testament occur throughout Hebrews.

Hebrews' interpretive style goes beyond typology to encompass various other Jewish methods of exegesis, some of which are similar to allegorical interpretation. Bruce is right when he states, "The Old Testament writings are treated by our author as a *mashal*, a parable or mystery which awaits its explanation and the explanation given in the pages of the epistle takes the form of Messianic typology."[32] Plainly, the valuable lessons of Hebrews will remain inaccessible so long as we restrict ourselves to classical grammatical-historical hermeneutics.

The Problem with the Warning Passages of Hebrews

For many believers, some of the major "stumbling stones" in the epistle to the Hebrews are the passages in which the author's warnings reach so high a tone that he seems to suggest that it is possible for a Christian to lose his or her salvation. In Heb 2:3 he warns, "How shall we escape if we ignore such a great salvation?" He becomes more explicit in Heb 4:11, "Let us, therefore, make every effort to enter that rest, so that no one will fall by following their example of disobedience." The warning becomes even more intense in Heb 6:4–6: "It is impossible for those who have once been enlightened, who have tasted the heavenly gift, who have shared in the Holy Spirit, who have tasted the goodness of the word of God and the powers of the coming age, if they fall away, to be brought back to repentance, because to their loss they are crucifying the Son of God all over again and subjecting him to public disgrace." And if this was not sobering enough, the author adds an imagery of "thorns and thistles" and being

---

32. Bruce, *Hebrews*, 27.

"cursed" and "burned"—descriptions that for many Christians evoke the thought of hell fire! That is not the end of his warnings; in Heb 10:26–27 he emphasizes again, "If we deliberately keep on sinning after we have received the knowledge of the truth, no sacrifice for sins is left, but only a fearful expectation of judgment and of raging fire that will consume the enemies of God."

Does the author of Hebrews teach that salvation is not eternally secure? Does he contradict the other parts of the New Testament? Are the people to whom these warnings were directed really saved Christians or were they "pretending to be saved"? What sort of sin results in this impossibility? And whose impossibility is it anyway? Is it the impossibility of the fallen Christian to repent, or the impossibility for other Christians to restore the fallen person to fellowship, or is it the impossibility for God to forgive the repentant apostate? And are these mere warnings, perhaps using a tinge of exaggeration to shock tempted Christians, without meaning that they could actually be eternally "lost," or did the author literally mean this would happen to apostate Christians?

These are questions that have been raised throughout the centuries about the warning passages in Hebrews. Martin Luther, for example, tripped on these "stones" and wrongly suggested that, though Hebrews should be part of the New Testament, it is of lesser degree of weight (together with the epistle of James) as compared to Paul's epistles. These sentiments remain common but unstated attitudes of many preachers today who would repeatedly preach from other books of the Bible over and over again but ignore or avoid Hebrews.

This study does not attempt to give full definitive answers to all of these questions.[33] It is clear that the warning passages are aimed at a congregation of born-again Christians (Heb 2:2–3), yet the author's words should be taken seriously and not be negated as if he was bluffing. Some studies have pointed out that the rhetorical nature of this sermon should serve to explain the severity of the passages.[34] It is argued that the author paints a severe picture of the consequences of backsliding, to achieve the

---

33. For a discussion of the warning passages, see DeSilva, "Exchanging Favour," 91–116; Gleason, "The Old Testament Background of the Warning in Hebrews 6:4–8," 62–91; Oberholtzer, "The Thorn-Infested Ground in Hebrews 6:4–12," 319–28.

34. Nongbri, "A touch of condemnation," 265–79, for example, points out, "The author of Hebrews employs threats of eternal condemnation using words and imagery familiar from apocalyptic literature, particularly 4 Ezra, to evoke a specific kind of fear in his audience."

intention of producing fear, shock, and warning against regression in their faith. This is correct insofar as we do not imply that he exaggerated the consequences of backsliding. He meant every word he said.

In sociological terms, the author of Hebrews is comparable to a driving instructor who is teaching a beginner how to drive. The instructor needs to warn the beginner about the dire consequences of careless driving, of losing one's concentration, and of driving while disoriented or under influence of alcohol. As we will explain in more detail in chapter three, every liminal state of transition, as was the case of the congregation in Hebrews, is dangerous. And it is important that the dangers inherent in liminality be highlighted to instill a positive sense of fear that sustains the focus and careful attention of the persons in that state. That is exactly what the author of Hebrews is doing with the warning passages. His severe warnings were all aimed at instilling godly fear that does not presume on the grace of God.

Hebrews was also persuaded that, though some members of his congregation were nearly backsliding, none had fallen into the state of which he warns them (Heb 6:9). In that respect, the warnings in the epistle to the Hebrews are even less severe than what Paul says about Hymenaeus and Alexander, whom the apostle "handed over to Satan to be taught not to blaspheme" (1 Tim 1:20). Indeed, the New Testament contains warnings and statements about apostasy similar to our author's. Jesus warned in Matt 12:31–32, "I tell you, every sin and blasphemy will be forgiven men, but the blasphemy against the Spirit will not be forgiven. Anyone who speaks a word against the Son of Man will be forgiven, but anyone who speaks against the Holy Spirit will not be forgiven, either in this age or in the age to come." John states in his epistle, "There is a sin that leads to death. I am not saying that he should pray about that. All wrongdoing is sin, and there is sin that does not lead to death" (1 John 5:16–17). Peter also speaks very severely about Christian apostates, whom he describes as "slaves of depravity—for a man is a slave to whatever has mastered him. If they have escaped the corruption of the world by knowing our Lord and Savior Jesus Christ and are again entangled in it and overcome, they are worse off at the end than they were at the beginning" (2 Pet 2:19–20). Viewed with all these other New Testament statements, Hebrews is indeed not at all isolated and these warning passages should not be "stones of offense" that turn us off from the epistle.

The Problem with the Uniting Theme of Hebrews

The final problem we need to discuss is the question of the uniting theme of Hebrews. As with many other issues in Hebrews, no consensus has been reached and some have therefore described the whole venture of identifying a uniting theme as unfruitful. Yet identification of a general idea that would help bring together the themes of the epistle is definitely helpful for application, study, teaching, and preaching purposes. Of the several proposals that have been made, we shall review four: the superiority of Christianity over Judaism, the high priestly ministry of Christ, the pilgrimage of the people of God, and some recent proposals.

The Superiority of Christianity over Judaism

Perhaps the oldest and commonest approach to Hebrews was to regard it as a sermon that extols the superiority of the Christian religion, its covenant, and spiritual benefits over that of Judaism. Since the author focuses, at least in the first ten chapters, on demonstrating the superiority of Christ as the mediator of the new covenant, and the better benefits that accrues from his superior ministry, it has been assumed that perhaps there was a major problem in this congregation related to understanding and accepting the nature of Christianity over against their former religion. The apostasy that the author so feared was imminent within his congregation and against which he desperately warns them, was basically a slide back into Judaism and its rituals. The whole sermon was therefore an enterprising effort to avert this defection.

On the surface of it, this argument is plausible. The author immediately plunges into comparisons. The former revelation is pitted against the new and final revelation in Christ. It was a common belief that the angels were the mediators of the Ten Commandments on Mount Sinai and are hence compared with Christ, the mediator of the new covenant law. Moses and Aaron were the first people through whom the former covenant was initiated and are also similarly compared with Christ. In addition, it is clear from other parts of the New Testament, the epistle to the Galatians in particular, that there were defections of Christians back into Judaism during the first century. It is therefore quite possible that there was a similar scenario that our author addresses with his sermon. If this was the purpose of Hebrews, then we could assume that the uniting theme of Hebrews is to show how Christianity is superior to Judaism.

Despite its popularity, this approach to Hebrews does not do the whole book adequate justice. Though the comparisons are strong, they do not seem to suggest at all that Judaism was what the author was pitting Christianity against. If that were so, then by ignoring some of the major faults of Moses and Aaron in these comparisons, he would not have sufficiently achieved his purpose. Rather than denigrating Judaism, the author actually saw many of its giants as heroes of the same faith as Christianity (Hebrews 11). His language of comparisons does not sound as those of a person who was attempting to exclude Judaism but rather seeking to include it under the "new faith" in Jesus. He took pains to demonstrate that Jesus and Moses were in the same household together with his hearers (Hebrews 3), and even though Jesus, being the Son over the house, has obtained more glory than Moses, Moses was also of some glory.

Moreover, the author's warnings in the exhortational parts are so severe in tone that his rather mild treatment of Moses and Aaron would suggest that the comparisons were not aimed at showing the inferiority of Judaism rather than its continuity into Christianity. Then also, the author's concerns in the exhortations, especially in Hebrews 11–13, are to spur his congregation on to move forward in faith, persevering to the end, rather than warning against backsliding. He does not pit Christianity against Judaism in these crucial parts of the sermon. This approach is therefore not sufficiently adequate to account for the epistle's themes.

The High Priestly Ministry of Christ

A second approach is to regard the high priestly ministry of Christ as the uniting theme. Though the doctrine of the intercessory ministry of Christ at God's right hand is not unique to Hebrews, the title and the sustained exposition of it are distinctive to the epistle, and hence it has been suggested that the whole endeavor was to expound on this doctrine. According to Moule, this doctrine "draws together the theology of the Epistle and gives it its distinctive character."[35] The author signals his intention to do this exposition as early as Heb 1:3 where he refers to the "purification of sins" by the Son. He does not, however, call Jesus high priest until Heb 2:17, briefly and in passing, and then again in Heb 3:1. Not until Hebrews 5 does he start to systematically deal with this subject.

It does, therefore, appear that if this was his central theme, he was being cautious and careful in approaching it. The doctrine was perhaps the "solid food" (Heb 5:12) that was hard to be explained to his hearers. In this regard, the main concern of Hebrews should be seen as that of worship, the Christian way of worship, which is different from that of

---

35. Moule, "Sanctuary and Sacrifice," 37.

Judaism. In emphasizing the high priestly ministry of Christ, Hebrews teaches the new and confident access that our Lord provides us into God's very presence. The glorious honor of Christ is being expounded so that we who follow him will continue to have confidence and "worship God acceptably" (Heb 12:28). The epistle's extensive use of the Jewish Psalms of worship, Ps 95 and 110 in particular, indicates this emphasis on worship in Hebrews. Thus Pfitzner's comment is right, "Every climactic point in the Letter is a statement about worship."[36]

If however, the high priestly ministry of Christ was the author's central motif, what connection does it have with the exhortations and the harsh warnings? How should we also connect Hebrews 11–13 to the theology of the high priesthood of Christ? These questions and many more have not been adequately answered.

The Pilgrimage of the People of God

A third approach is to employ the theme of pilgrimage of the people of God to heaven as the uniting theme of Hebrews. This idea was long recognized by the early eastern Christians as predominant in Hebrews and in a culture where the concept of the soul's journey through this world to God has always dominated its theology, Hebrews was very much loved in the eastern world. This theological consideration was, however, not that popular in western Christianity until 1938 when Ernst Käsemann first noted that the "*Wandering People of God*" is "the principal motif"[37] in Hebrews. His argument was particularly centered on Hebrews 3–4 where there is a sense of lack of progress in Israel's charge toward the promised land and in its place, an aimless wandering in the desert. However, Käsemann's postulate that Hebrews derived this concept of wandering from a Gnostic theology was clearly incorrect.

Barrett refined this concept and noted that the epistle emphasizes the eschatological *movement* of believers toward heaven.[38] Hebrews 11–13 in particular is filled with this theme. Terms and phrases like "stranger in a foreign country" (Heb 11:9), "promised land" (Heb 11:9), "from a distance" (Heb 11:13), "aliens and strangers on earth" (Heb 11:13), "looking for a country of their own" (Heb 11:14), "longing for a better country—a heavenly one" (Heb 11:16), "reward" (Heb 11:26), "wandered in deserts and mountains" (Heb 11:38), "promise" (Heb 11:39), "run with persever-

---

36. Pfitzner, "*Hebrews*," 28.
37. Käsemann, "*Wandering People of God*," 1984.
38. Barrett, "The Eschatology of the Epistle to the Hebrews," 1954.

ance" (Heb 12:1–3), "you have come to Mount Zion" (Heb 12:18–24), "here we do not have an enduring city, but we are looking for the city that is to come" (Heb 13:14), and "outside the camp" (Heb 13:12–13) all reinforce this theme of pilgrimage in Hebrews.

Even though the movement motif is prominent in Hebrews, it is not clear that this is best represented by the pilgrimage metaphor. The cultic events that are emphasized by Hebrews, unlike those of pilgrimage, have already occurred. And even when some elements of rituals are referred to, they involve what Christ has done on behalf of the cultic community rather than what the community was supposed to do. Theirs was merely to enter the *space* where Christ ministers and receive the grace and help that accrues from his cultic achievement on their behalf. Similarly, whereas in Hebrews the major event for which the movement begun (i.e., the sacrificial death and exaltation of Jesus) was in the past, in the pilgrimage motif the major event is usually in the future. In addition, the people of God will also not return from their pilgrimage but will forever be in the eternal presence of God at the end of their movement.

The major drawback to seeing pilgrimage as the uniting motif is that it does not adequately fit the expositions with the exhortations. Even though Isaacs has suggested that the expositions deal with the pilgrimage of Jesus, whereas the exhortations deal with the pilgrimage of the people of God,[39] the expositions are too static to demonstrate any movement or pilgrimage motif. In addition, how do the comparisons within the expositions fit with the pilgrimage theme in the exhortations? What roles do sacrifice, covenant, and tabernacle have to play in the pilgrimage theme?

The movement motif of Hebrews, as we shall demonstrate in chapter five, is best represented by the notion of migration rather than pilgrimage. The author of Hebrews has employed the migration of the camp of God's people as a parable, with Jesus as its "Moses" and "Aaron," leading them to the promise. This approach will also explain the significance of the rituals of sacrifice and covenant in the epistle.

Some Recent Proposals

New interpretive approaches in biblical studies have helped uncover some other themes in Hebrews that have been suggested as uniting the theology of Hebrews. Using insights from rhetorical criticism, Koester has suggested that the theology of "Perseverance in Suffering" could unite the teaching of the epistle. He proposes that the comparisons in the expositions point

---

39. Isaacs, *Sacred Space*, 1992.

to the greater glory of Christ who also persevered and is now seated at God's right hand.[40] The exhortations are therefore aimed at encouraging the despondent believers to continue in faithful perseverance. This is a helpful approach, but does not sufficiently explain the comparisons and the emphasis of the high priesthood of Christ. By what criteria has the author chosen the angels, Moses, Joshua, and Aaron as persons to be compared with Jesus? Why did the author compare Aaron with Jesus, for example, since he makes no clear reference to Aaron's suffering?

DeSilva has, on the other hand, employed concepts from social anthropology to examine the epistle. He has suggested that because first-century Mediterranean societies were honor based and operated according to a patron-client paradigm, the author of Hebrews exhorts the congregation to look unto Jesus who despised the shame of the cross and follow his example.[41] The higher "court of heaven," in DeSilva's words, assessed Jesus and exalted him to God's right hand. We should similarly despise this world's shame and honor, and rather seek the glory that comes from the heavenly court. By being at God's right hand, Jesus provides us with the ultimate access to God's blessings and despite the various covert and overt pressures that believers are subjected to, there is no reason to conform to this world. Notwithstanding the ingenuity of DeSilva's proposal, a number of scholars[42] have rightly pointed out that the patron-client paradigm does not fit the way the theology of Hebrews is shaped and thus his application appears strained.

Isaacs employed the phenomenological approach to examine the references to various spaces in Hebrews.[43] With the basic assumption that Hebrews was written after the destruction of the Jerusalem temple in AD 70, Isaacs argues that the epistle was designed to show that Christ our high priest ministers in a better, permanent, and indestructible sacred place in heaven. The epistle at once consoles the dejected Jewish Christians who have lost the temple and at the same time points them to the eternal tabernacle above. Jesus, who has progressed through his own pilgrimage on

---

40. Koester, "Hebrews, Rhetoric and the Future of Humanity," 103–23.

41. DeSilva, *Perseverance*, 2000.

42. For example Malina, in his review of DeSilva's, "Despising Shame," 378–9, comments that DeSilva's interpretation of the patron-client paradigm as applied to Hebrews does not take into full consideration the "social systems, institutions and values, much less the specifics of social sanctions and patronage" of the community behind the epistle.

43. Isaacs, *Sacred Space*, 1992.

earth, now invites us to follow him to enter into the presence of God in this tabernacle above.

We will return to Isaacs' intriguing thesis later, since it employs the concept of spatiality, just as our methodology does. Although her assumption that Hebrews was written in response to the destruction of the temple is plausible, it remains unproven. References to the temple per se are completely absent from the epistle. In addition, the theory that spaces are either sacred or profane, though it remains a popular concept in religious and biblical studies, as we shall later demonstrate, is very much disputed and regarded as an outdated interpretation in the social sciences today.

Conclusion

Evidently questions remain unanswered with regard to this epistle. Hebrews' historical, social, and cultural background is not clearly delineated, even though the developmental history of the congregation is now better understood. There is a general agreement regarding its literary genre as a sermon and its literary structure as composed of alternating expositions with exhortations. It does appear to me, however, that the theological and interpretive significance of Vanhoye's identification of the chiastic structure of Hebrews has not been sufficiently explored. In this book, we propose that this structure does indeed provide some indication of how we may understand and interpret the epistle.

The warning passages have also remained a matter of theological challenge, even though the epistle, in that regard, is clearly within the mainstream of early Christian theology. The challenges the epistle throws up are nevertheless to our advantage because they have stimulated more and more inquiries and re-examination. This study is another of those inquiries, which perhaps takes advantage of all the previous proposals, but approaches the epistle by examining its spatial references. In the next chapter, we will detail the methodology of spatiality and how we may apply it in biblical studies.

3

Spatial Analysis of a Biblical Text

MOST OF the thought units of the epistle to the Hebrews are expressed using spatial references, expressions, and metaphors. In Hebrews 1, the author compares Jesus to the angels in heaven. In the expositions of Hebrews 2, Jesus is compared with the angels in relation to the devil, the whole creation, and humanity in the "world." In Hebrews 3, he is compared with Moses in the "house of God," and in Hebrews 5–10, he is compared with Aaron in the Holy of Holies. In each of these sections it is the *space* concerned that controls the argument and theology of the author.

The exhortations of Hebrews are similarly expressed with language that depicts *movement* (combination of space and time) and *orientation* in the direction of movement. In Heb 2:1–4, he warns the congregation not to "drift away"; in Heb 3:7–4:11, he encourages them to "enter" or "go in"; in Heb 5:11–6:12, he chastises them for not "leaving" to "go on" to perfection; in Heb 10:19–39 he exhorts them again to "enter" and "draw near" and not to "shrink back." His intense warnings and frequent reminders of their past history are all aimed at realigning or *re-orienting* them in the correct direction of movement.

Though the exhortations of the later half of the epistle in Hebrews 11–13 are framed by the Christian virtues of faith (Hebrews 11), hope (Hebrews 12), and love (Hebrews 13), these virtues are also expressed with spatial language and movement metaphors. Faith is explained as a "movement" toward God (Heb 11:6), while one is "looking forward to" (Heb 11:10) or "thinking of" (Heb 11:15) or "longing for" (Heb 11:16) the "city" (Heb 11:10) and "the country" (Heb 11:15) that God has prepared for his people. Hope is similarly expressed as "running the race with perseverance" (Heb 12:1), while the "eyes" are fixed on Christ. Similarly in Hebrews 13, the church is depicted as a community of priestly followers of Christ who are exhorted to "go to him outside of the camp" (Heb 13:13).

Ideas of "*space*" and "*movement*" clearly permeate and dominate the whole language of the epistle to the Hebrews. Understanding these spatial and movement references is the key to unlocking the epistle to the Hebrews. This is not surprising, for human thought is often patterned according to spatial, as well as temporal, coordinates. Immanuel Kant, the nineteenth century philosopher, described space as an *a priori* concept that humans employ (together with other *a priori* concepts such as time) to structure, systematize, and understand their experiences.[1] Stephen Toulmin, the British sociological philosopher, has similarly described *space* as the "intellectual scaffolding" on which people build their understanding of the world.[2]

In line with modernity's way of thinking, however, Christian theology has tended to privilege the temporal sequencing of arguments and narratives over their spatial arrangement. Needless to say, this contributes to inadequate understanding and appreciation of the richness of the Bible. This lack of appreciation is one of the reasons why the spatial phenomenon in the argument of Hebrews has not attracted much attention. Yet the spatial references in Hebrews act as the framework, the "intellectual scaffolding," on which the author unfolds his argument. We will best be able to understand the epistle if we have the methodological tools[3] that are able to analyze how spatiality operates in a Bible passage. Spatiality is the paradigmatic framework which employs several theories on spaces and places from different academic disciplines, spanning philosophy, physics, archaeology, architecture, anthropology, sociology, political science, geography, linguistics, literary criticism, mathematics, critical theory, film and theater studies, theology, and biblical studies, to name just a few, to study

---

1. Kant, *Critique of Human Reason*, 1929.

2. Toulmin, "Cosmopolis," 116–17.

3. In biblical studies, methodology is very crucial because it describes the assumptions and the steps that the Bible student intends to use in order to answer particular questions. Spatiality as a methodology is a subtype of sociological exegesis that employs models from the social sciences to answer questions in the Bible. Like all other methodologies, it has its drawbacks—in particular because it tends to use generalized theories to apply to what is sometimes a unique circumstance in the Bible. This generalization paradoxically also constitutes its distinctive advantage because sociological exegesis presents its assumptions "up front" and uses comparisons to tease out the answers from the Bible. In so doing, it makes the methodology and conclusions much open for assessment by others. For more on sociological exegesis, see Domeris, *Sociological and Social Historical Investigations*, 215–34.

the nature of the relationships and interactions between people and objects and their places. I propose that by applying this framework to biblical studies, and in particular to the theology of Hebrews, we will be able to understand the epistle better.

In this chapter, we shall explore the use of spatial analysis for detailed study of biblical passages. We will clarify some of the sociological theories that explain the way human beings relate with their places and with each other within a given space. We will demonstrate that despite the numerous theories from different disciplines in spatiality, there is a general trend that defines the nature of humanity's interactions in spaces. We shall also explain how authors represent spaces in their works and some of the theories that will help us follow their thought patterns. Based on all these, we shall formulate a model by which we can study the spatiality of a Bible passage. References will also be made to Bible passages and scholarly work that employ the theories in this chapter.

Definitions in Spatiality

The best working definition of *space* for centuries was proposed by Aristotle, who defined it as "the innermost motionless boundary of what contains."[4] Though this definition is not adequate, it provides us with some useful characteristics of "space" worth highlighting. First, a space has *boundaries* that define it and by which it interacts with adjacent spaces. Indeed, we tend to define a space by delineating what its boundaries are and thus distinguish it from other spaces. Second, a space is always defined by "what contains"; in other words, it is what is "inside" the space that defines the character of that space. In fact, as future theories in spatiality were to emphasize, there is a very close dialectical relationship between the space and the object within it, such that the nature of the space is determined by the nature of the object contained within it. In return, the space imposes its characteristics on the object. For example, a person would normally behave differently in his or her living room as compared to when he or she is in the library.

The interaction that exists between a space and the object within it transforms it into a place. *Place* therefore describes the dialectical relationship between a space and its object. Place gives the object its position, location, and identity in space. *Position* is the loose connection that exists between the object and its place at a particular moment, whereas *location* describes the relative position of an object in relation to another object.

4. Aristotle, *Physica*, 1930 Bk. 4 Chp. 4 G3r.

Identity is the higher degree of attachment that develops between the object and its place. As we shall find in the next chapter, all these concepts are heavily utilized in the spatial language of Hebrews.

Third, Aristotle's definition demonstrates the relationship between space and time through the concept of *motion*. Motion occurs when space (and its object) changes its position and *time* is a measure of this motion. Time and space are therefore frequently used interchangeably, even in ordinary conversations. For instance, when we refer to the year, we are indicating the time that it takes for the earth to travel the distance of its orbit around the sun. The time is an indirect measure of the space of travel. The understanding of this relationship is important, for we shall find that when Heb 6:5 states that believers have tasted "the powers of the coming age," for example, the phrase "coming age" is a fusion of space and time. Similarly, in Hebrews 3–4, the author typologically interprets the *space* of the Holy of Holies as representing Sabbath rest, which describes "time eternity." Language of space and time are closely related and often used interchangeably.

Aristotle's definition of space is inadequate for a number of reasons. First, it only describes what we may call, "absolute space"; that is, it accounts only for physical and tangible spaces that we can experience with our senses. There are other types of spaces that are not material, such as the spaces on an architect's building plan or those in our imaginations and dreams. These types of spaces, what may be called imagined or virtual space or "utopia," are also very important because they constitute the way human beings think and communicate and therefore will require our competence to analyze them. In addition, "absolute space" is never really absolute, for the appreciation of a space depends on who the observer is. Different observers experience different aspects of a space. Put in a more elegant way, our perceptions of space depend on our conceptions of it. This phenomenon would be even more pronounced were we to be the "objects" within the space. Human beings relate to their spaces in different ways and this is reflected in different degrees of attachment (identity) and social relationships (locations) with each other in that space. So, for example, whereas a teenager may regard the home as a restrictive "prison," his or her parents may regard it as a place of security from the harshness of the external world.

A fuller working definition of space therefore is: *A space is an aspect of human reality that involves ideas of distances, directions, boundaries, orientation, location, and time that intimately interacts with human perceptions and conceptions of it and their relationships with each other.*

Spatiality is the academic discipline that analyzes the conditions and practices of persons and their social life in addition to their relative positions and locations with one another. What this definition of spatiality means is that to study a place, one needs to first define it by delineating its boundaries, distances, and directions and examine the conditions and practices of the persons within the place, their social relationships, relative positions and locations, and their perceptions and conceptions regarding the space. This is clearly not an easy process, especially when what you are trying to analyze is a Bible passage. It is therefore more useful for the analysis to be organized in a systematic way. The tools by which the discipline of spatiality achieves such systematic analysis of spaces are called *theories* and *models*.

Theories and Models in Spatiality

A *theory* is a statement or principle that is used to explain a group of observations and which can in turn be used to make generalized predictions about the same observations elsewhere or at another time. Though spatial theories from mathematics and physics, such as Newton's laws of motion or Einstein's law of relativity are good and employed by scientists, they do not easily transfer to analyzing human spatiality. Other theories, such as anthropological spatial theories, help to demonstrate how human beings relate to their spaces in their "primitive settings"; geographical theories highlight the relationship of physical places with each other and also of human beings with their places; philosophical theories help to analyze human ideas, conceptions, and imaginations of their spaces; sociological theories help to analyze the nature of human social relationships within spaces; and literary theories help us to analyze how spatiality influences the nature of the narratives and arguments in a text.

A *model* is a collection of theories that are related to the same phenomenon and are grouped together to construct a framework so that the phenomenon can be studied in its entirety. Instead of examining the theories in spatiality from each academic discipline, therefore, it is easier to organize the theories into four models:

1. Theories that help analyze the human-place relationship
2. Theories that help analyze the movement of human beings between places
3. Theories that help analyze human-to-human relationships within a place
4. Theories that help analyze the spatiality of a text

Theories on Human-to-Place Relationship

The two major theories discussed below, those of Mircea Eliade and Bollnow, are largely anthropological and enable a general analysis of the manner in which human beings relate to their environments in their "primitive setting."

Mircea Eliade's Sacred and Profane Spaces

Mircea Eliade (1907–1986) was a professor of history of religions whose phenomenological theory of sacred and profane spaces has, for the last fifty or so years, significantly influenced the analysis of the human religious behavior in varying environments. Eliade postulated that ancient human beings basically related to their environment in a predictable manner based on their religious beliefs. The space in which they were at a particular time was to them either sacred or profane. This distinction between spaces was fundamental to their behavior and differentiates ancient from modern human beings, who experience places as uniform, with no distinction between the sacred and the profane.

According to Eliade, a sacred space has three main characteristics. First, it is identified and isolated by the deity through a special miracle or revelation from the deity, what Eliade called a *hierophany*. Second, to indicate his or her meeting place with the deity following the revelation, ancient persons would build a special monument, usually a vertical structure such as a pole, pillar, tree, or temple, whose top is near the sky, which they believed was the usual home of the deity. This place, which Eliade called the *axis mundi*, is "the meeting point of heaven, earth and hell."[5] On occasions, the top of a mountain, being near the sky, may be the *axis mundi*; and in places where there are no mountains, the religious person builds sacred pyramids such as those of Egypt or the Babylonian ziggurats as the *axis mundi*.

Third, a sacred space, according to Eliade, is also characterized by order, which he called the *cosmos* to differentiate it from the surrounding *chaos*. The *axis mundi* becomes the center of the world for the religious person—a place of holiness, purity, and frequent pilgrimages and encounters with the deity. The religious person's world becomes organized around this cosmos in a threefold ring of temple-city-country; the temple is at the center and the country is at the periphery. To the Jew, for instance, the temple of Jerusalem, the city itself, and the whole Holy Land characterizes their cosmos. All other lands outside this cosmos were regarded as

---

5. Eliade, *Sacred and the Profane*, 12.

profane and constituted chaos. Holiness, purity, and defilement make up a radiating ring pattern from the center, so that the closer one was to the central sacred place, the holier and purer one was. In Judaism and according to Malina, "In this arrangement, the Holy of Holies marks the center of the Temple Mount, which marks the center of Jerusalem, which marks the center of the holy land, which marks the center of the world. At the center of centers, God's holy people have the opportunity to interact with God."[6]

Eliade's theory that spaces are either sacred or profane has found wide application in the theology of worship and biblical studies. It has, for example, been employed to analyze and explain the theology of the Garden of Eden, the paradise where God first revealed himself and fellowshipped with human beings. Humanity's disobedience resulted in the defilement of this space and was therefore banished to the profane and chaotic periphery. Levenson investigated the parallels between the Jewish temple and the Garden of Eden and suggested, "It is reasonable to assume that some in Israel saw in Zion the cosmic mountain which is also the primal paradise called the Garden of Eden."[7]

Indeed, this explains the many cosmic names that the Old Testament gives to Jerusalem—it is "the city of our God, his holy mountain . . . Mount Zion, the city of the Great King" (Ps 48:1–2). From here, "perfect in beauty, God shines forth" (Ps 50:2). Psalm 46:4 even suggests a link between the city of Jerusalem and the Garden of Eden: "There is a river whose streams make glad the city of God, the holy place where the Most High dwells." Moses' experience with the burning bush is another typical illustration of this concept. God's instruction to Israel regarding the proper place of worship in Deut 12:13–14, "Be careful not to sacrifice your burnt offerings anywhere you please. Offer them only at the place the LORD will choose in one of your tribes, and there observe everything I command you," is also easily explained using Eliade's theory.

In the same way, Seth Kunin examined sacred space in Judaism from an anthropological structuralist perspective and categorized them into two types: the static (e.g., the temple or synagogue) and dynamic (e.g., the tabernacle) that is detached from location and is based more on objects, people, and activities.[8] In both cases the concept of a center of worship, which focuses the entire religious quest of people, is fundamental. Isaacs

6. Malina, *The New Testament World*, 184–85.

7. Levenson, *Sinai and Zion*, 131.

8. Kunin, *God's Place in the World*, 1998.

has also employed Eliade's theory to examine Hebrews, on the assumption that the epistle was written after the destruction of the temple of Jerusalem with the aim of projecting the new and eternal sacred space in heaven where Christ ministers. In so doing, the author aimed "to move the Christians away from the hope for a restoration of the old order"[9] and to redirect their vision to an alternative sacred place (i.e., the heavenly tabernacle). To Isaacs, the theological emphases of Hebrews were an attempt to find a way to continue the faith without the sacred temple of Jerusalem.

Eliade's theory runs into major difficulties when applied to the New Testament as a whole. Bruce Malina has, for example, argued that in the New Testament church, sacred spaces were no longer fixed, impersonal spaces. "Sacred space is located in the group, not in some impersonal space like a temple. The group is the central location of importance, whether the Body of Christ, the church . . . the story of Jesus . . . becomes the portable exportable focus of sacred space."[10] That the New Testament Christian community was characterized as "house," "household," and "temple" (e.g., 1 Cor 3:16; 2 Cor 6:16; Eph 2:19, 21) illustrates how the Old Testament notion of sacred space had been replaced in the New Testament. Eliade's emphasis on the *hierophany* as the major feature of a sacred space has also been questioned by Smith who believes that, frequently, sacred spaces were chosen by human beings (rather than by deities), who through rituals consecrated them for religious use. "Within the temple, the ordinary (which to any outside eye or ear remains wholly ordinary) becomes significant, becomes sacred, simply by being there . . . there is nothing that is inherently sacred or profane."[11]

In addition, the teachings of Jesus that the true worship of God was unrelated to place as much as "in spirit and truth" make Eliade's theory less useful. "Jesus declared, 'Believe me, woman, a time is coming when you will worship the Father neither on this mountain nor in Jerusalem . . . a time is coming and has now come when the true worshipers will worship the Father in spirit and truth, for they are the kind of worshipers the Father seeks'" (John 4:21–23). When Jesus told his disciples that "where two or three come together in my name, there am I with them" (Matt 18:20), he effectively reclassified a sacred place as defined by his presence. Indeed, even in the Old Testament God continually drew his people's attention to the fact that he chooses to dwell in places, but he could not be

---

9. Isaacs, *Sacred Space*, 67.

10. Malina, "Christian Origins and Cultural Anthropology," 38.

11. Smith, *To Take Place*, 104.

contained in these or any other places. He is everywhere and all places are open to him. Solomon got his theology right when at the dedication of the temple he pointed out, "Will God really dwell on earth? The heavens, even the highest heaven, cannot contain you. How much less this temple I have built" (1 Kgs 8:27). In other words, God cannot be captured and held in one place. Eliade's theories are therefore inadequate in accounting for human-place relationships.

Space as Dwelling

In contrast to Eliade, a number of spatial theories view human conception and relationship with space as derived from its utility and human psychosocial connections to it. The German philosopher and phenomenologist, Otto Bollnow, argued that human conception of spaces originates from the complex psychosocial interaction with it as a "dwelling" or "home."[12] He defined space as a "medium" which is dialectically constructed between human physical, social, cultural, and psychological nature and their environmental conditions. This interaction produces an attachment that defines the place as dwelling or home and provides the primary spatial orientation for human beings. The daily routine in this "home," including even the bed in which people sleep, contributes considerably to this spatial attachment and orientation. Where the interaction with the space produces negative sentiments, such as fear, guilt, sadness, or disgust, a feeling of detachment toward the place results and people respond by behavioral avoidance.

A new settlement of people in a place would initially establish a central point for orientation, which Bollnow calls the "zero or fixed point." From here humans would depart and return. Other markers such as paths, rivers, and roads also provide directions in this general psychosocial orientation in space. He argued that there may be more than one zero point in a community which serve as reference points—perhaps a church building, post office, and a market—but these points are hierarchically conceived, so that one zero point is more important than the others.

Abraham's movement in the promised land using Hebron as "zero point" is one biblical illustration of this concept. It was near Hebron that God first promised Abraham to give him and his descendants after him the land (Gen 13:15). Here, his name was changed to Abraham (Gen 17:5), and this particular spot was the only place, the only piece of the promised land that he owned—where he "pitched his tent," traveled to and fro

---

12. Bollnow, *Mensch und Raum*, 1963.

from, and where Isaac and Jacob spent most of their lives (Gen 35:27, 37:14). Here Abraham, his wife Sarah, and most of the other patriarchs and their wives were buried (Gen 23:17–20, 49:30, 50:13). Abraham and his descendants therefore developed a psychosocial attachment to Hebron so that this town always carried the connotation of "home" to his descendants. This is one reason why the future generation turned Hebron into a "city of refuge" (Josh 20:7, 1 Sam 30:31). Therefore, when one reads in Num 13:22 that the spies of Israel came to Hebron and met the Anakim there, the underlying message is that Israel's soldiers came "home" to their father's house and found it occupied by strangers.

Bollnow also suggested that human psychological conception of space goes through four developmental stages: There is an initial primary spatial confidence, followed by fear of homelessness that gives the feeling of being lost. The institution of the "house" is hence established to provide the needed security and protection from this fear. This "home" phase is then followed by a higher organizational type of security in the wider environment such as the city or country. Security, therefore, is at the heart of humankind's psychosocial relationship with places.

Bollnow's theories have recently been mirrored in the work of human geographers such as Tuan[13] and Johnston.[14] Concepts such as "dwelling," "home," "homeland," "place of birth," and therefore "identity" are fundamental determinants of human-place relationship and have been subsumed under the all-encompassing term, the *sense of place*. The sense of a place is defined by three key characteristics: the intrinsic character of the place that differentiates it from other places, the sentiments of attachment or detachment that it induces in individuals, and the communal sharing of these sentiments in relation to that place. Thus the sense of a place is a major factor in the development and stability of a society.

The concepts of dwelling and home are indeed common in both the Old and the New Testaments. In his everlasting covenant with David, God promised, "I will provide a place for my people Israel and will *plant* them so that they can have a *home* of their own and no longer be disturbed" (2 Sam 7:10, cf. Ps 132:11–14; emphasis added). This promise by God to give his people a *home* defines the whole theology of the Old Testament, for in Brueggemann's words, "Land is a central, if not the central theme

---

13. Tuan, *Space and Place*, 1990.

14. For a more extensive discussion of the nature of human-place interaction, see de Blij and Murphy, *Human Geography*, 2000 and Johnston, et al., *Dictionary of Human Geography*, 2000.

of biblical faith."[15] At its core, the theology of the Old Testament is about the promise of land to the patriarchs, the *migration* of the Israelites toward this "promised land," their initial possession of it, their struggle to keep it, their loss of it, their exile to another land, their continued reflection on it and *orientation* toward it while removed away from the promised land, and their return to it. Dwelling in this land was the basic idea that shaped and reshaped the theology of Israel so that on occasions the land related to the physical promised land where God also dwells with his people, and at other times is related to a heavenly land which is God's permanent abode and into which he beckons his people to come and fellowship with him. He himself had commanded Israel earlier on in their wilderness migration, "Have them make a sanctuary for me, and I will dwell among them" (Exod 25:8). And when Solomon eventually built the temple, he confessed in his confusion, "The LORD has said that he would dwell in a dark cloud; I have indeed built a magnificent temple for you, a place for you to dwell forever" (1 Kgs 8:12–13).

John's Gospel therefore expressed the incarnation of God in terms of this dwelling: "The Word became flesh and made his dwelling among us" (John 1:14). In Christ, God came to dwell with his people, and so became, in effect, an "immigrant" just like them, while he leads them toward his permanent heavenly home. Jesus' words, "In my Father's house are many rooms; if it were not so, I would have told you. I am going there to prepare a place for you. And if I go and prepare a place for you, I will come back and take you to be with me that you also may be where I am" (John 14:2–3) therefore makes good sense when understood this way.[16]

The sense of a place also helps to define other spatial ideas such as *urbanization, city, country, citizenship, strangers, or foreigners*. These concepts are relevant to the study of the epistle to the Hebrews. An urban area (to be distinguished from a rural area) is a geographical district that has a high concentration of human dwellings and other infrastructures, high population density, complex and varied economic activity, and more often than not a sophisticated political and cultural system. Though the ancient Mediterranean cities were nothing like the modern western city, they were clearly distinguishable from the surrounding rural agricultural settlements. As noted by Malina, "The first century Mediterranean city was really a large ruralized central place in which properly pedigreed 'farm-

---

15. Brueggemann, *The Land*, 4.

16. For other applications of space as dwelling, see Matthews, "Physical space, imagined space, and lived space," 12–20; Balch, "Rich Pompeiian Houses," 27–46; and Santiago, "Domestic Space" 69–81.

ers/ranchers' displayed and employed their unbelievable wealth in competitions for honor among one another."[17] They contained large houses, temples, palaces, theaters, gymnasia, warehouses, and libraries. Because of its higher development, cities may (though not always) continue to attract more populace, either on temporary bases for employment and other reasons or even permanent residence, thus resulting in continued expansion.

The countryside surrounding a Mediterranean city was more or less the territory of that city, with frequent movement of people between the two. Moreover, because of its complex political, cultural, and economic organization, many residents of the city develop strong attachment, pride, and shared identification with it that is equivalent, at least in the ancient Mediterranean sense, to citizenship. In addition, some of the larger cities, such as Rome and Jerusalem, acquired primacy over other cities, and were thus described as "metropolis," (i.e., "the mother city,") to which every citizen, wherever they were in the empire, belonged. The metropolis was the nerve center of the ethnic and religious identity of a people. Philo, for example, described Jerusalem (in contrast to Rome) as a metropolis for the several million Jewish immigrants scattered all over the Roman Empire[18] (see also Acts 2:11). The psychosocial attachment to a city hence constitutes the citizenry's vision or ideal, and becomes the philosophy that drives its people. A city is, for that matter, always a combination of real, imagined, and utopic space, and represents the civilization, aspirations, and dreams of its citizens. A city is symbolic and defines its people.

The concept of the city has important relevance in biblical studies. It is remarkable that the first human settlement to be called a city was built by Cain (Gen 4:17), after he had renounced God and "went out from the LORD's presence and lived in the land of Nod, east of Eden" (Gen 4:16). The Bible is here noting how Cain's rejection of God's government was complete. The Garden of Eden was the "City" that God had built for humanity, where his presence (i.e., his government) was to be perpetually. Cain instead chose to leave God's presence and go to the land of Nod, East of Eden. The name Nod is derived from the Hebrew word which means "wandering" and "East of the Garden of Eden" was where God had earlier placed the cherubim with the flaming sword to prevent access to the garden (Gen 3:24). Cain's building of a city was therefore a symbol of humanity's open rejection and defiance in the face of God's rule.

---

17. Malina, *The New Jerusalem* Minnesota, 31.
18. Philo, *Flaccus*, 281.

Similarly, God had good reasons to view with apprehension the decision of the people of Babel after the flood in Gen 11:4, to "build ourselves a city, with a tower that reaches to the heavens, so that we may make a name for ourselves and not be scattered over the face of the whole earth." These men and women of the plains of Shinar were attempting to set up a civilization whose aspirations and philosophy opposed and affronted Jehovah God. Abraham, on the other hand, rejected this human quest for a civilization whose ethos was against God's, and instead, in the next chapter of Gen 12, he began "looking forward to the city ... whose builder and architect is God" (Heb 11:10). Abraham moved in the opposite direction to Cain.

Human psychosocial attachment to a city represents an attachment to an ideal, to a culture, civilization, and social vision, to a philosophy, and to a system of government. Christians, by their commitment to the Lord Jesus Christ, consequently look for a different kind of city and so live in this world as strangers whose citizenship is from heaven (Phil 3:20) while "looking forward to the city with foundations" (Heb 11:10). This is the city that, according to Rev 21, has the "Lord God Almighty and the Lamb are its temple" (Rev 21:22) and which "only those whose names are written in the Lamb's book of life" (Rev 21:27) will enter.

The concept of "city" also transfers to the metaphor of kingdom, which the author of Hebrews, following Jesus' example, employs to explain the realm of God's rule.[19] According to Hebrews, therefore, Abraham and the other faithful migrants of Hebrews 11–12 set for themselves a different agenda to search for a different life in God's presence, a different city that God himself has built. It is evident from the above discussion that spatial concepts heavily influence the language of Hebrews.

Theories on Human Movement between Places

Another aspect of spatiality that influences the language of Hebrews is in relation to human *movement* between places. Indeed, a large amount of religious concepts are expressed with the use of metaphors of movement. The most powerful, memorable, and often repeated sayings of Jesus are active movement verbs such as go (e.g., Matt 28:19), send (e.g., John 20:21), follow (e.g., Matt 4:19), come (e.g., Matt 11:28), etc. Similarly, metaphors of spatial orientation such as up (e.g., Matt 5:1), down (e.g., John 6:33), left and right (e.g., Matt 20:21), below and above (e.g., John 8:23), and orientation prepositions that connect people and places such as between

---

19. See Moxnes, *The Economy of the Kingdom*, 1988.

(e.g., Luke 16:26), with (e.g., Matt 12:30), through (e.g., John 1:17), into (e.g., John 3:19), unto (e.g., Rom 1:16), from (e.g., 2 Tim 2:19), and in (e.g., John 10:9) are all very common *movement* and *orientation* terminology that are used to express biblical faith and powerfully influence our response to the word of God.

One of the reasons why the epistle to the Hebrews is a very forceful, inspiring, and motivating epistle is the abundance of *movement* and *orientation* metaphors such as "come boldly" or "approach" (Heb 4:16), "draw near" (Heb 10:22), "leave" (Heb 6:1), "go on" (Heb 6:1), "enter" (Heb 4:11), "high" (Heb 1:3), "right hand" (Heb 1:13), and "higher" (Heb 7:26). We therefore need a consistent system that will enable us to interpret these movement metaphors in order to grasp the epistle's message. We shall briefly examine the nature of human movement, from the cognitive and the sociological perspective, in order to understand how such metaphors operate. Following that, we shall discuss two commonly employed root metaphors of movement (i.e., pilgrimage and migration).

Movement and Spatial Orientation

The movement of a person may be defined as his or her change of *location* relative to other places over time through the use of spatial *direction* and *orientation*. Location refers to the relative position of the person in space in relation to other persons and places. Direction of movement, on the other hand, refers to a specific route between the person's original position and his or her intended destination. The spatial orientation of a moving person refers to the process of *alignment* in relation to the specific direction of movement. Orientation is a way of describing how the moving person is progressing toward the destination and where he or she is in relation to the specific route that he or she should take. Orientation therefore requires the mental processing of *sensory perception* from the environment.

Since the moving person's location constantly changes, *orientation* is required as a continuous process of alignment (by constantly responding to the sensory perception from the environment) to enable the person keep to the *direction* of travel and to arrive at the intended destination. The role of sensory perception in this spatial orientation is, for that matter, fundamental. In humans, all the input from the five major senses—sight, hearing, taste, touch, and smell—are processed in the brain to provide this alignment. The first two of these sensations (i.e., sight and hearing) in particular serve as rich sources of biblical metaphors related to the orientation of the believer as a person on the move. The Bible, for example, expresses revelation with the metaphor of sight or insight (e.g., Matt 13:14–15) and obedience to God as "hearing" or paying "heed" to God's word (e.g., Rev 13:9). These metaphors of sensory perception demonstrate the essential orientational roles of the word of God and faith in the life of a Christian.

The lack of sufficient sensory input or wrong interpretation of any of these sensations results in disorientation. Darkness is therefore a disorienting environment and is commonly used as a biblical metaphor for being lost and lacking God's enlightenment (e.g., Matt 6:23, Luke 11:36, 2 Pet 1:19). Similarly, blindness is used as a metaphor for spiritual ignorance (e.g., Matt 23:24), so that in parts of the Gospels (e.g., Mark 10, John 9), the healing of blind persons is linked with Jesus' call to discipleship. Being a disciple of Christ is a call to follow him who is "the way" by looking to him and listening to his voice. In Hebrews we shall find that our author emphasizes the role of God's word in providing specific direction and faith in providing orientation in relation to this direction in the believer's journey to the promise.

Movement and Liminality

From the sociological point of view, human movement may be analyzed by employing the concept of liminality. Arnold van Gennep, who analyzed rituals and rites of passage using the metaphor of movement, first proposed this concept.[20] Liminality, he pointed out, accompanies any change of place, state, or even age. He also indicated that all such transitions might be analyzed in three sequential phases: the separation or pre-liminal phase, the liminal phase itself, and the aggregation or the post-liminal phase.

The social anthropologist, Victor Turner, developed these concepts further and defined liminality as a transitional phase in life, during which a person abandons his or her old identity and dwells in a threshold state of ambiguity, openness, and indeterminacy. The word "liminal" is derived from the Latin "*limen*," which means threshold. "During the Liminal stage, the between stage, one's status becomes ambiguous; one is 'neither here nor there, one is betwixt and between all fixed points of classification . . .'"[21] People in liminality tend to experience a sense of togetherness, comradeship, lowliness, and non-hierarchical homogeneity, which Turner called *communitas*. They also tend to be marginalized in society, either as minority groups or certainly separated by some means from the wider community.

---

20. van Gennep, *Rites of Passage*, 1961.
21. Turner, "Margins and Poverty," 232.

The liminal phase is particularly dangerous because of the disorientation, ambiguity, and instability it produces. It is filled with difficulties, fragility, risks, and hazards because the ambiguities are not well tolerated. As stated by Douglas, "Danger lies in transitional states, simply because transition is neither one state nor the next. The person who must pass from one to another is himself in danger and emanates danger to others . . . To have been in the margins is to have been in contact with danger."[22] The instructions that are given before one enters the liminal period therefore tend to underscore these dangers and are aimed at instilling a positive sense of fear that will help *liminas* to maintain their concentration and therefore orientation during the movement. To the uninitiated, these warnings may sound as if they are exaggerations, but attention to them is fundamental for survival during the movement.

In an examination of 1 Cor 10:1–12, where Paul discusses the experiences of the Exodus generation, Oropeza has cogently argued, "It was during the Israelites' wilderness trek that the conceptions of liminality and *communitas* affected the social and religious values of the people in a religious way," and that Paul's stern warnings of apostasy were a reflection of the liminal status of the Corinthian believers.[23] It is suggested in our study of Hebrews that the same sociological situation of liminality also applied to the congregation who first received the epistle.

Pilgrimage and Migration as Root Metaphors

Two types of human spatial movement that are most commonly employed as religious metaphors are pilgrimage and migration. A pilgrimage is a journey by a person to a sacred place or shrine for religious or cultic purposes. In Eliade's terminology, therefore, pilgrimage is a journey from the profane chaotic periphery to the cosmic sacred center for an encounter with God. Partin, using the Muslim *hajj* as template, has noted four constituent elements of a pilgrimage: (i) separation from the origin, (ii) journey to a sacred place, (iii) a fixed cultic purpose for the pilgrimage, and (iv) experience of hardship as part of the journey.[24] The pilgrim's voyage itself may be conceived of in four stages: the initial *separation* or leaving "home" is followed by a period of *liminality* that precedes *entrance* to the sacred place for encounter with the deity and then the pilgrim's *return* as a transformed person back home.

22. Douglas, *Purity and Danger*, 119–20.
23. Oropeza, "Apostasy in the Wilderness," 75.
24. Partin, *The Muslim Pilgrimage*, 1967.

As pointed out in the previous chapter, the theology of Hebrews has been interpreted using the concept of pilgrimage. From Käsemann to Barrett and Isaacs, it has been stressed that the exhortations of Hebrews 3–4 and Hebrews 11 are dominated by this pilgrimage theme. Isaacs's interpretation goes further to suggest a historical context (i.e., the destruction of the temple of Jerusalem in AD 70) as the reason for the author's emphasis on the theology of pilgrimage.

Though it has generally been assumed that pilgrimage theology does indeed exist in Hebrews, commentators have emphasized that this does not act as the uniting theme. Johnsson has, for instance, pointed out that despite the presence of the pilgrimage theme in Hebrews, the epistle also contains other features. "In at least three significant points—the figure of Jesus, the nature of the goal, and the concern with an event in the past—Hebrews cuts its own path . . . Christianity in Hebrews is set forth in a variety of ways and we should not claim too much for the pilgrimage idea."[25] For the Christian in Hebrews, the major transformation that encapsulates the pilgrimage theme has already occurred, and the movement is not aimed at seeking a transformation as much as moving toward a permanent place from which there will be no return. Plainly, Hebrews contains considerable data depicting movement, but this is not sufficiently explained by the metaphor of pilgrimage.

We suggest that it is the geographical model of *migration*, not pilgrimage, which better explains the movement theme in Hebrews. According to *The Dictionary of Human Geography*, migration is a "permanent or semi-permanent change of residence of an individual or group of people."[26] Of the several theories of migration that examine the separation of immigrants from their origins, the simplest is Lee's theory in which he delineated the factors influencing migration as dependent on various "pushes" and "pulls" from the origin and destination.[27] "Push" forces such as war, famine, forced human trafficking, flooding, etc., combine with "pull" forces such as liberation, better climate, employment and socioeconomic lifestyle, and family factors to influence the flow of people from one place to another. Like the pilgrim, the migrant goes through the stages of separation, liminality, and entrance into a host country where he or she resides. Unlike the pilgrim's separation, however, the departure of the immigrant, in most cases, is a complete physical severance from the source

---

25. Johnsson, "The Pilgrimage Motif," 247–48.
26. Johnston et al., *The Dictionary of Human Geography*, 504.
27. Lee, "A Theory of Migration," 47–57.

with no intention of return. It is true that the pilgrim's departure from home may be accompanied by ceremonies that resemble funeral rites, but the immigrant's separation from origin constitutes an actual transformation in status. The immigrant may thus be truly said to have died to his or her origins.

The stage of liminality during migration is similar to that of pilgrimage, even though in the case of the immigrant, liminality may extend throughout the period of settlement in the host country and perhaps may never terminate. In addition to the immigrant's social status of liminality—of *communitas*, marginality, and indeterminacy—the migrant experience is also characterized by a peculiar sense of place, of disorientation and consciousness that has been described by social scientists as "diasporic." The migrant may feel "in place" but not at "home." The term "Diaspora" has in recent times acquired significant metaphoric connotations and, according to Safran, is now used "more and more for displaced people who feel, maintain, invent or revive a connection with a prior home."[28] This connection with a prior home tends to orient their psychological, social, and cultural behavior in the host country so that in many respects, the immigrant maintains a different identity from the native person.

The maintenance of this identity also relies, to a large extent, on a *collective memory* linked to the historical experience of the separation from origins by the founders and the journey so far. Often this collective memory is in the form of a historical narrative of the circumstances of separation and the challenges and difficulties of liminality. The collective memory is a primary resource for the community's identity and orientation.[29] Communities of immigrant people seek to maintain this collective memory with repeated telling of the narrative of the separation and the experiences during the migration, and in some cases, the erection of commemorative monuments or instituting festivals to serve as *aide memoirs* for future generations. We shall later on find these concepts very useful in explaining parts of the exhortations of Hebrews.

Generally, the immigrant may not intend to physically return to the land of origin. Nevertheless he or she maintains an idealized vision of a symbolic geographical place far away that he or she regards as home and to which he or she may return. This symbolic place is often the perfect idealized form of the land the immigrant has left behind and is called "home-

---

28. Safran, "Diasporas in Modern Societies," 86.

29. For more on the role of collective memory in identity formation among immigrants, see Noiriel, "Amnesia and Memory," 367–80.

land." This homeland therefore acquires the connotations of "the city," attachment to which may define the immigrant's identity. It is important to stress that this idealized "homeland" is anchored in reality, but it is also utopic in the sense that it is an idyllic form of the immigrant's origins to which he may dream of returning. The notion of "returning home" to the immigrant is therefore an eschatological concept that provides orientation during the journey.

Throughout their history, the Israelites have been very familiar with this diasporic migrant consciousness. They were conscious of and, to some extent, idealized the nomadic migrant lifestyle of their founding fathers, the patriarchs, who lived in lieu of a future homeland that they bought into but never fully possessed during their lifetimes. The Israelites became immigrants in Egypt till their liberation under Moses. In their journey to the promised land, they had the most profound spiritual, cultural, political, theological, and social experience that constituted them as a nation in Diaspora. This experience was forever to serve as the template of the idealized liminal migrant spirit—both positive and negative for the Jews.

Their settlement in the promised land was not permanent and they soon became exiled again from this land. In exile, this diasporic migrant consciousness remained very strong and they constantly retrojected their experience into that of the wilderness. To the Jew in exile, therefore, life was always very much equivalent to that in the wilderness; being tried, tested, and prepared by God for the promised land, which was their home. Jews understood their various dispersions and migrations as "a transitory, miserable and unfavourable stay. It was understood as a preparation, an intermediate situation until the final divine gathering in Jerusalem."[30]

The first century Mediterranean region was well known for its millions of displaced Jewish immigrants. According to Elliot, "the attraction of educational opportunities (such as the university at Tarsus) and health spas (at the renowned Asclespian spring shrines) and athletic and dramatic festivals, religious pilgrimages, mass movements of deported groups, the banishment of individuals, and the peregrinations of assorted itinerant philosophers and missionaries," all resulted in significant flows of immigrants during the time.[31] The migrant and diasporic consciousness was therefore a common phenomenon among the earliest Christians, most of whom were Jewish. That the Jewish people were intimately familiar with the experience of migration and Diaspora throughout their history conse-

---

30. Baumann, "Diaspora," 317.
31. Elliot, *A Home for the Homeless*, 67.

quently made the concept a very potent root metaphor for their religious life—a concept that spilled over into Christianity.

The earliest Christians, because of the non-recognition of their religion at the time, were even more marginalized and had the worst of the "migrant condition." Christians were sometimes "excluded from voting and landholding privileges as well as from the chief civic offices and honors, they enjoyed only limited legal protection while . . . they still shared full responsibilities with the citizenry for all financial burdens, such as tributes, taxes, and production quotas."[32] It is in this sense that they developed three main migration-related terminologies to describe their diasporic state: as strangers (or aliens), foreigners, and sojourners. These metaphors themselves had double meanings, for in some respects, Gentile Christians were no longer "excluded from citizenship in Israel and foreigners to the covenants of the promise . . . but [became] fellow citizens with God's people and members of God's household" (Eph 2:12, 19). And yet on the other hand, they were to consider themselves "like a stranger in a foreign country . . . looking forward to the city with foundations, whose architect and builder is God" (Heb 11:9–10).

The Christian condition is clearly a diasporic migrant condition whose orientation is toward the heavenly homeland. A quote from *The Letter to Diognetus*, which was an anonymous letter written sometime in the second or third century AD in reply to an equally unknown inquiry about the Christian religion, fittingly describes the Christian's "migrant" condition:

> For Christians cannot be distinguished from the rest of the human race by country or language or customs. They do not live in cities of their own; they do not use a peculiar form of speech; they do not follow an eccentric manner of life . . . Yet, although they live in Greek and barbarian cities alike, as each man's lot has been cast, and follow the customs of the country in clothing and food and other matters of daily living, at the same time they give proof of the remarkable and admittedly extraordinary constitution of their own commonwealth. They live in their own countries, but only as aliens [*paroikoi*]. They have a share in everything as citizens [*politai*], and endure everything as foreigners [*xenoi*]. Every foreign land is their fatherland, and yet for them every fatherland is a foreign land . . . It is true that they are in the flesh, but they do not live according to the flesh. They busy themselves on earth, but

---

32. Elliot, *1 Peter*, 94.

their citizenship is in heaven. They obey the established laws, but in their own lives they go far beyond what the laws require.[33]

Theories on Human-to-Human Relationship in Places

Having constructed a general model on how humans relate to their spaces in terms of defilement and also in terms of dwelling, and how they move between places, we now investigate how they relate to each other in a given space. The question we want to answer is this: is there a way of predicting, in general sociological terms, how human beings would relate to each other when they are in a given place? There are several theories to aid in this investigation, but two that we will find useful and applicable to the spatial phenomena in Hebrews are by Michel Foucault and Robert Sack.

The Spatial Theories of Michel Foucault

Michel Foucault (1926–1984) was a French philosopher and one of the doyens of postmodernism whose influential works are widely applied across several disciplines such as philosophy, cultural studies, history, education, architecture, sociology, urban design, theology, literary studies, and management studies. It is important to point out from the outset that Foucault was an atheist and application of his theories to biblical studies always needs to be done with a significant degree of discernment and caution. Yet his theories have been considerably influential in shaping the social science discipline of spatiality and are of particular interest to us for two reasons: his interesting classification of spaces and his development of the social theory that links space with human interaction and relationship with each other through knowledge and power.

In his *Of Other Spaces,* Foucault classified spaces into three categories:

i. Real Places—the physical and social environment of humans
ii. Utopias—the imagined, visionary, and virtual space that is perfect and often aspirational
iii. Heterotopias—Places such as cemeteries, libraries, museums, brothels, monasteries, military camps, and theaters where real places come into contact with utopias. Heterotopias are "effectively enacted utopias in which the real sites, all the real sites can be found."[34]

33. Richardson, *Early Christian Fathers*, 217–18.
34. Foucault, "Of Other Spaces," 22–27.

Heterotopias also account for the concept of hybrid spaces (i.e., the fusion or interface between real and virtual spaces). Thus, for example, when a person stands in front of a mirror, the perception of space the person acquires is a combination of the real space in which he or she is standing and the virtual space that is at the other side of the mirror. Cyberspace is one such example of a hybrid space, where people who are logged on to the Internet connect their spaces through a virtual space. Similarly, when people conduct meetings through webcams and videoconferencing, they are interacting through a hybridized space.

The concept of heterotopia may be used to explain several Bible passages. Hebrews 12:22–24, for instance, depicts Christian worship in a hybrid space that includes living Christians, angels, and dead righteous people of God in an assembly: "You have come to Mount Zion, to the heavenly Jerusalem, the city of the living God. You have come to thousands upon thousands of angels in joyful assembly, to the church of the firstborn, whose names are written in heaven. You have come to God, the judge of all men, to the spirits of righteous men made perfect, to Jesus the mediator of a new covenant, and to the sprinkled blood that speaks a better word than the blood of Abel" (Heb 12:22–24). We shall later on use this concept to explain the comparison of Jesus with Aaron in Hebrews 5–10.

Foucault also postulated that the nature of human-to-human relationships within a space is hierarchical and is based on power and knowledge. He regarded space as "fundamental in any exercise of power" and in his major work, *The Archaeology of Knowledge*,[35] he discussed the ways in which the positioning and arrangement of individuals and groups within a space can lead to the empowerment of some to the disadvantage of others, resulting in hierarchies of power within the space. Though the exact arrangement may differ from one culture to another, each society has a way of encoding the power relationships among people gathered together in a place through this arrangement and positioning. In many societies, people nearer the "center" or "fixed points" would tend to have greater advantage and power compared to those who are in the periphery.

Foucault's understanding of "power" is much debated among sociologists,[36] but there is evidence that it changed during his lifetime from a rather negative, coercive view of power to a more positive understanding

---

35. Foucault, *The Archaeology of Knowledge*, 1969.

36. For an in-depth discussion of Foucault's view of power, see Dreyfus & Rabinow (Ed.), *Michel Foucault*, 1982.

of it. Power in the latter sense is the means by which individuals influence each other to perform certain tasks or change behaviors. It is this view of power that guides our approach in this study. Power, in this sense, is the way an individual influences other persons—the authority to effect a change in a person and so provide for that person resources that would not otherwise be available. The power that operates within spatial dimensions, according to Foucault, is coded in a hierarchical system based on proximity, distance, inclusion, and exclusion, and it is often expressed in terms of contests among the people in that space. The nearer one is to the center of power, the more access one has to that power.

When Hebrews describes Jesus as "sat down at the right hand of the Majesty in heaven" (Heb 1:3), several expressions of the spatial dimensions of power come to mind. Jesus' elevated, prominent, and right-hand position, his seating, and nearness to God are all expressions of the power relations in the heavenly realm. His power in that realm makes him ultimately the one able to effect change and influence the others there. Similarly, when he is described as Son "over" the house, whereas Moses is servant "in" the house (Hebrews 3), the greater powers of Jesus are being expressed through spatial language. Equally, by "drawing near" to the exalted Jesus in the center of power, believers are able to receive all the resources they need to effect change in their lives and circumstances.

Foucault also links the power relationship between human beings in spaces to knowledge. According to him, people use and manipulate knowledge and information to control the power dynamics in human relationships. It is here that the ideological tone of Foucault's work becomes very obvious and draws several criticisms.[37]

All spaces, to Foucault, are "simultaneously represented, contested and inverted." The contest for power among individuals is not necessarily through open confrontations but is observed, sometimes subliminally, in their behavior, attitude and the manner in which they speak with each other in public. In the Palestinian and Mediterranean societies in which the Bible was written, the most important cultural expression of the contest for power between human beings is through the *riposte* or challenge of honor and shame. This pivotal value system controlled how the ancient Mediterranean conducted his or her interactions with others in spaces. David DeSilva explains honor and shame *riposte* this way:

---

37. For criticisms of Foucault's work, which includes his exclusion of human determinism and agency, and his earlier negative interpretation of power dynamics in human relationships, see Janicaud, *Rationality, Force and Power*, 1992.

The challenge-riposte is essentially an attempt to gain honor at someone else's expense by publicly posing a challenge that cannot be answered. When a challenge has been posed, the challenged must make some sort of response (and no response is also considered a response). It falls to the bystanders to decide whether or not the challenged person successfully defended his (and, indeed, usually "his") own honor.[38]

DeSilva employed this concept to examine the theology of Hebrews and suggested that the major root of the problem with the community behind Hebrews was one of loss of honor. These Christians had "adopted a lifestyle that, in the eyes of their pagan neighbors would have been considered antisocial and even subversive." This led to their ostracism and in turn resulted in their demoralization. By providing a Christian "counter-definition" of honor and shame, the writer of Hebrews aimed at revitalizing the faith and witness of the discouraged Christians. Neyrey has also pointed out that this concept also pervades the whole of the Gospels.[39]

There have been several applications of Foucault's spatial theories to biblical studies.[40] The encounter between Adam and Eve and the serpent in the Garden of Eden (Gen 3), for instance, may be studied using these theories. Our first parents' desire for power through the tree of knowledge in the garden became a source of temptation and, ultimately, their fall from God's glory. The devil had earlier on himself been thrown out of heaven because he had desired to "ascend to heaven; I will raise my throne above the stars of God; I will sit enthroned on the mount of assembly, on the utmost heights of the sacred mountain. I will ascend above the tops of the clouds; I will make myself like the Most High" (Isa 14:13–14). Height, prominence, position, proximity to the center of power, and power itself are inextricably linked and as I shall demonstrate more fully in chapter four, they may be employed to explain the comparisons in the Christology of Hebrews. In Hebrews 1, the comparison of Christ with the angels is described in spatial terms. Whereas Jesus is "brought" (Heb 1:6), the angels are "sent" (Heb 1:14) from God's presence, and whereas the Father speaks to the Son as "you" and "I," the angels are described with third person pronouns such as "they" (Heb 1:14 KJV), as if they were not present at all

---

38. DeSilva, *Honor, Patronage, Kinship & Purity*, 29.

39. Neyrey, *Honor and Shame in the Gospel of Matthew*, 1998.

40. For example, see Strenski, "Religion, Power, and the Final Foucault," 345–67; Castelli, *Imitating Paul*, 1991; Beaudoin, "Foucault Teaching Theology," 25–42.

in this space. Likewise, the tense encounters between Jesus, the Sanhedrin, and Pilate depicted in John 18 may be usefully analyzed with aspects of Foucault's theories.[41]

Robert Sack's Theory on Human Territoriality

Robert Sack is a human geographer whose work on how human beings relate with each other in places using the concept of territoriality has found wide application, not only in human geography, but also in international relations, conflict management, geo-politics, and biblical studies.[42] Sack defines territoriality as "the attempt by an individual or group to affect, influence, or control people, phenomena, and relationships, by delimiting and asserting control over a geographic area." This phenomenon has been extensively studied in animal behavior, especially in the way birds control their nests, and is also evident in any family by the way parents exercise control of their children. By delimiting areas such as the bedroom as out of bounds to their children, parents employ territoriality to assert their authority within the boundaries of the house.

People commonly use a system of social classification and ordering in space to organize and manage the power relations. This ordering in spaces is done with the use of cultural rules (e.g., who sits where and has access to which and what information), boundary setting (e.g., certain places may be entered only by people with the requisite power and passwords), and social organization (e.g., people may be organized into different classes in a culture so as to delineate how much power is available to whom and where). Jerome Neyrey has, for instance, applied this concept to John's Gospel[43] and to explain the cultural connotations of Paul's statement that he had taught the Ephesians from house to house (Acts 20:20).[44]

Sack's model has three features. First, the way space itself is classified in a particular society has territorial undertones. Binary and opposite classifications such as private against public, mine against yours, black against white, adult against children, sacred against profane, male spaces against female spaces, etc., are all systems that enable people to claim control of their territories where they wield power. Second, the way these classifica-

---

41. For more of post-modern theories in spatiality, see Lefebvre, *The Production of Space*, 1991 and Soja, *Thirdspace*, 1996.

42. Sack, *Human Territoriality*, 1986.

43. Neyrey, "Spaces and Places," 60–74 and Neyrey, "What's Wrong With This Picture?" 77–91.

44. Neyrey, "Teaching," 69–102.

tions are communicated to outsiders also has territorial undertones. The name of the place itself, signals (such as crests and emblems), symbolic gestures, and other such behavior and attitudes all serve to communicate who has territorial claims to a place. Third, control of access to places with such devices as gates, fences, rock piles, walls, and doors helps maintain the delimitation of the space from other persons who have no power to cross the boundary and enter. We shall find, for example, that the veil of the Holy of Holies served such a function for the Aaronic priesthood, and Jesus' sacrificial death grants his people the power and the "confidence to enter the Most Holy Place by the blood of Jesus, by a new and living way opened for us through the curtain, that is, his body" (Heb 10:19–20).

All these theories on how human beings relate to their spaces and each other will enable us to fruitfully analyze a space. In biblical studies, however, we are not dealing with space as we tangibly experience it in daily practice; instead, we are seeking to analyze a literary depiction of that space. A space in reality could be different, in subtle or significant ways, when it is represented in a textual form. The situation is therefore not that simple and we need other theories that will help us analyze the representation of spaces in literature.

Theories on How Spaces Are Represented in Texts

In applying spatial theories to a text, we need to appreciate the nuances and peculiarities by which authors represent and depict spaces. Three literary phenomena need highlighting for our purposes: the phenomena of spatial historiography, spatial form devices, and spatial symbolisms (also called spatial semiotics).

Spatial Historiography

Spatial historiography describes the phenomenon whereby an author narrates an event based not so much on the chronological sequence, but rather on a series of spaces. It may serve the purposes of a historian, journalist, or a writer of fiction, for example, to ignore the actual temporal sequence of an event and rather narrate it in a spatial sequence or series. Instead of describing the haphazard movement of the actors and characters between sites, scenes, rooms, territories, or different places in the story, something that can destroy the structure and plot of the story, the writer may choose to narrate all the events that occurred in one place, then move to the next place, etc. The narrative then acquires a sense of smooth progression that is readable and understandable but which is not necessarily the actual chronological sequence in which it occurred.

The series of places serves as the theme that enables the whole story to be fully grasped rather than its chronological progression. The wilderness itinerary of Israel from Egypt to the promised land is, for instance, repeated in three ways in Numbers 20–21, Deut 1–3, and Judg 11, because, in each case, the concern was to provide a theological theme of the nature of the migration journey of God's people to the covenanted land of promise.[45] Equally, though, it has been common for the book of Numbers to be structured in temporo-spatial terms, so that Numbers 1–10 occurred at Mount Sinai, Numbers 11–21 occurred on the journey from Sinai to Moab, and Numbers 22–36 is located in the Transjordan, the whole book itself defies such a structure. The author is not so much concerned with chronological sequence as much as on the nature of the relationship between the Exodus generation and Jehovah before they rebelled and the development of the new generation to replace the old. In fact, this will prove to be one of the many similarities between Numbers and Hebrews—the first part develops the theme of failure to move on, and the second part develops the theme of faith for arriving at the promised land.

In the New Testament, Luke's narration of the historical details of the ministry of Jesus (Luke 9–19), according to a series of geographical territories that ends in the climatic events in the temple of Jerusalem, is another illustration of this phenomenon.[46] According to Luke, Jesus traveled from the region of Galilee, through Caesarea Philippi and Samaria into Judea, to Bethany in and around the region of Perea, and then, in the final weeks, he rides triumphantly into Jerusalem and heads toward the temple to cleanse it before his death. It is clear from John's Gospel, however, that Jesus made several trips to Jerusalem. Luke, on the other hand, organizes the storyline according to a "journey to the temple of Jerusalem" motif. Similarly in the Acts of the Apostles, he organizes the expansion of Christianity in radiating fashion from "Jerusalem and in all Judea and Samaria, and to the ends of the earth" (Acts 1:8), and stops his narrative in Rome, which was the center of the political world at the time. To Luke, geography was as important as history and we need to always remember that space and time have a close relationship, and one must not be privileged above the other.

---

45. See Kallai, "The Wandering-Traditions," 175–84.
46. See Filson, "The Journey Motif in Luke–Acts," 1970.

Spatial Form Devices

Another literary theory that describes the relationship between space and time in a text is Yuri Lotman's (1922–1993) concept of spatial form devices.[47] These are spatial techniques used by the author to delay or even disrupt the chronological progression of the narrative, in order to enable the writer develop the plot and characters more fully. Spatial form devices temporarily suspend the forward movement of the narrative and help expand its setting or spatial aspects. Dozeman has employed this theory to explain the way the narrative at Mount Sinai, as recorded in Exod 19–34, is "disrupted" by repetitions and interruptions by various laws and spatial descriptions, with Moses repeatedly moving up and down the holy mountain.[48] The forward movement of time is disrupted in such a way that the unappreciative Julius Wellhausen described the situation as "intolerable . . . because the course of history is interrupted."[49]

Ironically, this "interruption" is indeed the desired effect of the spatial form device used in the narrative. The reader is forced to take notice of the spatial setting of the story and not its forward chronological movement. Thus Moses' repeated movement up and down the mountain of God draws one's attention to the spatial relationships between God, Moses, and Israel. Dozeman describes the effects of spatial form devices in a narrative as comparable to an orange; "like an orange, such a narrative is structured into individual pieces—similar segments of equal value—in which the movement is circular, focused on the single subject, the core."[50]

Another example of spatial form is illustrated by the role of the Sea of Galilee in the narrative structure of the first half of the Gospel according to Mark. Mark records rapid and frequent movement of Jesus to and from this lake; from here he calls his disciples (Mark 1:16, 19, 20) and teaches and heals the crowd (Mark 4:35, 5:1, 18, 21, 6:53, 54, 8:10, 13). He made frequent trips across it (Mark 4:35, 5:21, 6:32, 8:10), and this location served as the center of Jesus' movements in this half of Mark's Gospel (Mark 7:31). Jesus' power over the elements is very much illustrated in Mark by his power over the Sea of Galilee, to walk on it (Mark 6:48) and to still its raging storms (Mark 4:39). The Sea of Galilee is evidently a spatial form in Mark and any interpretation of that Gospel needs to bring

---

47. Lotman, *The Structure of the Artistic Text*, 1977.

48. Dozeman, "Spatial Form in Ex 19:1–18a," 87–101.

49. Wellhausen, *Prolegomena to the History of Ancient Israel*, 342.

50. For more of spatial form devices, see Smitten & Daghistany, *Spatial Form in Narrative*, 1981.

its significance to the religious and socio-cultural setting of Galilee to bear on the gospel. In other words, according to Mark, the Sea of Galilee played a very important symbolic role in the ministry of Jesus.

Lotman argued that spatial form devices can have semantic and symbolic significance: "These language of spatial relations (within narrative) turns out to be one of the basic means of comprehending reality . . . the structure of the space of a text becomes a model of the structure of the space of the universe of possible meanings of signs in the narrative." Spatial form devices may consequently hold an important key that elucidates the general theme of the text in question. In Exodus 19, the stress that the spatial form makes on Mount Sinai evidently demonstrates the centrality of this cosmic mountain in the theology of Exodus and its relationship to the repeated laws. Equally, Mark's utilization of the Sea of Galilee as a spatial form alludes to Jesus as the Lord of the seas, just like his Father (Ps 107 and Job 38:8).[51] Mark has therefore highlighted the ministry of Jesus around this lake in order to provide a theme for his narrative.

In Lotman's words, a spatial form or semiosphere, as he called it, is "the universe of possible meanings of signs in the narrative." In other words, they define and circumscribe the direction in which the text should be interpreted. To put it another way, if an author focuses on the spatial depiction in a way as to disrupt the chronological progression of the narrative, it is fair to assume that the spatiality of the narrative holds the key to interpreting the text.

In this study, it is proposed that the expositions of Hebrews are spatial forms or semiosphere, which, when studied correctly, confirm that the author has used the camp of Israel as depicted in the book of Numbers as a type to convey his message. The wilderness camp and tabernacle, with its people and ministry, provided the author and us also "the universe of possible meanings" for interpreting Hebrews. If we grasp this concept, the interpretation of the epistle to the Hebrews will become less difficult.

Spatial Symbolisms

If the spatiality of a text may serve as the symbolic key to interpreting it, then we need a consistent and systematic method on how to approach this symbolic interpretation. In addition, since authors frequently employ spatial terms and phrases as metaphors and other figures of speech, we need to have an organized scheme for analysis. Take Heb 1:13 as an example, where God the Father tells the Son, "Sit at my right hand until I

---

51. See Malbon, "The Jesus of Mark and the Sea of Galilee," 363–77.

make your enemies a footstool for your feet." It is clear that "sitting" at the "right hand" of God, "feet" and "footstool" are not literal but are figures of speech, spatial signs or metaphors needing interpretation that are of semantic, cultural, theological, and biblical significance. Semiotics is the academic discipline that provides a system for interpreting and understanding the dynamics of signs and figures of speech.

Two aspects of the discipline of semiotics are important for our study in Hebrews. First, Hebrews employs the phenomenon of *intertextuality* whereby the author makes references to the Old Testament using direct citations or indirect allusions and echoes. Many of these intertextual references are spatially expressed and hence we need to understand intertextuality as is operational in Hebrews. The second aspect is the use of *spatial metaphors* in the epistle. An author does not choose one metaphor in favor of another by chance but is purposeful and deliberate in his or her choices. In choosing "heavenly city" as a metaphor for eternal life with God, or "draw near" as a metaphor for prayer, the author of Hebrews is being deliberate, and our duty as his interpreters is to find out why he chose that metaphor.

Metaphors contain clues to understanding the intentions of an author. Lakoff and Johnson have argued that human thought pattern is "fundamentally metaphorical in nature . . . the way we think what we experience and what we do every day is very much a matter of metaphor."[52] Metaphors are frequently not just replacing one group of words with another or being merely analogical constructs, but serve as guides to the rhetorical intentions of the writer. The spatial term "up" in some cultures, for example, is associated with positive sentiments such as goodness, virtue, happiness, consciousness, health, life, the future, high status, and having control or power, whereas "down" is associated with badness, depravity, sickness, death, low status, being subject to control or power, and with negative emotions. Similarly, upper parts of the human body, such as the head, are regarded more positively in some cultures than the lower parts, such as the feet.

Table 3.1 (next page) summarizes some of the commonest spatial metaphors and symbols in the Bible. Several spatial depictions also have symbolic meanings. The wilderness, for instance, has a symbolic connotation of testing and refinement, whereas the sea has the connotation of danger, chaos, and destruction.

---

52. Lakoff & Johnson, *Metaphors We Live By*, 1980.

Table 3.1: Examples of Spatial Symbols and Metaphors in the Bible

Symbol	Meaning	Biblical Examples
Tabernacle	Presence of God with His people	John 1:14
Garden of Eden	Paradise, God's presence, heaven	Isa 51:3, Ezek 28:13
Head	Leader, high esteem, honored	Deut 28:13, Isa 9:15
Race	Life in general, Christian life in particular	Eccl 9:11, 1 Cor 9:24, Heb 12:1
Way	Lifestyle, avenue, access, opportunity	John 14:6, Heb 10:20
Door	Access, opportunity	Matt 25:10, Jn 10:7, Rev 3:20
Wilderness	Test, liminality	Matt 4:1, Acts 13:18
Mountains	Revelation, divine communion, honor	Exod 19:20, Heb 12:22, 2 Pet 1:18
Valley	Judgement, decision-making, humility, danger	Luke 3:5, Joel 3:14
Right Hand	Honor, power	Matt 25:33–35, Heb 1:3–4, 13
Up	Exalted, honor	Luke 16:23, 18:31
Down	Humility, abasement	John 3:13, 2 Cor 10:4

A Model for the Spatial Analysis of a Bible Passage

Using the spatial theories that have been discussed, we now propose a model for conducting a spatial analysis of a Bible passage[53] that involves three essential steps:

53. There is a critical methodological question that needs mentioning but in passing. Is it methodologically correct to impose twenty-first century postmodern spatial theories on scriptures that were written in a different context several millennia ago? This is a fair question, which actually goes to the heart of

1. Foreground the spatial references in the text
2. Spatial analysis of the text by applying the model to the foregrounded references
3. Assessment of the influence of spatiality on the theological argument of the passage.

Table 3.2 (next page) is a summary of all the theories of spatiality that have been discussed, and together, they constitute the model to be used for spatial analysis of the Bible in our study. For illustrative purposes, I will use Numbers 13 as an example to demonstrate the model. Numbers 13 records the fateful spy mission to Canaan that eventually resulted in thirty-eight years of wilderness wandering and is important for the study of Hebrews because it is discussed at length in Hebrews 3–4. The author of Hebrews, like the author of Numbers 13, regarded the dangers facing the Exodus generation as equivalent in magnitude to apostasy. The writer therefore warned his congregation not to follow the example of the Israelites, "See to it, brothers, that none of you has a sinful, unbelieving heart that turns away from the living God" (Heb 3:12). A study of Numbers 13 will help us understand this aspect of the background of Hebrews and the nature of the Exodus generation's unbelief that made it equivalent to apostasy.

Foregrounding the Spatial References in a Text

Before conducting a spatial analysis of a passage, one needs to tease out or foreground (i.e., make prominent) all the references to spaces in that text. This requires a thorough and careful study because it is easy to skip spatial references. Place names, geographical features, and markers such as mountains, hills, rivers and lakes, weather, climate, boundaries, and bordering places are important and should be marked out. Note references to settlements, villages, towns, and cities, together with their nature and symbolic values. The use of a Bible map is invaluable in spatial studies, and to follow the narrative or argument more fully, it may be necessary to diagrammatically map out the movements of the people or the argument

the nature of sociological exegesis and has been dealt with elsewhere. Flanagan, "Ancient Perception of Space," 15–43, has, for instance, noted that the Bible-making communities, having lived in "segmentary societies," would have had similar conceptions of spaces as post-modern people, even more than their "modern" counterparts. Even if they didn't, as Cook & Simkins, "Introduction," 1999, have cogently argued, the comparativist nature of sociological studies, despite its tendency to generalize and be reductionistic, actually enhances our understanding of the Bible.

or narrative itself. Even when spatial terms are being used as metaphors or symbols, it is essential at this early stage to nevertheless highlight them.

Table 3.2: Summary of Spatial Theories of Relevance to Biblical Studies

1. The Nature of Spaces
    a. Types of Spaces: Real, Absolute, Imagined, Virtual, Relational, Visionary, Hybrid Spaces, Heterotopias, and Utopias
    b. Boundaries, Relationship with other spaces, Interchangeability of Space and Time, Motion
    c. Orientation markers such as mountains, rivers, etc.
    d. Locations, Positions, Identity, Place names, and their significance.

2. Human Relationship with Spaces
    a. Eliade's theory of Sacred and Profane Spaces
    b. Bollnow's Concept of Dwelling and Home
    c. Movement of people between places: pilgrimage and migration metaphors

3. Human Relationship with Each Other in Spaces
    a. Foucault's Concept of Contested Space based on Power and Knowledge
    b. Sack's Concept of Territoriality

4. Representation of Spaces in Literature
    a. Concept of Spatial Historiography
    b. Lotman's Concept of Spatial Form Devices
    c. The Role of Spatial Semiotics: Intertextuality and Spatial Metaphors

Also, take serious note of the people and their spaces—who they are and whether there are any particular references to the nature of their relationship with the space (i.e., any references to their positions, locations, and identity, and the nature of the discourses between them). Is the space their usual dwelling, or are they strangers in that space? Do they have particular attachment to that space? Identify references to time, spatial orientation, and movement, for they also refer to spaces. Occasionally, no direct reference will be stated in the passage about which space the author is dealing with. This is not uncommon because frequently, a space is taken as given by the author and so is not directly mentioned. Yet a serious consideration of the nature of the depiction will indicate which space the author has in mind. Take, for example, Hebrews 1 where the author does not directly mention the space, which circumscribes the comparison between the angels and Jesus. The themes of royalty, the nature of the discourse between God the Father and the Son, the references to worship, and the use of the word "sent" in Heb 1:14 all indicate that the space the author had in view in Hebrews 1 was heaven.

Table 3.3 (next page) shows how the spatial references are identified in Numbers 13. We realize immediately that the chapter is replete with these references. We have not highlighted the references to persons and their discourses to keep the table tidy, but it is important that identification of the persons and the discourses be part of the foregrounding process. The chapter can also be divided into three parts: the sending of the spies (Num 13:1–20), the description of the spy mission itself (Num 13:21–25), and the report by the spies (Num 13:26–33).

Having identified all the spatial references the next step in the foregrounding process is to collate the data together before analysis. It is clear that the chapter is dealing with the land of Canaan and how different "persons," God, Moses, the spies (both the minority and majority groups), the inhabitants of Canaan themselves, and the assembly of Israel perceived (i.e., saw, felt, and experienced) it and conceived (i.e., imagined, related to, and attached themselves to) it. The land is described in several different ways in this chapter. It is described physically in terms of its geography,[54] agriculture, economics, inhabitants and climate, and politically in terms of its occupation by other people. Conceptually it is described in terms of the way the different groups of spies identified and attached themselves to it. Theologically, it is described in terms of God's interest in it. Note,

54. See the excellent geographical analysis of this narrative in Beck, "Geography and the Narrative Shape of Numbers 13," 271–80.

in addition, the other place names in the passage, and also the references to the location of the camp of Israel in the Desert of Paran, which are not accidental information.

Table 3.3: Spatial References in Numbers 13

References to Spaces are in **Bold**, Times are *Italized*, and Movements are Underlined

13:1	The LORD said to Moses,
13:2	"Send some men to explore **the land of Canaan,** which I am giving to the Israelites. From each ancestral tribe send one of its leaders."
13:3	So at the LORD's command Moses sent them out from **the Desert of Paran**. All of them were leaders of the Israelites.
13:4 –15	These are their names: The list of spies [omitted]
13:16	These are the names of the men Moses sent to explore **the land.** (Moses gave Hoshea son of Nun the name Joshua.)
13:17	When Moses sent them to explore Canaan, he said, "Go up through **the Negev** and on into the **hill country**.
13:18	See what **the land** is like and whether the people who live there are strong or weak, few or many.
13:19	What kind of **land** do they live in? Is it good or bad? What kind of **towns** do they live in? Are they unwalled or fortified?
13:20	How is the **soil**? Is it fertile or poor? Are there trees on it or not? Do your best to bring back some of the fruit of **the land**." (It was *the season* for the first ripe grapes.)
13:21	So they went up and explored **the land** from the **Desert of Zin as far as Rehob, toward Lebo Hamath.**
13:22	They went up through **the Negev** and came to **Hebron**, where Ahiman, Sheshai and Talmai, the descendants of Anak, lived. (Hebron had been built *seven years* before **Zoan in Egypt**.)
13:23	When they reached the **Valley of Eshcol**, they cut off a branch bearing a single cluster of grapes. Two of them carried it on a pole between them, along with some pomegranates and figs
13:24	That **place** was called the **Valley of Eshcol** because of the cluster of grapes the Israelites cut off **there**.
13:25	At the end of *forty days* they returned from exploring **the land.**

13:26	They <u>came back</u> to Moses and Aaron and the whole Israelite community at **Kadesh in the Desert of Paran**. There they reported to them and to the whole assembly and showed them the fruit of **the land**.
13:27	They gave Moses this account: "We <u>went</u> into **the land** to which you <u>sent</u> us, and it does <u>flow</u> with milk and honey! **Here** is its fruit.
13:28	But the people who live there are powerful, and **the cities** are fortified and very large. We even **saw** descendants of Anak there.
13:29	The Amalekites live in **the Negev**; the Hittites, Jebusites and Amorites live in **the hill country**; and the Canaanites live near **the sea and along the Jordan**."
13:30	Then Caleb silenced the people before Moses and said, "We should <u>go up</u> and take possession of **the land, for we can certainly do it**."
13:31	But the men who had <u>gone up</u> with him said, "**We can't** attack those people; they are stronger than we are."
13:32	And they spread among the Israelites a bad report about **the land** they had explored. They said, "**The land** we explored devours those living in it. All the people we saw **there** are of great size.
13:33	We saw the Nephilim **there** (the descendants of Anak come from the Nephilim). We seemed like grasshoppers in our own eyes, and we looked the same to them."

The details of the itinerary of the spies are not provided but the borders of the land they explored are given; and the Valley of Eshcol is equally important to this story. The reference to Hebron is pivotal information, for as we have noted earlier, this spot was Abraham's "home" that he purchased—his zero point. The spies' stop in Hebron has an important theological meaning, for they actually came "home" to their ancestral land. As part of the foregrounding, note all the significant persons who are referred to in this chapter as well: God, Moses, the inhabitants of Canaan, the Anakim in particular, the assembly of Israel, and the spies (the order of their names that are listed in Num 13:4–15 is itself interesting, for this is peculiar and may well have some theological significance. So also is the cryptic reference to Joshua's change of name). Note the manner in which they speak with each other as well as what they say. The repetition of the spies' itinerary and their report should be compared for similarities and differences.

The references to movement in the chapter should also be noted. Reflect on how many times the word "sent" occurs in this passage. In addition, note how the movement toward Canaan is always described as "going up." Is that meant to describe a physical northward or uphill movement, or there is a symbolic interpretation to it? It could be both. There are very few references to time in the chapter, such as the reference to the season and the forty days. Is forty days symbolic?

Spatial Analysis of Numbers 13

After collating the foregrounded spatial references, the next step is to analyze it. Since "the land" is the spatial focus of Numbers 13, analyze how it is perceived and conceived in the narrative. God describes the land as "the land of Canaan, which I am giving to the Israelites" (Num 13:2). Not only is the land a gift from God to Israel, God was intending to forcibly take it away from the Canaanites and give it to Israel. Putting it another way, in God's "mind," in God's "geographical imagination," the land of Canaan was a contested space and he had his own battle to win in this matter.

The spies also described the land as one that "flows with milk and honey" (Num 13:27). What does this phrase mean? Noth's dismissive statement that this way of portraying the promised land was an empty "stereotype" is incorrect.[55] Three more sober levels of meanings have been suggested. On a superficial level, some think of it as referring to the agricultural fertility of that land. It has therefore been common for the statement by the spies in Num 13:27 to be interpreted as a wholly accurate report. We should, however, remember that, at this time, the Israelites were not agrarian farmers but herdsmen, and therefore an agricultural land was not primarily what they were looking for. On the other hand, it has been suggested that the expression refers to grassland suited for pasture, with thickets where wild honey was freely available. As pointed out by McCarter, the phrase had this pastoral connotation that implied "the raising of livestock and beekeeping, staple economies of the central Israelite hills."[56] When the spies therefore lifted the grapes and declared, "Here is its fruit," they were not so much confirming their expectation as much as sarcastically declaring how the land was unsuitable for the raising of livestock and beekeeping! In this respect, the grassland of the Desert of Paran from where the spy mission was launched was far better for their subsistence than a fertile agricultural land.

On a theological level, the expression describes the nature of the national rivalries, for which the land was well known. Levine has expertly shown that "the phrase is invariably used with reference or allusion to the

---

55. Noth, *Exodus*, 41.
56. McCarter, *Exodus*, 89.

Covenant" between God and Israel.[57] In Stein's words, this description of the promised land is an "evidence of a struggle, a Yahwistic counter slogan, as it were, in the continuing battle to attach Israel to Yahweh and to ward off the attraction of archrival Baal."[58] The contested nature of this land is also indicated by its occupation: "The Amalekites live in the Negev; the Hittites, Jebusites and Amorites live in the hill country; and the Canaanites live near the sea and along the Jordan" (Num 13:29). It was fully occupied. If we remember that in this culture, land was always regarded as a gift from the occupants' deity, we would appreciate that what is being described here is that the spies came into contact with various deities occupying the land that Jehovah had promised them. Coming from the lips of the spies, the statement that "the land indeed flows with milk and honey" should have infused renewed faith to join in with God in his battle against the false gods of the Canaanites. The mission of the spies was not just a military reconnaissance or a geographical exploration. They were ambassadors of Jehovah, "sent" out to prepare the ground for the transformation of the region into a citadel for the worship of God. Unfortunately, they did not perceive their duty that way.

This is why the stop at Hebron is so important to this story. The spies visited what they could truly call "home," for Abraham's cemetery in Hebron epitomized all the promises of God to the spies and their ancestors. Hebron, however, was not just, in Foucauldian terms, "represented and inverted," it was also contested. The spies "came to Hebron, where . . . the descendants of Anak lived" (Num 13:22). The descendants of Anak, or the Anakim, have been traditionally understood as giants descending from Anak who dwelt in South and West of Canaan. They are mentioned fifteen times in the Old Testament[59] and, as in our passage, were believed to be the descendants of the Nephilim. The association between the Anakim and the Nephilim brought enormous fears to the heart of the people of the ancient world who met them. This was because the Nephilim were thought to be the giant-sized offspring of the rebellious angels who were largely responsible for God's exasperation with humanity before the flood (Gen 6:3–4) when he declared, "My spirit shall not always strive with man."

---

57. Levine, "The Land of Milk and Honey," 57.

58. Stein, "The Land Flowing with Milk and Honey," 555–6.

59. Num 13:22, 33; Deut 1:28, 2:10, 11, 21, 9:2; Josh 11:21, 22, 14:12, 15, 15:14, 21:11; Judg 1:20.

A link therefore exists between Hebron, the descendants of Anak, the Nephilim, and striving with God. In perceiving themselves as grasshoppers before these giants, were the spies expressing surrender to the mythical creatures? Spiritual cowards that they were, they could not face up to what they themselves thought were demonic powers. Or were they on the other hand employing that mythical link to foment fear and rebellion among the Israelites? Perhaps the two scenarios are not disconnected. Their unbelief was related to their striving with God, Moses, and Aaron.

This "striving" with God and Moses becomes more noticeable to us when we analyze the nature of the relationships between the persons in the narrative. The passage portrays a hierarchical relationship based on power and knowledge from God, down through to Moses and Aaron, the tribal leaders, the spies, and the congregation of Israel. Moses receives instructions from God, which he duly relays and performs. He instructs the spies, but there is subversion and a power struggle, as Numbers 14 later shows. The majority group of spies manipulated knowledge and used it as a weapon in their power struggle with Moses. Among the spies themselves, we see two types of knowledge striving with each other. The majority group of spies based their report on mere physical sight: the large cities, the grapes, and the Anakim they saw. Their report had no reference to the spiritual imagination or spiritual sight that is based on God's word. They divorced their physical perception from God's promises and so did not see what God had "imagined." Their knowledge was fed purely by the natural senses, which often conflict with the spiritual. They therefore behaved like mere geographical scouts, whose interest was to use their knowledge in their perpetual struggle against Moses.

The minority group, made up of Caleb and Joshua, had a different kind of knowledge (i.e., revelation-knowledge, the knowledge that comes from God's word and feeds the life of faith). Joshua said, "If the LORD is pleased with us, he will lead us into that land, a land flowing with milk and honey, and will give it to us" (Num 14:8). Caleb and Joshua's assessment of the promised land was done through a spiritual imagination that is linked directly to God's promise and not by looking at grapes. They saw with the eye of faith what God had "imagined" and so believed his promises. In the words of the author of Hebrews, "they were longing for a better country—a heavenly one" (Heb 11:16), the promised land that God had given them to possess, and saw it ahead. The differences in perceptions of the promised land between the majority and minority group spies depended on their different conceptions of it.

Assessment of How Spatiality Influences Numbers 13

Some scholars have pointed out the "flat" nature of the narrative in Numbers 13. It gives a matter of fact presentation without making a clear-cut theological commentary on the behavior of the spies. God in Numbers 13 is said to appear silent until Numbers 14. Hence many have insisted that Numbers 13 should always be read together with Numbers 14. The matter of fact presentation, however, is only superficial. By exploring the spatiality of Numbers 13, we begin to see how it lays a strong foundation for Numbers 14. The rebellion by the congregation, God's anger in Numbers 14, and his excommunication of the Exodus generation from the promised land are now explicable.

Commentary on the incident in Numbers 13 became part of the subsequent liturgical language of Israel. Hence, in Ps 95:7–8, a temple liturgical "call to worship," the Bible admonished later generations of Israelites: "Today, if you hear his voice, do not harden your hearts as you did at Meribah." The unbelief that stemmed from striving with God, surrender to other gods, and living by carnal sight and not by the spiritual imagination of faith based on God's word was at the root of the people's failure to possess the land. The spies can therefore be said, in the words of the author of Hebrews, to have departed from the living God. Hebrews had good reasons for warning his congregation to eschew an "unbelieving heart that turns away from the living God." (Heb 3:12), for the unbelief that chooses not to be on the side of Christ is rebellious, striving, and is departing from the living God. Faith, like space, is always contested, and those who do not choose to be on God's side, who do not spiritually "look for God's country," (to borrow from Hebrews) have chosen the opposing side. This is the element of apostasy in the narrative of Numbers 13.

Conclusion

The social science discipline of spatiality has only recently been applied to biblical studies and hence in this chapter, we have deliberately chosen to be elaborate. In particular the four concepts of *spaces, orientation, movement,* and *migration* will prove to be essential to understanding Hebrews. It is hoped that this rather long detour will also become valuable for understanding and applying several other passages of the Bible in which concepts of space dominate.

Not all passages are open to spatial analysis; however, in those that spatial references dominate, a careful, systematic, and thorough approach to spatial analysis will yield much fruit. The model we have set out in this chapter uses several theories to enable this analysis to be done. Foregrounding the spatial references in the passage, exploring the various perceptions and conceptions of the spaces, and also the nature of the social relationships, the discourses, and the intertextual references to other parts of the Bible may provide beneficial information and insight. References to spatial orientation and movement are also important indexes of the spatiality of the text. In the next two chapters, we shall apply our methodology to the epistle to the Hebrews, but undoubtedly this is a model that may also be valuable to the study of other passages.

4

The Camp of God's People Around the Tabernacle

Spatial Analysis of the Expositions of Hebrews

THE AUTHOR of the epistle to the Hebrews was faced with a major challenge in writing his sermon. His congregation, who in times past had seen the powerful hand of God at work among them, was now faced with various difficulties, persecution, and harassment from the larger society, and had become despondent and lethargic in their faith. Some among them were now tempted to abandon the faith altogether. Others were at loggerheads with the fellowship and its leaders and, in their dejection and spiritual malaise, had refused to join the meetings. How does the author of Hebrews address this looming spiritual disaster among a Jewish Christian community in Diaspora in such a way as to capture their spiritual imagination, re-invigorate their faith, and so shake away their malaise and cause them to strive on toward their heavenly calling?

Insightfully, Hebrews discerned that there was a typological correspondence between his congregation and the migrant camp of Israel surrounding the wilderness tabernacle and moving toward the promised land. He therefore constructed a sermon that employed a Christological reading of this camp to draw out principles and lessons for application to the pastoral problems of his congregation. He achieved his aims in three ways. First, he structured the sermon in such a way that it followed a step-by-step typological exposition of the wilderness camp of Israel. In other words, the camp served as the "intellectual scaffolding" or "semiosphere" upon which the writer framed his message and thus made it easier for his listeners and readers to follow the argument. Second, he imaginatively placed Jesus in each of the spaces of this "virtual" camp, highlighting his status, relationships with others in the spaces, and functions. Third, this provided the basis for the "word of exhortation." He intertwined the expositions with exhortations, warning his listeners and readers not to behave as the camp of Israel did. Instead, they should re-orient themselves toward the direction of their calling and move forward to enter God's promised salvation, rest, and perfection—the heavenly city and the unshakeable kingdom. This movement was to be through faith derived from obedience to God's word, perseverance derived from hope in what God has prepared ahead for his people, and love derived from the fellowship of God's people. The whole of the epistle to the Hebrews can therefore be studied using the model of spatiality explained in the previous chapter.

In this chapter, we will demonstrate how we can best understand the manner in which the expositions of Hebrews fit together in the author's scheme by employing spatiality as our analytic tool. For ease of analysis, we have separated the expositions from the exhortations. As stated in chapter two, whereas the spatiality of the expositions of Hebrews is static and focuses on the camp of God's people, that of the exhortations is dynamic and focuses on movement (or the lack of it) of the camp. The exhortations will therefore be separately analyzed in chapter five.[1]

The expositions of Hebrews are located in Heb 1:1–14 where the space in the author's scheme is heaven; Heb 2:5–18 where the space is the world; Heb 3:1–6 where the space is the "house of God"; and in Heb 5:1–10 and 7:1—10:18, where the space is the Holy of Holies. We will demonstrate that in the author's typological scheme, the world corresponds to the camp, the house of God corresponds to the priestly courtyard and the Holy Place (both of which the author regarded as one unit), and the Holy of Holies corresponds to heaven. We will follow our three-step methodology, namely foregrounding the spatiality, spatial analysis of the passage, and assessment of the theological significance.

The Son in the Heavenly Assembly (Hebrews 1)

In Vanhoye's proposed structure of the epistle, he regards Heb 1:1–4 as an introductory statement or prologue and then groups the whole of Heb 1:5—2:18 in one section dealing with eschatological matters with the title "Christ's Situation." In its details, however, he recognizes three sub-divisions to the section, which essentially agree with George Guthrie's divisions

---

1. Of course, the whole epistle may be studied in series as it is, but separation of the expositions from exhortations makes it easier to demonstrate the author's scheme. As we suggest in chapter five, the alternating structure follows the style of the book of Numbers, in which the laws tend to be static and focused on the camp and tabernacle and the narratives deal with the movement of God's people.

of the epistle: Heb 1:5–14 is an exposition that expands on the prologue; Heb 2:1–4 is an exhortation; and Heb 2:5–18 is another exposition. Thus the whole of Hebrews 1 is an exposition, which in terms of spatiality is focused on heaven.

There is a general consensus among biblical scholars that the catena of Heb 1:5–14 is an explanation of the statement in Heb 1:4 that Jesus "became as much superior to the angels." Lane, for example, notes that there is correlation and "synthetic parallelism" between Heb 1:1–4 and Heb 1:5–14.[2] Similarly, Koester argues that the whole of Heb 1:1–2:4 is a long exordium dealing with "God's manner of speaking," of which Hebrews 1 is an expository subdivision, which is separate from the exhortatory Heb 2:1–4.[3] The whole of Hebrews 1 should therefore be considered as an extended introduction to the epistle in which the author summarizes the existing knowledge of his congregation about the status of Christ in heaven.

The Prologue of Hebrews

In Montefiore's words, the carefully constructed and alliterative prologue of Hebrews is a very rich "sonorous and distinguished prose style" that is paralleled in the Bible only by the beautiful prologue of John's Gospel and Paul's Col 1:14–20.[4] Its immediate and arresting statement of the speech of God through his exalted Son, to whom he has given a more excellent name, serves to prepare the listeners to be attentive to the coming message, and at the same time, anticipates many of the topics that will occupy our author's attention. Its allusion to Num 1:1 will also be highlighted later on in the study.

In the prologue, the author does not propose his premise or the hypothesis that he aims to explore. He only gives some clues as to what would be the major themes of the sermon. One of these major themes is the relationship between salvation history, spatiality, and God's revelation (knowledge). "In the past God spoke to our forefathers through the prophets at many times and in various ways, but in these last days he has spoken to us by his Son, whom he appointed heir of all things, and through whom he made the universe" (Heb 1:1–2). "Salvation history" (i.e., the progressive history of the saving deeds of God from the Old Testament times through its consummation in Christ and the coming eschatological

---

2. Lane, *Hebrews 1–8*, 22.
3. Koester, *Hebrews: ABC*, 85.
4. Montefiore, "Hebrews," 33.

age) heavily influences the typological interpretation of Hebrews. Scott Jr. notes, for instance, how, according to the prologue of Hebrews, "in Christ salvation history has taken a quantum leap forward. You cannot go back. To turn away from Christ is to attempt to push salvation history backwards, to reject the reality of 'the age to come' (6:4 ff)."[5]

When it comes to the narration of this salvation history, however, the author of Hebrews often does not present events in their chronological sequence but in what may appear on the surface to be rather unsystematic. The whole of the prologue is one such example of a non-linear arrangement of temporality in Hebrews. Meier has, for instance, pointed out that in setting out the "career" of the Son in the prologue, the author moves back and forth in time: "the train of thought begins with Christ's exaltation (1:2b, 1:5–6), moves back to creation (1:2c, 1:7), moves further back to pre-existence, divinity and eternal rule, (1:3a, 1:8bc), moves forward again to creation as well as governance and guidance of creation (1:3b, 1:10–12), moves all the way up to exaltation (1:3d, 1:13) and draws a final conclusion comparing Christ's exalted status to the angels' inferior role."[6] This manner of handling "literary time" in a nonlinear fashion is characteristic of an author whose interest is more on "space" than "time." Hence, in the prologue, salvation history is being narrated through "spatial" historiography rather than in a sequential chronological order. We therefore get a first indication of the prominence of spatiality in Hebrews. "Time" will be utilized to serve the author's "spatial" purposes in this epistle. This principle will be very important when he later stresses that Christ's redemptive work became completed only in heaven. In these parts of the sermon, the author freezes "time" in order to focus on space.

This is not to say that the author of Hebrews had no interest in chronological sequence of events. Indeed, in certain parts of his sermon, he is going to rely on chronological sequence to make his argument. In Hebrews 7, for instance, our author will emphasize that since the divine oath that declared Jesus as "Priest forever in the order of Melchizedek" (Ps 110:4) was made through David in the Psalms, and therefore was *after* the Levitical system had been established, this meant that the Levitical system was deemed ineffective and imperfect even at the time of David. In this particular segment of Hebrews, the time sequence was important for the argument. It is hence vital to pay close attention to our author's use of space and time throughout the whole of the epistle.

5. Scott Jr., "Archegos," 48.
6. Meier, "Symmetry," 523.

In the prologue, Hebrews makes spatial references to the Son's creative work and his territorial claims to "all things." The universe was made through him and he is now "sat down at the right hand of the Majesty in heaven" (Heb 1:3). He sits in exaltation having completed his work; he sits at God's right hand with all the power and authority of the Godhead; he sits at God's right hand in heaven, in the very presence of God; and "since that time he waits for his enemies to be made his footstool" (Heb 10:18). It is when we study the spatiality of the catena of Old Testament quotations in Heb 1:5–14 that these spatial emphases become even more evident.

Spatial Analysis of Heb 1:5–14

To buttress his point that the Son is superior to the angels, the author makes use of seven Old Testament quotations that he puts together in order to portray a scene in heaven, in which God the Father speaks to the Son in the presence of his worshipping angels. Throughout this section, the author restrains himself from commenting and lets the Old Testament speak for itself. Thompson has noted that the catena has three parts: Heb 1:5–6 contains three citations (Ps 2:7, 2 Sam 7:14, and Deut 32:43) and deals with the royalty of the Son; Heb 1:7–12 also contains three citations (Ps 104:4, Ps 45:6–7, and Ps 102:25–26) and deals with his power and divinity; and Heb 1:13–14 contains one citation (Ps 110:1) dealing with his exaltation.[7] Consideration of the Old Testament contexts of the citations is helpful. Ultimately, however, the author has employed the texts to depict a scene that blends the theology of divine sonship with messianic kingship in Christ's exaltation. The presence of these themes in Hebrews 1 has therefore led to the general consensus[8] that the catena of Heb 1:5–14 is describing the "drama" of Christ's post-resurrection enthronement, in which God presents his Son to the angels in heaven and enthrones him.

The catena not only focuses on events but also focuses on the place where the events occur (i.e., heaven). In so doing, the passage provides us some clues on the spatiality of heaven. The manner in which the Old

---

7. Thompson, "Structure and Purpose of the Catena," 352–63.

8. See Commentaries by Ellingworth, Lane, Koester, and Isaacs. This consensus is, however, a recent one. Older commentaries by Chrysostom, Augustine, Calvin, Gregory of Nyssa, Käsemann, and Attridge, for example, suggested that the catena depicts several different events in the "career" of the Son. Whether it is a single or several events, the spatiality of the catena is however the same—focused on heaven.

Testament verses are woven together without many explanations and introductions suggests that the first recipients of the epistle were already familiar with them. It appears, however, that it is the spatial significance of these already familiar Old Testament verses that may have escaped them. The author's plan, good teacher as he was, was to use this summary of familiar Old Testament verses to accentuate the spatial aspects of heaven. Even though he does not describe a vision of heaven, and neither does he detail the topography of the heavenly realm, he nevertheless points to some of the spatial features of the heavenly realm that were relevant to his purposes.

First, Hebrews portrays heaven as having territorial boundaries, whose crossing by the Son is accompanied by angelic worship. Hebrews 1:6 states, "when God brings his firstborn into the world, he says, 'Let all God's angels worship him.'" The penetration of the heavenly boundary is a common theme in both the Old[9] and New[10] Testaments. During Jesus' earthly life, it was penetrated on at least seven occasions: by the Holy Spirit (at his baptism), by angels (at his birth, transfiguration, death, and resurrection), in revelations (Mary, Joseph, the shepherds), and by Jesus himself at his ascension. Many of these breaches were also accompanied by declarations by God and angelic worship.[11] The catena also refers to another breach of the heavenly barrier by the angels (Heb 1:14), but unlike that of the Son's, this was unaccompanied by any fanfare. The breaching of the heavenly boundary will later be an important component of the author's overall message.

Second, heaven is portrayed as a throne room in which God addresses his Son as God (Heb 1:8) and praises him for his eternal creative work and his royal scepter of righteousness. The depiction of heaven as an imperial palace is another common theme in both the Old[12] and New[13] Testaments and will, again, later on be very important to the author's message. Here in Hebrews 1, the aim of the author was simply to highlight it. Shortly, he would characterize this throne as a "throne of grace" where mercy and help is always available to those who approach it (Heb 4:16). Heaven is hence not just an imperial palace, but also an imperial temple. The Hebrews con-

---

9. Gen 5:24, 28:12; 2 Kgs 2:11; Ps 24:7–10.

10. John 1:51, 3:13, 20:17; Eph 4:8; Rev 7:2.

11. Schmidt, "Penetration," 229–46.

12. Exod 17:16; 1 Kgs 22:19; Job 26:9; Ps 9:4, 7, 11:4, 47:8, 103:19; Isa 6:1, 66:1; Ezek 1:26; Dan 7:9.

13. Matt 5:34, 19:28, 23:22, 25:31; Rev 1:4, 3:21, and 4:2 ff.

gregation, it appears, did not know this cultic function of God's throne, and so the author does not elaborate on it in the catena.

Regarding the "persons" in the heavenly realm, the theme of royalty colors the manner in which the angels are depicted in Hebrews 1 as servants and messengers who worship the Son (Heb 1:6) and are sent out from his presence to minister to the spiritual needs of believers (Heb 1:14). This portrayal of a heavenly royal court of God, with his attending angels as royal servants and members of the senate or *familia*, occurs frequently in the Bible and is a common motif in the Jewish inter-testamental literature.[14] As described by Barclay, the Jews distinguished the angels of God's presence (i.e., the hierarchy of higher angelic beings, "the seraphim, the cherubim and the ofanim . . . always around the throne of God") from those who are sent out to perform various tasks.[15] Though these distinctions may have been in the author of Hebrews' mind, he was careful to include all angels in his description. None escapes the characterization as changeable royal servants and worshippers of the Son. Christ, on the other hand, is described as God, eternal king, heir, and creator of all things.

The relationship between the persons in this heavenly space is therefore hierarchical and is based on territoriality and power. In declaring the Son as firstborn and heir (Heb 1:5), God "is delimiting and asserting control over a geographic area" and at the same time is communicating "the social ordering" in this space, to borrow from Sack's terminology. This social ordering is best demonstrated by the manner in which God speaks in the catena of Hebrews 1. The Father does not speak directly to any angel in this catena, hence the author's two rhetorical questions in Heb 1:5, 14. When the Father speaks in relation to the angels, it is as a command or declaration (Heb 1:6), and is a description of the nature (Heb 1:7) and function (Heb 1:14) of angels. God refers to the angels with the third person pronoun, "they," and never with the Son's "my" and "you." In other words, the angels are talked about but never spoken to. This is one of the characteristic features of discourse that portray power relations in the Greco-Roman society. As Seneca points out, for example, slaves in this

---

14. See Gen 1:26; 1 Kgs 22:19–23; Ps 89:5–7; Exod 24:9–10; Isa 6:1–8; Jer 23:18–22; Job 1:6–12; Ps 103:19–22; Job 15:8; Ezek 1; Zech 3:1–5; Exod 15:11; Deut 32:8, 33:2; Ps 29:1; Neh 9:6; Dan 7:9–14; Job 38:1–7 and in apocryphal books such as Jubilees 30:18, 1 Enoch 71, Ascension of Isa 6–11, Songs of Sabbath Sacrifice.

15. Barclay, *Hebrews*, 21. The other functions of angels in Hebrews include mediating the delivery of the law of Moses (Heb 2:3), administering the nations in the present age (Heb 2:5), and visiting the saints (Heb 13:2).

society and especially in public functions "were normally required to curb their tongue."[16]

The authority of the Son is far superior, as he sits at God's right hand (Heb 1:4, 13). Power is being expressed here in terms of proximity and orientation. God's "right hand" is powerful (Exod 15:6; Ps 118:15–16) and protective (Ps 80:17) and it is from this privileged location that intercession is made and answered (1 Kgs 2:19). That Jesus sits at God's right hand is therefore a symbolic statement of his divinity and power. His location should induce in the angels, "a state of conscious and permanent visibility that assures the automatic functioning of power," to borrow from Foucault. Heaven, like all spaces, is "hierarchical," and God through the catena provides the reasons why the Son is better than the angels in this space. He is better because he is begotten of the Father—the firstborn Son who inherits the Father (Heb 1:5–6)—and that is why the angels are commanded to worship him. He is better because he is divine Son, everlasting king (Heb 1:8), and creator of all things (Heb 1:10), whereas the angels are created servants (Heb 1:7). He is better because he is immutable, unchanging, and unchangeable (Heb 1:11–12), whereas the angels are mutable.

The Contribution of Hebrews 1 to the Argument of the Epistle

Any proposed explanation for the flow of the argument of Hebrews must grapple with defining the role of Hebrews 1 in the epistle. Because of the relentless comparisons of Jesus with the angels, it has been suggested[17] that there was a heretic angelomorphic Christology, similar to what was prevalent in Colossae (Colossians 1–2) that our author was attempting to correct. This is an unlikely explanation since there is no clear-cut polemic against angels or any injunctions against their worship in Hebrews. On the contrary, the author's attitude toward angels was positive, even suggesting that some believers had entertained angels (Heb 13:2) in their homes. If there were a danger of angel worship in this community, such a statement would have defeated his supposed polemic purpose.

Others have asserted that the angels are one of several mediators, messengers, or "apostles" of the old covenant (including the prophets, Moses, and Aaron) against whom the writer compares Jesus. This view may seem to be supported by the reference in Heb 2:2 to the "the message spoken by

---

16. Seneca, *Epictetus*, 47.3.

17. Charles, "Angels, Sonship and Birthright," 171; Gleason, "Angels and the Eschatology," 90–91.

angels," but its premise that there was a wide divide between Christianity and Judaism at the time that Hebrews was written is unproven. Since such a wide divide was not very likely, even at the end of the first century, the polemic interpretation makes the argument of Hebrews appear "overdone,"[18] to quote from Dahms. Unlike Paul's polemics in Galatians, the author of Hebrews does not point to any specific rituals or practices of Judaism (except possibly the cryptic reference to "ceremonial foods" in Heb 13:9).

It is when we highlight the spatiality of Hebrews 1 that the significance of the comparisons to the whole epistle becomes much clearer. The manner of the presentation, with the use of a catena of Old Testament citations and very little explanations by the author, shows that, as a good teacher, our author begins his sermon by restating what was already known to his congregation. This summary acted as a foundation of what was to follow. Indeed, there is evidence that some of these Old Testament verses were employed together in those times. Thus Montefiore has suggested that the author was quoting from a "testimonia" that was previously existent in the congregation.[19] O'Neill has likewise identified the similarities between Hebrews 1–2, John 3:13, and two Cave 4 Dead Sea Scroll fragments ($_4Q_{491}$ and Fragment 11 [$_4Q_{491C}$]), all of which are made up of originally disconnected texts put together to describe an ascended man, "exalted to heaven to receive an incomparable name."[20]

It is therefore likely that the Hebrews congregation was familiar with these testimonia. They knew that Jesus is exalted and enthroned on God's right hand, and they knew the angels who are his royal servants eternally worship him. What they did not yet appreciate were Jesus' functions, as king-priest at God's right hand. Hebrews 1 lays a solid foundation that Jesus is indeed in heaven, enthroned at God's right hand, and worshipped by the angels. And this heaven should be understood, from the Old Testament scriptures, as an imperial temple. From now on our author is going to carefully demonstrate the full implications of this king-priest function of Jesus in heaven. He will demonstrate to them that heaven is the antitype of the Holy of Holies in which the Lord ministers as high priest in the order of Melchizedek, and that he has made this *space* also accessible to "those who come to God through him, because he always lives to intercede for them" (Heb 7:25). It is through foregrounding and

---

18. Dahms, "First Readers of Hebrews," 365.
19. Montefiore, *Hebrews*, 40.
20. O'Neill, "Who Is Comparable to Me in My Glory," 38.

analyzing the space of Hebrews 1 that this theological function of the catena in the epistle becomes more obvious.

The Son in the World (Heb 2:5–18)

After an interlude of exhortation in Heb 2:1–4, the author resumes his exposition in which he boldly describes the humanity of the God-man Jesus as humankind's substitute, representative, sanctifier, captain, champion, hero, pioneer, example, kinsman-redeemer, senior brother, and high priest. Donald Miller rightly titles Heb 2:5–18 "Why God became Man," for the passage expresses the complex nature of all the possible permutations of relationships between the angels, creation, human beings, the devil, and God, who for a little while became "lower that the angels." Many of the important themes that follow in the epistle—sacrifice, atonement, high priest Christology, suffering, fear, perfection, sanctification, fellowship of the brethren, and migration—are introduced in a fascinating account and proposition in Heb 2:5–18.

The passage is easily divisible into three parts: Heb 2:5–9 describes the temporary positional abasement of the Son to the angels, Heb 2:10–16 describes the purpose of this abasement (i.e., that Jesus will suffer and die), and Heb 2:17–18 states the benefits of his death. There is a comparison of Jesus with the angels in Heb 2:5 and Heb 2:16, but this is set in an overall context of the other combinations of relationships in the "inhabited world": Jesus' relationship with humanity, to the devil, and to all creation. Spatial analysis of the passage will demonstrate that not only is the passage discussing the finished work of Christ in this world, but also that the author typologically saw a correspondence between the wilderness camp of Israel and the world.

The Spatiality of Heb 2:5–18

It is clear from Heb 2:5 that the author's attention in his argument shifts from the heavenly realm in Hebrews 1 to the "inhabited world." In line with the apocalyptic nature of New Testament speeches, throughout the whole of Hebrews, the author's discussion of the state of the present world is largely limited to its creation and sustenance by the power of the word of the Son (Heb1: 3), its redemption by Jesus (Heb 2:10), and its imminent disappearance and replacement (Heb 1:11–12, 9:26, 12:27). In the meantime, his focus in Hebrews 2 is on how the Son became human to lead his brothers and sisters from this "inhabited world" and into "the world to come, about which we are speaking" (Heb 2:5).

Our analysis begins by identifying the boundaries of this *space*. And the first boundary, which actually dominates the concerns of the author and which is presented in several different aspects throughout this section, is death. First, death is portrayed as the limiting boundary to humanity's glory. That is one of the implications of the sad reality stated in Heb 2:8—"Yet at present we do not see everything subject to him." Regardless of humanity's achievements in this created world, we will all one day succumb to death. It is indeed the ultimate nemesis of humankind, and its defeat, according to Hebrews 2, is beyond even the abilities of the angels who are in temporary charge of this world. Second, death is depicted as an exploited boundary. The fear of death, according to Hebrews, has become the instrument with which the devil subjugates human beings. Death, in the eyes of fallen humanity, is not a passage "to glory" (Heb 2:10), but a prison fence that instills "terror" (Job 18:24) and "horror" (Ps 55:5). This is why human beings will do anything to avoid dying. Achilles spoke for all fallen humanity when he said in the Odyssey (XI: 488), "Say not a word in death's favor; I would rather be a paid servant in a poor man's house and be above ground than a king of kings among the dead."

Third, Heb 2:5–18 portrays the crossing of the boundary of death in military and cultic terms. It is militaristic because it involved the defeat of the devil, and it is ritualistic because the crossing was through sacrifice. Jesus "suffered death, so that by the grace of God he might taste death for everyone . . . that by his death he might destroy him who holds the power of death—that is, the devil—and free those who all their lives were held in slavery by their fear of death" (Heb 2:9, 14–15).

Regarding the author's seemingly pointed focus on death and the fear of it in this section of his homily, Gray has suggested, "The author [of Hebrews] has an apologetic interest in addressing the perception that Christianity is a superstition."[21] Hebrews' discussion of death in this passage should not, however, be seen only as a way of dealing with superstitions but as necessary for his typological scheme in which sacrifice was required before the high priest could pass from the camp of wilderness Israel into the realm of the holy. We will see the significance of this shortly.

Five "persons" are identified in this space: the angels, humanity, the devil, creation, and the Son. The angels are portrayed as temporary governors in administrative charge of the present world, a belief supported by Old Testament passages such as Dan 10:21, 12:1, and 2 Kgs 19:35–36 and which was elaborated by first-century Jewish literature. William Barclay

---

21. Gray, *Godly Fear*, 6.

describes some of the first-century speculations on the role of angels in the world: "There were 200 angels who controlled the movement of the stars and kept them in their courses. There was an angel who controlled the never ending succession of the years and months and days." An angel controlled the sea, frosts, dew, rain, snow, thunder, lightning, etc. Some were wardens of hell; others were destroyers who executed God's punishment on the world. "So many were the angels that the Rabbis could even say: 'Every blade of grass has its angel.'"[22] The author of Hebrews does not go into such details, but at least implies that without the angels, the plight of God's creation would have been terrible indeed.

Yet the functions of the angels in this "inhabited world" are only to *preserve* this world "until the world that is to come," and to continue the stewardship that man has abysmally failed to give to this present world. The angels are also here in the world to minister to the saints who would inherit the salvation to come (Heb 1:14). Despite these important functions, however, the angels cannot do anything to reverse the spiritual condition of fallen human beings who remain prisoners under the devil's power. It is Jesus alone who, through his death, would reverse the wretched state of fallen humanity.

Humankind is portrayed in a number of ways in this inhabited world. They are first described as "son of man," with a glorious potential at the inception of creation (Heb 2:6–8). As curator of God's creation, humanity's glorious potential filled David with awe, as he penned Ps 8, which our author quotes here. Humanity, according to David, was supposed to be the custodian of God's wonderful creation. Territoriality therefore colors this portrayal. Humanity is secondly described as a disastrous steward, whose frustrated, disorderly, and appalling failure is simply put by our author as evident to all: "Yet at present we do not see everything subject to him" (Heb 2:8). Humanity is also depicted in its bleakest condition, not just as a failure but even worse, as a captive slave—they "all their lives were held in slavery by their fear of death" (Heb 2:15). The devil is depicted here as a brutal slaveholder who uses death as a "henchman in the devil's service and the threat of death as an instrument with which he bludgeons humanity into submission."[23]

Through their association and solidarity with Jesus, humankind become "sons" to be brought to glory (Heb 2:10), members of the "same family" (Heb 2:11) with Jesus, and "brothers in the presence of the con-

---

22. Barclay, *Hebrews*, 22.
23. Lane, *Hebrews 1-8*, 61.

gregation" of praise (Heb 2:12). To Jesus, believers are "children God has given me" (Heb 2:13), "children" with whom he shared the same "flesh and blood" (Heb 2:14), and "Abraham's descendants" (Heb 2:16), who are the elect to whom God's promises belonged. Jesus' solidarity with human beings therefore reverses all the disastrous condition of fallen humanity. All creation, on the other hand, is portrayed as subject to humankind, under the aegis of the angels. The relationships portrayed in this space are therefore hierarchical and characterized by territoriality.

Careful attention must be paid to how Jesus is described in Heb 2:5–18. He is first made a little lower than the angels in solidarity with humankind. His lowering is both in terms of the shortness of the time and the hierarchical position in relation to the angels. The writer categorically denies that Jesus could have been an angelic being: "For surely it is not angels he helps, but Abraham's descendants" (Heb 2:16). Whereas the angels could not reverse the fallen state of humanity, Jesus, in sharing humanity's nature, did exactly that and so redeemed them from destruction. The relationship between Jesus and the angels is therefore depicted as an ironic contest, with a hint of subversion to it. In taking on the nature of humankind, Jesus achieved for humanity what the angels, though higher up in the hierarchical order, could not achieve.

A complex of depictions describes the relationship between Jesus and humankind. The title "Archegos" for Jesus in Heb 2:10 is not captured by any single English terminology but is a combination of the connotations of pathfinder, founder, and leader-ruler.[24] As a human being, Jesus is therefore the leader, captain, champion, pioneer, and author of our salvation. In addition, Jesus is portrayed in the terminology of redemption, as the liberator of humanity, whom he delivers (Heb 2:15), rescues (Heb 2:18), sanctifies (Heb 2:11), and leads into glory (Heb 2:10). A migration into glory motif is already developing at this early stage of the epistle.

The relationship between Jesus and the devil is, on the other hand, portrayed as a combat rather than a contest. This portrayal of the death of Jesus as a cosmic battle between him and the devil may be understood with the help of a number of allusions or parallels,[25] most important of which is the concept of the kinsman-redeemer that is described in Lev 25. The solidarity of Jesus with humanity makes him humankind's kinsman and so qualifies him to redeem enslaved humanity and lead them into glory.

---

24. Scott Jr., "Archegos," 47–54.
25. Koester, *Hebrews: ABC*, 239.

Jesus is also depicted through the sacrificial death by which he identifies with humanity. His death is the most significant event in this space and the author explores several dimensions of it. The author notes that Jesus' death was for his "perfection" (Heb 2:10). Lindars has noted that the idea of perfection occurs throughout the epistle and here in this space, perfection means the completion of God's plan rather than ethical perfection. "Though Hebrews is deeply concerned about the conquest of sin, he does not use the idea of perfection to denote the moral ideal, except in so far as that is entailed in the completion of God's plan."[26] Perfection of Jesus means that his death made him completely suitable as the sacrifice for our sins.

The notion of Jesus as sacrifice dominates the way the author of Hebrews describes his ministry and functions in this space. The author uses the spatial template of the wilderness camp of Israel as a model to emphasize that Jesus fulfilled the sacrificial rituals of the Day of Atonement. This sacrificial template involved a combination of the covenant confirmation ceremony in Exod 24:3–8 and the Day of Atonement rituals described in Lev 16, the Red Heifer ritual of Num 19, the sin offerings of Lev 4:1–6:7, and the daily sacrifices (Heb 7:27; Num 28:1–8). In all these sacrificial rituals, the regions of the wilderness camp of Israel were functionally divided into three (Fig 4.1), each corresponding to the stages of the sacrificial drama. As detailed by Nelson, the Jewish sacrificial drama "entailed three episodes: the death of the victim, passage by the priest into the realm of the holy, and the use of blood to effect purification and to create a covenantal relationship."[27] The ritual death of the animal victim itself occurred in the camp, at the worshippers' square in the eastern front gate of the tabernacle, near the altar for burnt offerings (Exod 27:13–16, Lev 4:4; in the case of the Red Heifer sacrifice, it was outside the camp).

The author of Hebrews therefore discusses the significance of the death of Jesus in such a way that it conformed to these three episodes. Jesus' death as victim, by which he identified with humanity occurred in the space of Hebrews 2. His passage as high priest through the courtyard and Holy Place will be discussed by the author in Heb 3:1–6, and his presentation of his own blood to God within the Holy of Holies will be the focus of Hebrews 5–10. The wilderness camp of Israel was separated from the courtyard and tabernacle by a boundary or fence, which apart from the priests, no other member of public was allowed to cross into the holy

---

26. Lindars, "Theology," 44.
27. Nelson, "He Offered Himself," 252.

Fig. 4.1: The Sacrificial Spaces Influencing the Spatiality of Hebrews

The Camp Death of the Sacrificial Victim (Heb 2:5–18)	*Courtyard and Holy Place* Passage of High Priest (Heb 3:1–6)	*Holy of Holies* High Priest Presents Blood (Hebrews 5–10)

realm. Any trespasser was put to death (Exod 19:20–24, 20:19–20; Num 3:38). This is why the author of Hebrews portrays death as the boundary of this space, which then became a means by which the devil subjugates humanity.

The author of Hebrews stresses that Jesus died so that "*he might* taste death for everyone . . . *he might* destroy him who holds the power of death . . . *he might* become a merciful and faithful high priest in service to God . . . *he might* make atonement for the sins of the people" (Heb 2:9, 14, 17, 18; emphasis added). It is here that one will run into major difficulties if temporality (i.e., chronological sequence) alone is used to examine the epistle, for the language here could be mistaken for implying that humanity's salvation was not completed on the cross but only after Christ's ascension to heaven. What concerns Hebrews here is not the chronological sequence of events but its spatial sequence. "He might" in Hebrews 2 is not a stress on future time, but a stress on the functions of Jesus in the successive spaces of the camp. It is a typical "spatial historiography" in which the spaces controlled the narrative and not chronology. Time, for all intents and purposes, was frozen in this part of the discussion, for it was the spatial sequence, controlled by the template of the sacrificial ritual, which mattered to our author.

The Contribution of the Spatiality of Heb 2:5–18 to the Argument of Hebrews

This wonderful passage of scripture, which indeed summarizes the good news of the redemption of fallen humanity by Christ, has also generated several perplexing questions that are unique to the theology of Hebrews. For example, why does the author focus so much on *death* in this chapter and not deal rather with the problem of sin, which is the cause of death, just as Paul, for instance, does in Rom 3–8? What priority does death have over sin and humanity's problem? Does his seeming emphasis that Christ died so that "he might become a merciful and faithful high priest . . . that he might make atonement for the sin of the people" imply that Christ could only deal with the issue of sin *sometime after* his death? If not so, then when did Christ become high priest—on the cross or after? Why, also, does the author split the sacrifice of Christ into stages that gives the impression that his work was not finished on the cross but only when he presented his blood to the Father after the ascension? And where does the resurrection fit in this storyline?

These questions have troubled past generations of theologians who have approached Hebrews with temporality and chronological sequencing as their analytic tools. Ernest Scott among them expressed his frustration that the author's method is "a highly artificial one. We cannot but feel, as the writer elaborates his analogy, that he is engaged in pouring new wine into old bottles, which are burst under the strain."[28] Such frustration, one begs to suggest, is of our own making, because we focus unduly on chronological sequence and immediately assume that words like "might" or "become" are dealing with "time" without noticing that it is the spatial sequencing that mattered to the author of Hebrews. We will arrive at the answers to some of the questions that have been asked of the author of Hebrews in relation his theology in this passage only after we have foregrounded and analyzed its spatiality.

The author takes the historical details of Jesus' death, resurrection, ascension, and exaltation for granted and rather "strings out" the significance of this history to fit the spatial template of the camp of Israel around the tabernacle that he has employed for his theological purposes. Héring's complaint that the author "unrolls as though Jesus went up to heaven immediately after death"[29] is therefore completely mistaken. That Jesus rose from the dead is the unstated bedrock assumption of the argument that enables the author to "roll on" into the subsequent space. In fact, had he overtly referred to the resurrection, his argument would have been more confusing, for then "time" would have been stressed to the point of making the argument ridiculous. Instead, what he has done is to freeze time and focus on the spaces of the camp.

The author's goal in Hebrews 2 was not to, in Long's words, "unpack the calculus of the atonement."[30] Rather, he aimed at demonstrating the fulfillment of the Old Testament sacrifices by Christ. To him, the problem of death is dealt with in the camp, through the death of the sacrificial victim. Sin, which is the cause of death and defilement of humanity, is, on

---

28. Scott, *The Epistle to the Hebrews*, 124–25.
29. Héring, *Epistle to the Hebrews*, xi.
30. Long, "Bold in the Presence of God," 55.

the other hand, only dealt with in the Holy of Holies where the blood is presented to God. This is the template that controls his argument.

Hebrews imaginatively uses the Bakhtinian phenomenon of the dissociation of space from time[31] for good socio-cultural and theological reasons related to the Jewish congregation to whom he writes. Chronology is for that reason being made to serve the purpose of the spatiality of Hebrews 2. The elaborate Day of Atonement ceremonies of Leviticus 16 and the spatial defilement rituals and the arrangement of the camp of the people of God in Numbers now acquires meaning to us as we study them through the lens of Christ's death. Whereas Paul spends several chapters in Rom 3–8 to explain how death and sin were dealt with by Christ's death, our author, on the other hand, uses these few verses, aided by the picture of the camp and tabernacle of the wilderness, to achieve the same explanation.

The fact is, throughout the New Testament, the significance of the dual aspects of the death of Jesus that are signified by the symbolism of the Lord's Supper (the body and the blood of Christ) is consistently emphasized separately, even though they refer to the same and single event. Jesus himself said in John 6:53, "I tell you the truth, unless you eat the flesh of the Son of Man and drink his blood, you have no life in you." The single act of putting one's faith in Jesus is depicted as eating his flesh *and* drinking his blood. Similarly Paul, in speaking about our salvation in Rom 5:6–10, states that we are "justified by his blood" and at the same time, "we were reconciled to him through the death of his Son" (cf. 1 Cor 10:21, Eph 2:12–16, Heb 9:16–18). The meaning of the single event on the cross is spoken of in these two ways so that one is related to the death of Christ's body and the other to the presentation of his blood. These are not separated by time but, according to Hebrews, they are separated by space.

In Hebrews, the body relates to Jesus' death and is discussed in relation to the camp of God's people, and the blood relates to his presentation of his own blood to the Father in the Holy of Holies and will be discussed by the author in Hebrews 5–10. As we shall shortly note, this presentation of Jesus' blood to God is not physical or material but spiritual. Since it is a spiritual presentation, it represents the same event of the death of Jesus on the cross but understood in two different spheres or spaces. Before he could discuss the presentation of the blood in the Holy of Holies, however,

---

31. Reed, *Dialogues of the Word*, 1993, analyzes "time" in Hebrews and suggests that "time" is sometimes frozen or "static" in parts of the author's argument.

the author discusses the spatial significance of the priestly courtyard and Holy Place in the form of "the house."

The Son in the House (Heb 3:1–6)

The spatiality of the argument of Hebrews, from Hebrews 3 onward, assumes a more metaphorical tone with the use of several figures of speech, puns, and plays on words, some with double or even triple meanings. We do well to pay careful attention to the author. The classification of Heb 3:1–6 as an exposition is itself not straightforward. Guthrie's proposed structure of Hebrews categorizes it as part of the whole exhortation of Heb 3:1—4:13, but the exposition on the greater glory and superiority of Jesus over Moses dominates Heb 3:1–6 so much that, despite the admonishments at its beginning and end, the doctrinal part cannot be overlooked. In fact, this passage illustrates the close relationship between the two genres in the epistle and represents the transitional nature of the themes that are discussed in the "house." It is reasonable, therefore, to treat this passage as largely an exposition with some exhortations.

Using texts from Num 12:1–8, and allusions to the oracles to Eli in 1 Sam 2:35 and Nathan in 1 Chron 7:14, the author discusses the faithfulness and glory of Jesus in relation to the "house." The resulting contrast between Jesus and Moses in Heb 3:1–6 has been pivotal to the school of thought that interprets the theology of Hebrews as a polemic against Judaism, and yet when we closely examine the passage, we realize that the emphasis is on continuity of the people of God more than discontinuity. Both Moses and Jesus are members of the same house of God. Jesus is the Son and heir, Moses is a servant in the house, and both are faithful to God. Jones, largely drawing from this passage, has suggested that the figure of Moses may be employed as a heuristic device to examine the pastoral theology of the whole of Hebrews. He points out that the author "conveyed the presence of Christ and cult by comparing the leader and cult of the old covenant with the leader and cult of the new covenant."[32] Jesus, like Moses, having liberated his enslaved people, leads them as pathfinder into "the house" and toward "glory." The passage is hence vital to the epistle's argument.

---

32. Jones, "The Figure of Moses," 96.

The Spatiality of Heb 3:1–6

The space that circumscribes the argument in this part of Hebrews is called "the house." The house is built by Jesus (Heb 3:3), "but God is the builder of everything" (Heb 3:4). This is another powerful statement in the epistle on the divinity of Christ, a fundamental belief the author shared with his hearers so much that he found it unnecessary to explain.

Three different forms of the Greek word for "house" are used, each one of which is repeated twice (Heb 3:2, 5; 3:3, 6a; 3:4, 6b) for emphasis. These Greek words were often used for a group of people such as a family or a nation, or for a spatial structure, especially for a cultic building such as the temple or tabernacle.[33] In the rest of Hebrews, the author uses the word "house" with these two connotations in mind. In Heb 8:8, 10, and 11:7, "house" refers to a nation or household, whereas in Heb 10:21–22 (where the exhortation parallels that of Heb 3:6), it is the cultic building that he has in mind—"since we have a great priest over *the house* of God, let us draw near to God with a sincere heart in full assurance of faith, having our hearts sprinkled to cleanse us from a guilty conscience" (emphasis added). Therefore, since the author points out in Heb 3:6 that "we are his house," the primary meaning of "house" in Hebrews 3 is that of a group of people. Nevertheless, his use of "house" in the passage also adds a secondary semantic connotation of a cultic structure that cannot be excluded from the meaning. Double meanings color several of the metaphors that our author uses and this is one of them.

These undertones of cultic structure of "the house" in Hebrews 3 are further buttressed by the use of the spatial terms "build" and "builder" in the passage. The Greek word used for "built" carries with it the nuance of erecting a house and preparing it for use. The house is built for the "glory" (Heb 3:3) of the one who constructed it.[34] Hence, not only does the author maintain the double meanings of the household and house in Hebrews 3, he also paints a picture of the erection of a transitional house for cultic use. He is therefore playing on words to keep both imageries of God's house, as God's people (family or nation), and a cultic building together in this passage.

The cultic connotations of the house are reinforced even further when we consider the boundaries of this space. God's people enter the

---

33. Vine, *Vine's Expository Dictionary*, 566.

34. There are several parallels between Heb 3:1–6 and 1 Pet 2:9–11 where believers are described as a royal priesthood and the holy nation of God migrating through a hostile world.

house through a "heavenly calling" (Heb 3:1), and are ritually separated unto him as "holy brothers" (Heb 3:1), for they have now been sanctified (cf. Heb 2:11) by Christ the apostle and high priest. On the other hand, the author does not elaborate the exit boundary of this house, but provides hints about it in the manner in which he uses the word "hope" in Heb 3:6—"we are his house, if we hold on to our courage and the hope of which we boast." Members remain in the house by maintaining their pride in "hope."

Speaking about this hope in Heb 6:18, the author states that members of God's house have left the world behind them and "we who have taken refuge might be strongly encouraged to seize the *hope set before us*" (NRSV; emphasis added). The house then, like any other dwelling, provides intermediate security and "hope" is ahead, "set before us." About this hope, he again emphasizes, "This hope as an anchor for the soul, firm and secure. It enters the inner sanctuary *behind the curtain*" (Heb 6:19; emphasis added). The hope that is ahead of the members of the house is described as *behind* the veil that is between the Holy Place and the Holy of Holies. The *veil* is therefore the exit boundary of the house, and "the house" typologically corresponds to the priestly courtyard and the Holy Place.

MacRae has observed that the author's peculiar use of "hope" and "faith" in the epistle is related to his movement theme such that "hope is the goal and faith is a means toward its full realization."[35] As a goal, hope is behind the veil and faith or faithfulness carries the believer through his or her life in the house, which therefore is represented by the priestly courtyard and the Holy Place together.

This interpretation of "the house" as the author's shorthand for the Holy Place and priestly courtyard together in Hebrews 3 becomes more pronounced when we examine the way the persons in the house are depicted. It is generally agreed among commentators that the community receiving this epistle was most likely a "house church" and the portrayal of believers in Heb 3:1–6, using cultic language such as "holy brothers" and "heavenly calling," would suggest some elements of the theology of the "priesthood of all believers" following after Christ in ministry in God's house. The members are holy because they have now been separated from the world and crossed the line from the death-defiled zone of the camp into the purity zone. The house therefore takes on Foucault's characterization of a heterotopia, as an enacted utopia in a real place. Oberholtzer has

---

35. MacRae, "Heavenly Temple," 179–99.

suggested that in the epistle, the congregation is addressed "as part of a worshipping community of believer-priests."[36] They all "have confidence to enter the Most Holy Place by the blood of Jesus" (Heb 10:19) and hence are exhorted to "consider how we may spur one another on toward love and good deeds . . . encourage one another" (Heb 10:24–25).

The relationship between Jesus and the members of the house is depicted in terms of leadership, as the one they should look up to and "consider." Apostle here means the "sent one," sent into another place as a representative. It is a motif which Hebrews shares with John's Gospel, though only Hebrews uses the title "apostle" for Jesus. As apostle and high priest of "our profession," Jesus is also our example in faithfulness and trustworthiness.

Moses is depicted in the house as a servant. The Greek word for "servant" in Heb 3:5 also has cultic connotations of a "temple servant." When God referred to Moses within the confines of the wilderness tabernacle as, "My servant Moses, he is faithful in all my *house*" (emphasis added) in Num 12:7, he used the same word for servant (temple servant) as in Heb 3:5. Moses in Heb 3:1–6 may therefore be seen as a servant who serves in God's tabernacle. Moses used the phrase, "temple servant" to describe himself elsewhere (Exod 4:10, 14:31; Num 11:11; Deut 3:24) and Hebrews consistently avoids using the other Greek words for servant in the rest of the epistle. Thus in Hebrews 3–4, a section where the author deals with the migration of the Old Testament people of God to the promised land, Moses is the leader to be compared with Christ. When our author therefore notes that Moses' faithfulness testified "to what would be said in the future," he was restating his typological style of interpretation.

Ellingworth's suggestion that it is Moses' "prophetic rather than a cultic role"[37] that is being referred to in Hebrews 3 seems therefore to be overly restrictive. The prophetic role of Moses is fused with his cultic priestly functions, as is seen in the dual titles of Jesus as apostle and high priest of our profession in this passage. In Hebrews 9, for instance, the author equates the Mosaic covenant to the Holy Place and describes the cultic functions of Moses that he performed in the priestly courtyard and the Holy Place with its vessels and furniture. He also notes the dominant role of Moses here in sprinkling the tabernacle and vessels with blood (Heb 9:21). He does not, however, describe any major functions performed by Moses in the Holy of Holies. Clearly, he took a serious view of the priestly

---

36. Oberholtzer, "The Kingdom Rest," 186.
37. Ellingworth, *Hebrews*, 207.

functions and leadership of Moses, and yet he restricted those functions to the Holy Place and the priestly courtyard. Consequently, the cultic connotations of the description of Moses as "temple servant" in the house cannot be discounted and the presence of the cultic imagery supports the view that the space which occupies our author's attention in Heb 3:1–6 has some relationship with the arrangement of the wilderness camp of God's people.

The writer of Hebrews therefore considered the house to correspond typologically to the parts of the tabernacle that were accessible only to the Levitical priests (i.e., the priestly courtyard and the Holy Place; Exod 29:42–43, 30:6–8; Num 18:1–8; Heb 9:6). The priests entered this area daily for ritual washings, sacrifices, dedications, and fellowship "to carry on their ministry" (Heb 9:6). In this sphere, Moses exercised considerable authority as he established and consecrated Aaron and his sons for the ministry (Lev 8).

Another indication of the author's spatiality in this part of his sermon may be found in Heb 13:9–14. The statement that believers "have an altar from which those who minister at the tabernacle have no right to eat" (Heb 13:10) indicates that our author metaphorically represented the people of God as the priestly community occupying the priestly courtyard and Holy Place, ministering at its altar and eating from its sacrifices. This region, which housed the altar, also served as the place of refuge (e.g., 1 Kgs 1:50) in the future temple, and it is there that the believers of Hebrews "have fled for refuge to lay hold of hope" (Heb 6:18, MKJV).

In this sphere, Jesus, their apostle and high priest, is compared with Moses of the wilderness camp and shown to have greater glory and honor. Comparison and contests are typical of typological interpretations. There is always an escalation or "heightening" between the type and the antitype. This house, like all other spaces, is therefore contested and the relationship between Jesus and Moses is hence presented as hierarchical. They were both appointed and sent by God. They were both faithful in the house. Jesus, however, "has been found worthy of greater honor than Moses, just as the builder of a house has greater honor than the house itself" (Heb 3:3). Jesus is greater than Moses because, as Son, heir, and builder, he has territorial claim to God's house. The superiority of Jesus is also expressed in spatial terms, so that whereas Jesus is Son "over" God's house, Moses is servant "in" the house.

The Contribution of the Spatiality of Heb 3:1–6 to the Argument of Hebrews

The exposition about the faithfulness of Jesus as Son and builder of the house in comparison to Moses as servant in the same house is strategically placed by our author at the beginning of his long exhortation on the failure of the Old Testament wilderness generation to "move on and enter" into the promised land. Paul Ellingworth was right when he mused, "To many modern readers this short section [Heb 3:1–6] may appear to be an anticlimax. If, as the author has demonstrated at length in chap. 1 Christ is higher than the angels, it would seem to go without saying that he is greater than Moses."[38]

It is nevertheless argued by some that the status of Moses in a number of first-century Jewish circles was so high that one can understand why the first readers would not have regarded such a comparison as redundant. Brett Scott, for example, explains that Moses was "held in almost God-like esteem, even higher than angels"[39] by many Jews, so much so that our author's comparisons were not a backward but rather a forward step in his flow of argument. Indeed Moses, like the angels, is viewed positively throughout this epistle and never denigrated. The common conclusion has therefore been that the comparison of Jesus with Moses in Heb 3:1–6 serves the author's overall scheme of showing that, as mediator of the new covenant, Jesus is greater than, but also in continuity with, the mediators of the old covenant.

While this may be so, it still leaves the question unanswered why our author refrained from pointing to any fault of Moses. He found fault with the old covenant all right, noting its ineffectiveness, repetitions, and earthly nature (Hebrews 9). Wouldn't it have served the purpose of such an explanation to point out that Moses, though faithful, was not faithful to the end, just as Num 20:12 does, particularly since the author exhorts the congregation in this passage to be faithful to the end (Heb 3:6)? It is this major omission by Hebrews that suggests that he is not at all interested in polemics against Moses or Judaism as such, but rather to show how Moses together with Judaism were types leading and merging into the greater and superior antitype, Christ.

The fact is, our author is not making an arbitrary selection of the greatest and good to compare with Christ, but was preconditioned by the spatiality of the section of his argument. In Hebrews 1, the space was

---

38. Ellingworth, *Hebrews*, 194.
39. Scott, "Jesus' Superiority," 203.

heaven, and hence the angels are the persons to be compared with Jesus. In Hebrews 2, the space was the world and hence though a comparison with the angels as the temporary administrators of this realm is made, the author also explores Jesus' relationships with other persons within the world. Here in Hebrews 3, the space is within the house of God—a double-edged metaphor for the whole congregation of God's people and the cultic building of the tabernacle. Within this space, Moses indeed is the leader of God's people in the Pentateuch, but our author would subsequently point to Joshua in Heb 4:8 as another servant in the house. The choice of Moses for comparison was not to address a false Moses Christology, neither was it arbitrary, but was preconditioned by the space that controlled the scheme of the author's exposition. This space incorporated the priestly courtyard and the Holy Place, where Moses wielded his authority. It did not include the Holy of Holies.

How does one handle the whole concept of "double meanings" when it comes to interpreting spatial metaphors? Several of the recent commentaries on Hebrews, after noting the nature of the cultic connotations and double meanings of the metaphors in this passage, surprisingly proceed to choose one meaning and ignore the others, resulting in a skewed interpretation of the message here. We need to reflect on this methodological question: is it correct to privilege one aspect of an author's deliberate choice of double meanings over against another one in our interpretation? It is evident that the author's primary meaning for the word "house" was a group of people, and yet with his emphasis on "built," cultic themes, and temple servant, he has brought sufficient connotations of a cultic building to it that a secondary inseparable meaning of a "house of worship" also reverberates in the background of the passage. Should we not take these connotations that seriously?

This is where our understanding of the nature of spatial metaphors is important. Authors do not choose their metaphors in an arbitrary fashion. Rather, metaphors provide us with an idea of the basis of the author's premises and thoughts. In so doing, they transfer the pictorial and imaginative elements of the figure of speech along with the ordinary meaning of the words that have been written. In other words, the denotations of the metaphor should not be dissociated from their connotations. By repeatedly using and maintaining a spatial metaphor of "the house," the author of Hebrews is speaking with typical double senses. He has consciously kept the two meanings of "house"—structure and people—together for a purpose.

Indeed, the division of the dual meanings of "house" from each other is more of a preoccupation of modern exegetes rather than our author's. In first-century Mediterranean societies, communities were defined more by the social network between the people than the structural buildings they occupied. This worked both ways so that a group of people was equivalent to the space they occupied. As Malina summarizes it, "People moved through other people, not through space."[40] Therefore, "house" as a community of people was equivalent in that society to "house" as a structure. There was no question of two different meanings in the mind of an ancient Mediterranean. The "house" in Heb 3:1–6 therefore represented the region of the priestly courtyard and the Holy Place, and from here, the author proceeds into the Holy of Holies.

Jesus the Great High Priest in the Holy of Holies (Hebrews 5–10)

Hebrews 5–10 constitutes the central and crucial part of the author's expositions in which he expounds the doctrine of Christ as our great high priest in God's presence and the benefits of his ministry in the form of the new covenant that his sacrifice inaugurates. Though the high priest Christology is universally qualified as the distinctive contribution of the author of Hebrews to New Testament Christology, the hesitant but elaborate manner in which he approaches it would suggest that this doctrine was a major theological innovation on the part of his first audience. Though Hebrews is the only epistle that uses the title of high priest for Jesus, the doctrine itself is not unique to the epistle but is also present in other parts of the New Testament. Hence Richard Longenecker has explained, "The fourth Gospel strikes a similar note in its presentation of Jesus as assuming the place of centrality in the nation's religious festivals . . . in the Pauline letters, the exalted Christ is spoken of as making intercession for his own . . ."[41] Despite its relentless exposition by our author, there is therefore no reason to regard the doctrine as strange. This doctrine was mainstream theological stuff that was being emphasized to its elaborate details for our benefit.

The long segment of Hebrews 5–10 is interrupted at a stage by an exhortation in Heb 5:11–6:17 that sternly warns the congregation about apostasy. The rest may be conveniently divided into three parts: Heb 5:1–

---

40. Malina, "Apocalyptic and Territoriality," 370.
41. Longenecker, *The Christology of Early Jewish Christianity*, 114–15.

10, Hebrews 7, and Hebrews 8–10. In Heb 5:1–10, the author elaborates the general qualifications of Jesus that makes him fit to be high priest. The passage discusses his appointment and calling by God, his human experience that prepared him for the ministry, his perfection, and his designation as high priest in the order of Melchizedek. A brief comparison is made with Aaron in Hebrews 5, which will later on be extended to include the two types of priesthoods in the rest of the expositions. Hebrews 7 may appear to a twenty-first century non-Jewish reader as a rather tortuous expositional interlude in which the author explains what the quoted prophecy from Ps 110 means by the "order of Melchizedek." If we were for a moment to put ourselves in the shoes of the first-century Diaspora Jew who first read this sermon, however, we would agree that explaining this "order of Melchizedek" priesthood was vital to the author's argument. The explanation serves to show the author's fulfillment theology and the king-priest nature of Jesus' ministry.

Hebrews 8–10 expounds the details of Jesus' ministry as high priest and at the same time shows its superior benefits in comparison to the Aaronic priesthood. It is here that the author fully unveils the spatial scheme of the tabernacle and wilderness camp which has until now controlled his exposition. Hebrews 8 introduces the *space* of Jesus' ministry: he "serves in the sanctuary, the true tabernacle set up by the Lord" (Heb 8:1). Hebrews 9 elaborates on it further by describing the details of the spaces of the wilderness camp and tabernacle and what functions were performed in each of its regions. Hebrews 10 explains the finality of Christ's sacrifice, for he "offered for all time one sacrifice for sins, he sat down at the right hand of God" (Heb 10:12).

The Spatiality of Hebrews 5–10

We must carefully tease out the spatiality of this section of Hebrews by separately examining the spaces, the persons and their relationships, and the events that occur in this section of the epistle.

The Hybrid of Spaces in Hebrews 5–10

The spatiality of Hebrews 5–10 deals with two spaces that our author regarded as mirror images of each other for typological comparison; one is the type and the other is the antitype. Aaron ministered in the Holy of Holies of the wilderness tabernacle, whereas Jesus, on the other hand, "has gone through the heavens" (Heb 4:14), where he is "sat down at the right hand of the throne of the Majesty in heaven, and who serves in the sanctuary, the true tabernacle set up by the Lord" (Heb 8:1–2).

The dissimilarities between the two spaces are fundamental to the author's argument, but they also serve as mirror images of each other. Aaron's space was earthly, fleshy, temporary, and ineffectual; Jesus' space is heavenly, eternal, and spiritual, and there he saves "completely those who come to God through him, because he always lives to intercede for them" (Heb 7:25). Jesus therefore performs an inverted and perfect form of the functions of Aaron's ministry in the Holy of Holies. Christ, Hebrews says, "did not enter a man-made sanctuary that was only a copy of the true one; he entered heaven itself, now to appear for us in God's presence" (Heb 9:24).

Clearly, the author of Hebrews uses Aaron's space as a heuristic device[42] to enhance his teaching on the nature of Jesus' ministry. Foucault's classification of hybrid spatiality is therefore a helpful scheme in examining Hebrews 5–10.

Fig 4.2: The Tabernacle According to Hebrews

Holy Place	Holy of Holies
Lampstand	Ark of the Covenant with Mercy Seat
Veil / Incense Altar	Π
Table of Loaves	

42. The word "heuristic" is derived from the Greek root word, "eureka," meaning discovery. Heuristic devices are conceptual devices that are employed by teachers to aid the explanation of difficult and abstract ideas. The simplest examples of such devices are figures of speech, metaphors, symbols, and parables. Complex examples are typology and allegory. Here in Hebrews 5–10, our author unveils how he has employed the wilderness camp and tabernacle as an allegorical scheme, a heuristic device, in order to explain the high priestly functions of the exalted and enthroned Jesus who provides access to God's people who are migrating to heaven.

To facilitate his congregation's understanding of this spatial scheme, our author explains some of the details of Aaron's earthly space in Heb 8:5 and 9:2–5 (Fig. 4.2). The wilderness tabernacle had two chambers. The Holy Place contained the lampstand and the table of showbread and was separated from the Holy of Holies by a veil. This veil was the entry boundary to the Holy of Holies that contained the Ark of the Covenant, whose golden lid was symbolic of the mercy seat (also called the throne of grace).

The author of Hebrews does not try and go into details about the symbolic meanings of all the contents of the tabernacle but explains that Moses built the wilderness tabernacle on strict instructions from God (Heb 8:5). This does not mean that Moses had a vision of a physical tabernacle in heaven, even though certain first-century Jewish groups interpreted Exod 25:9, 40 that way. What it means is that the plan for the wilderness tabernacle was purposely given by God to serve as type: "a copy and shadow" (Heb 8:5), "pattern" (Heb 8:5), and "illustration" (Heb 9:9). Consequently, to the author of Hebrews, the historical experiences of the migrant camp of Israel that is described in the book of Numbers, together with the Day of Atonement rituals and sacrifices associated with the tabernacle, were all analogical types and "examples" (Heb 4:11), heuristic devices whose meanings are fulfilled in the ministry of Christ.

Unlike Aaron's, Jesus' space is heaven itself. It is very instructive that contrary to the rich imagery of our author's language, he is so restrained when it comes to talking about the details of heaven. In fact, he refrains from describing any visual imagery of heaven in this book. Hebrews, unlike John's Revelation, is therefore not an apocalyptic or visionary literature and this is why any suggestion that the author of Hebrews depicts layers or tiers of heavenly regions because he uses the term "heavens" in Heb 1:10, 4:14, 7:26, 9:23, and 12:26 is incorrect. The plural "heavens" only serves as a respectful way of speaking about God's abode and the author simply depicts heaven as the place of God's very presence (Heb 9:24), as God's throne room (Heb 4:16 and 8:1), and as the place of Christ's ministry (Heb 8:1–2). We should therefore not push the interpretation of Hebrews to the extreme and imagine a physical tabernacle or material blood being sprinkled in it and so on.

The other metaphors that the author uses to depict heaven elsewhere in the epistle are the promised land (Hebrews 3 and 4), the city of God (Heb 11:10), the heavenly Jerusalem (Heb 12:22), and the unshakeable kingdom (Heb 12:28). This is why, again, it is not necessary to interpret the *veil* solely as depicting the sky, though evidently when the author stresses in Heb 6:19–20 that our hope "enters the inner sanctuary behind the curtain, where Jesus, who went before us," the veil is being interpreted as the sky through which our Lord ascended. In Heb 10:20, however, our author teaches that the veil also represents the body or flesh of Christ and he emphasizes that even now we can "enter the Most Holy Place by the blood of Jesus" (Heb 10:19), implying that the veil is also the spiritual access into God's presence, the living Christ. In other words, when we truthfully pray "in the name of Jesus," we are entering through the veil. Hebrews thus employs multiple interpretations of the wilderness tabernacle complex, as we shall discuss in more detail in the next chapter.

Table 4.1: Contrasting Features of the Two Spaces of Hebrews 5–10

Aaron's Space	*Jesus' Space*
"on earth" (Heb 8:4)	"in heaven" (Heb 8:1)
"an earthly sanctuary" (Heb 9:1)	"heavenly sanctuary" (Heb 9:24)
"set up by man" (Heb 8:2)	"set up by the Lord" (Heb 8:2)
"of this creation" (Heb 9:11)	"not a part of this creation" (Heb 9:11)
"man-made sanctuary" (Heb 9:24)	"heaven itself" (Heb 9:24)
"a copy and shadow" (Heb 8:5)	"the true tent" (Heb 8:2)
"a copy" (Heb 9:24)	"the true sanctuary" (Heb 9:24)

As a mirror image of Aaron's space, Jesus' space is not just opposite but also far superior to Aaron's space, just as an antitype is far more superior to its type. As table 4.1 shows (above), the fundamental difference between the two spaces is the dualism between what is spiritual and what is not spiritual, between that which is virtual and what is material. This basic difference does, however, escape some interpreters who get caught up with the details and intricacies of Hebrews' portrayal of Jesus in heaven and imagine that in heaven there exists a physical tabernacle, which is an exact replica of the one in the wilderness with a material throne of grace in heaven, ritual liturgy with sacrificial blood, etc. This way of interpreting and applying the author's teaching on the tabernacle not only presses them too far but also in the process defeats his point that the two spaces are completely opposite to each other. Martin Luther's warning about the spiritual nature of the imagery in Hebrews is helpful at this point:

> Again, in the new order, the tabernacle or house is spiritual; for it is heaven, or the presence of God. Christ hung upon a cross; he was not offered in a temple. He was offered before the eyes of God, and there he still abides. The cross is an altar in a spiritual sense. The material cross was indeed visible, but none knew it as Christ's altar. Again, his prayer, his sprinkled blood, his burnt incense, were all spiritual, for it was all wrought through his spirit.[43]

It is thus not correct for us to go beyond the spiritual allegorization of our author to imagine a substantive tent, tabernacle, and sanctuary in heaven with a priestly courtyard and a separate Holy of Holies and material blood being sprinkled. The heavenly counterpart is all spiritual.

The flexible language of Hebrews 8–10 may admittedly contribute to some extent to this misunderstanding of the author's typology. The interchangeable use of "sanctuary" and "tabernacle" in Hebrews 8–10 may give an impression of a full tabernacle with a priestly courtyard, a Holy Place, and Holy of Holies in heaven. At other points, however, the author clearly states that the whole of heaven corresponds to the Holy of Holies. MacRae has therefore suggested that both interpretations of the tabernacle are present in the epistle so that Heb 8:1–5, 9:11–12, 23 portrays heaven as the Holy of Holies (the whole of God's creation being his tabernacle/temple) but Heb 9:24 and 10:19–20 depict a separate and full tabernacle in heaven.[44] He suggested that the first is a Jewish Apocalyptic interpretation and the second is a Hellenistic Platonic interpretation.

MacRae did not, however, consider the flexible nature of the author's language in these chapters, a flexibility that, according to Koester, "is similar to the way the LXX uses terms in relation to the tabernacle."[45] The very fact that our author does not discuss any ministry of Christ in relation to the Holy Place and regards this part of the tabernacle as representative of the obsolete covenant (Heb 9:8–9) associated with the sphere of Moses' ministry (Heb 9:19–22) but not of Aaron's, demonstrates that even if our author thought of a full tabernacle in heaven, this tabernacle had no priestly courtyard or Holy Place. It has no veil either, for Christ, by his death, has rent the veil, which is his flesh, and opened the access for all to enter (Hebrews 10).

43. Luther, *Sermon for Fifth Sunday in Lent on Hebrews 9:11–15*.
44. MacRae, "Heavenly Temple," 179–99.
45. Koester, *The Dwelling of God*, 156.

Consequently, even if there is a tabernacle in heaven, it is a single-chambered, spiritual Holy of Holies, without a veil! As the argument proceeds, it becomes much more obvious that Hebrews conceives of the whole of heaven as this Holy of Holies without compartments. In this respect, our author completely concurs with John's vision of the heavenly Jerusalem, which he saw descending from God. "*I did not see a temple in the city,*" John says, "because the Lord God Almighty and the Lamb are its temple" (Rev 21:22; emphasis added). This is exactly the teaching of Hebrews about heaven. The whole of heaven is the spiritual tabernacle of God, the Holy of Holies.

The Persons in the Spaces of Hebrews 5–10

The author's theological discussions in Hebrews 5–10 are focused on the ministry and functions of two persons: Aaron and Jesus. Aaron as progenitor of the Levitical priesthood is compared with Jesus the great high priest "in the order of Melchizedek." Moses' ministry in inaugurating the old covenant is briefly mentioned (Heb 9:18–22) and Abraham is similarly mentioned as part of the development of the author's argument that the priesthood in the order of Melchizedek is superior to the Levitical priesthood. The focus in these chapters, however, is on Aaron and Jesus.

For all intents and purposes, according to Hebrews, Aaron was fully qualified to be high priest in the wilderness camp of Israel. He was an eligible human representative who was appointed and called by God to offer gifts and sacrifices on the people's behalf to God (Heb 5:1–4). God confirmed his appointment as high priest when his staff sprouted and budded in the contest with elders of the other tribes in the wilderness (Num 17). Hebrews alludes to this when he refers to the budded staff in Heb 9:4. Aaron's several failings in the Pentateuch are well known, especially in relation to the golden calf incident in Exod 32, and yet our author does not give any hint of criticism. The polemical approach to the interpretation of Hebrews meets a major weakness here, for what more opportunity could our author have wished for than to have compared a deeply flawed Aaron with Jesus. On the contrary, Hebrews depicts an ideal Aaron, one who held his office in high esteem. For whereas the comparison between Moses and Jesus was based on faithfulness, that between Aaron and Jesus is based on effectiveness of ministry.

We also see Jesus in a new light in this section. The author explains in detail that he was, like Aaron, called and appointed by God to be our high priest in the order of Melchizedek. "Christ also did not take upon himself the glory of becoming a high priest. But God said to him . . . You are a priest forever, in the order of Melchizedek" (Heb 5:5–6). This designation of the high priesthood of Jesus holds a very important key to the nature of his work and hence our author takes the time and effort to develop it in the whole of Hebrews 7. He had mentioned Melchizedek earlier in Heb 5:6, but many Bible readers understandably take a deep sigh when they read the first words of Hebrews 7, which sound like a tangential digression.

Hebrews 7 is not a digression, however, for our author is going to demonstrate to us why Jesus' priestly order is far superior to Aaron's Levitical order. The argument in Hebrews 7 goes in four stages. First, in Heb 7:1–3 the author argues that by virtue of the meaning of his name and his sudden "appearance and disappearance" in the narrative of Gen 14, Melchizedek is a type (or even perhaps theophany) of Jesus the Son of God. Second, in Heb 7:4–10, the author argues that because he blessed Abraham and received tithes from the great patriarch, Melchizedek was superior to Abraham and therefore superior to Aaron. Third, in Heb 7:11–22, he argues that by appointing a separate priesthood to the Levitical system and sealing it with his own oath, God replaced the old order with the new order, "by which we draw near to God" (Heb 7:19). Finally, in Heb 7:23–28, Hebrews argues that Jesus' priesthood is forever, "because Jesus lives forever, he has a permanent priesthood" (Heb 7:24). Explaining the nature of the priesthood of Jesus in the order of Melchizedek is therefore necessary for understanding the outcome of his ministry.

The Events (Ministries) in the Spaces of Hebrews 5–10

In addition to comparing the spaces and the persons, Hebrews 5–10 also analyzes the ministries associated with the Holy of Holies. Two main historical events provide the loci for the author's analysis: the *Covenant Inauguration* and the *Day of Atonement* ceremonies. Hebrews 9:19–21 makes reference to the initial inauguration of the Sinai covenant by Moses as recorded in Exodus 24 (the description is also influenced by Numbers 19). This was to emphasize the role and function of ritual sacrificial blood during the inauguration of the old covenant. Even though at the time of the inauguration of the covenant the tabernacle was not yet erected, Moses set up what can rightly be regarded as a "primitive tabernacle" for the ceremony. The mountain of God, where the elders of Israel received a theophanic revelation and the altar below it, was representative of the tabernacle and the people separated by a safe distance from the mountain represented the rest of the camp complex.

The inauguration of the old covenant was not only associated with cultic blood but also with sacrifices, but these sacrifices were offered not in the holy zone below the mountain, but elsewhere in or outside the camp and the blood was then brought into the holy zone for the sprinkling ceremony by Moses (Exod 24:5). Because our author was focusing on the Holy of Holies in the discussion of Hebrews 5–10, it is the significance of the sprinkling of blood that he uses as analogy of Jesus' ministry in heaven.

With reference to the covenant inauguration ceremony, therefore, the typological comparison is between the blood of the covenant and the blood of Jesus. Just as "without the shedding of blood there is no forgiveness" (Heb 9:22), Christ "entered the Most Holy Place once for all by his own blood, having obtained eternal redemption" (Heb 9:12). This difference lies at the heart of the comparison between the old and the new covenant. The promise of a new covenant in Jer 31:31–34 is quoted in full by our author (Heb 8:7–13) and is demonstrably superior to the old, just as an antitype is superior to its type. Whereas the worship associated with the old covenant was weak, earthly, ineffective, repetitive, and "can never take away sins" (Heb 10:11), the new covenant, on the other hand, is spiritual, effectual, and permanent. The comparison does not mean the two coexisted along each other, as the Platonists would have argued. In fact, to our author, the old covenant is mentioned because of its historical past and the fact that the new covenant has now replaced it.

With regard to the Day of Atonement ceremonies, it is the high priest's functions in the Holy of Holies on that day that are also compared with Jesus' ministry in heaven. The Day of Atonement rituals were mandated in Lev 16 and involved once a year entrance of the high priest into the Holy of Holies with blood for atonement and intercession on behalf of the people. Jesus fulfilled this typology when "he entered heaven itself, now to appear for us in God's presence. Nor did he enter heaven to offer himself again and again . . . But now he has appeared once for all at the end of the ages to do away with sin by the sacrifice of himself" (Heb 9:24–26). There, he also intercedes permanently on behalf of his people (Heb 2:17–18, 4:14–16, 6:18–19).

Table 4.2: Comparison of the Functions of the Levitical with Christ's Priesthood

Functions of the Levitical High Priesthood	Functions of Christ's High Priesthood
In the wilderness Holy of Holies	In heaven
Atonement repeated once every year	Atonement once and for all
Ministers with the blood of animals	Ministers with his own blood
Stands in ministration	Sits at God's right hand
High Priest dies and is succeeded	Lives forever in intercession

The two ministrations are again fundamentally different, just as a type is a shadow of its antitype, and this is what our author draws out in his concluding expositional remarks in Hebrews 10. Whereas the Levitical high priest does his functions annually, repetitively reminding the people of their sins (Heb 10:3), Jesus has once and for all fulfilled his functions (Heb 10:14). Whereas the Levitical high priest enters with the blood of animals (Heb 10:4), Jesus entered with his own blood as part of his obedient sacrifice (Heb 10:7). Whereas the Levitical high priest stood to perform his rituals, Jesus is "sat down at the right hand of God" (Heb 10:12). Whereas the Levitical high priest died and had to be replaced, Jesus ever lives to make intercession on behalf of his people. The comparison with the Levitical system (see fig 4.2) therefore helps to enhance our understanding of the eternal work of Christ as our sacrifice and high priest sat down at the right hand of Majesty on high.

The Contribution of the Spatiality of Hebrews 5–10 to the Argument of Hebrews

Hebrews 5–10 is both literally and metaphorically central to the epistle, and yet, because its argument is elaborate and seems repetitious, the description is rather static. This sense of lack of movement results from the author's focus on the space of the Holy of Holies, and the issues that he highlights are all related to this *space*. It is in relation to the Holy of Holies that he unveils three themes that are important to the whole argument of the epistle: the new covenant and its benefits, the functions of the high priest on the Day of Atonement, and the eternal effects of the sacrifice of Christ. These are all framed using the spatial framework of the wilderness camp and tabernacle and hence spatial analysis of Hebrews 5–10 helps in their exploration.

Because his first readers were perhaps not fully acquainted with the details and complexities of the Levitical ministrations within the camp and tabernacle, the author approaches the subject cautiously and in stages in Hebrews 1–4. It is in Hebrews 5 that he explains the details of Jesus' ministry as high priest in God's presence. Heb 8:1–2 is in effect a true summary of the expositions of the epistle: "Now the main point in what we are saying is this: we have such a high priest, one who is seated at the right hand of the throne of the Majesty in the heavens, a minister in the sanctuary and the true tent that the Lord, and not any mortal, has set up" (NRSV).

The Greek word *kephalaion* rendered as "main point" by the NRSV or simply as "point" by the NIV, is literally translated as "sum." It occurs on only two occasions in the New Testament: in Acts 22:28, where it is used for "sum of money" and here in Heb 8:1. The KJV therefore gets it right when it translates Heb 8:1, "Now of the things which we have spoken this is the *sum* . . ." What we have in Heb 8:1–2 is the summary of the exposition and not just a "point" (contra the NIV) or even "main point." Whether *kephalaion* is "main point" as most of the recent commentaries[46] prefer, or "summary," it is clear that for the author of Hebrews, the central issue, the gist, the summary of his expositions is this: Jesus ministers as high priest in the heavenly tabernacle. And yet, it is only after we have foregrounded the spatiality of expositions that this "main point" or summary becomes much more obvious. In the author's patient and careful exposition from Hebrews 1–7, he used the camp and tabernacle as "the intellectual scaffolding" for the expositions, so that the functions of Jesus as our high priest will be much clearer. Now in Hebrews 8–10, he demonstrates how the wilderness camp and tabernacle is the semiosphere, which then provides him the "universe of the possible meanings" of the whole homily.

---

46. Three possible shades of meanings of *kephalaion* have been proposed in the recent commentaries based on its use in antiquity: (i) as principal or chief point, (ii) as crowning affirmation on top of other points, and (iii) as a summary of the argument (see Koester, *Hebrews ABC*, 375). On all three counts, Heb 8:1–2 constitutes the gist of what our author has been saying from Hebrews 1–7. This refers not only to the Lord's high priesthood on God's right hand, but also his ministry in the heavenly tabernacle. Spatiality of the wilderness camp and tabernacle serves therefore as the framework or semiosphere of our author's argument.

Another important indicator in Heb 8:1–2 of the author's spatial scheme is the relationship the passage has with the Balaam oracles of Numbers 22–24. When Hebrews qualifies the heavenly sanctuary as a "tabernacle, which the Lord *pitched*" (emphasis added) in Heb 8:2, he is alluding to Balaam's description of the wilderness camp of Israel that the odd prophet saw and described in Num 24:6 as "aloes planted by the LORD." As Balaam stood on a hill and saw the beautiful encampment of Israel around the tabernacle in the valleys, the Spirit of the Lord came upon him and he burst into a profound prophecy that is unparalleled elsewhere in the Pentateuch.

What Balaam saw at the time was the concentric arrangement of the tribes of Israel pitched in their tents around God's tabernacle, and he described Israel as "planted" or "pitched by the Lord himself." He perceived that from among the encamped people of God around the tabernacle, "a star will come out of Jacob; a scepter will rise out of Israel. He will crush the foreheads of Moab" (Num 24:17). Though the primary referent of the "star" was David, in a secondary sense this prophecy referred to the Messiah. Balaam thus "saw" and prophesied that the Lord Jesus would be among the migrant people of God, pitched in a concentric manner around the tabernacle on their way to the promise. It is this exact imagery that has controlled the author of Hebrews' expositions. In saying that Jesus served in the tabernacle "that the Lord pitched," the author of Hebrews expected his hearers to adopt the imagery that Balaam also saw and perceived in his prophecy.

Until recently, the author of Hebrews' construction of the argument in Hebrews 8–10, especially his use of words like "pattern," "copy and shadow" (Heb 8:5), and "illustration" (Heb 9:9), had been interpreted by some scholars as shaped by Platonic philosophy. This concept, simply and briefly stated, asserts that all material objects have a real, ideal, and unchanging counterpart, which is abstract but far superior to it. What we perceive on earth are therefore merely "shadows" of their superior realities. The two are in parallel and no crossover exists, except through development of the human intellect to higher levels of thinking. Our author's statement that Moses erected a wilderness tabernacle "according to the pattern shown" (Heb 8:5) to him on the mountain has therefore been interpreted as evidence of Platonism in Hebrews. Ceslas Spicq's suggestion that the author's argument that the ministry of Jesus in the heavenly tabernacle results in the "parallel cleansing of the conscience on earth" (Heb 9:9, 14) is a reflection of such Platonic interpretation of Hebrews.[47]

What we have in Hebrews, however, are not two parallel worlds but a hybrid one in which Christ crosses over as the resurrected and exalted God-man to fulfill the functions of the great high priest on behalf of humanity. The comparison by the author of Hebrews is between a historical space of the wilderness tabernacle and the eternal space of heaven and not between two parallel worlds. There is therefore no element of Platonic thought at all in these parts of the epistle.

The concept of hybrid spaces (combining material and virtual spaces) is also a useful scheme when analyzing an event that simultaneously occurs in two or more spaces. Jesus' death on the cross and the spiritual presentation in heaven of himself and his blood before God is one and the same event that the author of Hebrews analyzed in two separate spaces. With the wilderness camp and tabernacle as his heuristic tool, the ministry and benefits from the death of Christ are now elaborately laid bare for our understanding.

Conclusion: The Wilderness Camp and Tabernacle as Semiosphere

It cannot be denied that Hebrews is a very well structured argument that applies the exposition of scripture to address real practical pastoral issues. This exposition focuses on comparing Jesus with the angels, Moses, Aaron, and the Levitical covenantal system. What is not clearly understood, however, is the criteria that controlled the selection of these persons for comparison by the author of Hebrews and how the expositions contribute to addressing the challenges of the congregation that are dealt with in the exhortations.

Commentators have noted also that each of the stages of the exposition is also focused in particular spaces. The angels are compared with Jesus in relation to heaven and then the world. Moses is compared to him in the "house of God" and Aaron and the Levitical high priesthood are compared with Jesus in relation to the Holy of Holies of the tabernacle. What has not been seriously explored is the possibility that these spaces act as the setting for the argument of Hebrews and therefore control the author's selection of persons for comparison.

---

47. Spicq, *Hébreux*, 72.

Some commentators have suggested that the spatial setting amounts to the cosmology of the author of Hebrews and that the movement from one space to another is a reflection of the pilgrimage theology expounded by the exhortations. The author, it is argued, portrays Jesus' ministry as moving from heaven to earth and back to heaven in pilgrimage into the presence of God, setting us example of perseverance that we should follow. The progression of the argument, it is pointed out, starts from the pre-existence of Christ, through his life on earth, his death, and to eternity in the future. Marie Isaacs, who employed the concept of sacred space to examine this phenomenon, concluded that the spatial "movement" in Hebrews is an expression of the author's eschatology being reflected by the pilgrimage motif.

Though there is indeed a movement motif in the epistle, this is located in the exhortations and the comparisons within the expositions are largely static. The progression of the argument of the expositions from heaven to the world, to the house and to the Holy of Holies (which to our author was a metaphor for heaven) was not time dependent. As we have previously stressed, time is frozen between the argument of Jesus' death in the camp and the presentation of his blood to God in the Holy of Holies. The same event that occurred on the cross is described in two different spaces. To press the argument of the expositions into a time-related movement motif creates the kind of difficulties that have been mentioned previously.

The expositions of Hebrews also begin from the end of Jesus' earthly career, now "sat down at the right hand of the Majesty on heaven" (Heb 1:3), and not from his pre-existence. It then goes back in time to his earthly life in the world and then moves forward in time to his function as our heavenly high priest. In terms of chronology, this is not an expression of pilgrimage motif. The spatiality of the "house" in Hebrews 3 has not also been adequately explored as playing a crucial function in the author's spatial framework. And yet, the author employs it as a double-edged metaphor that indicates that in addition to denoting the people of God, "the house" also connotes the space of the tabernacle courtyard and Holy Place.

What is clear from this study is that our author has employed the camp of Israel as the spatial scaffolding for the exposition. The camp of God's people around the tabernacle was the semiosphere in the epistle's expositions. In other words, the rest of the epistle to the Hebrews may be better understood using the camp of Israel arranged around the tabernacle as depicted in the book of Numbers as the interpretive key. Our author has imaginatively constructed a sermon along the lines of this picture of God's people on their way to the promised land, with Jesus as their leader and high priest, and has used it to draw out lessons that help deal with the pastoral problems of the congregation.

An examination of the exhortations of Hebrews in chapter five will demonstrate how as the camp of God's people migrate to the promise, the author warns against retrogressing back into the former way of life or standing still in unbelief, refusing to move on and enter God's promise. He rather encourages them to press on and persevere as God's people, drawing their strength from their great high priest and look forward to what God has prepared ahead of them.

5

The Migration of the Camp of God's People to the Promise

Spatial Analysis of the Exhortations of Hebrews

WE NOW turn our attention to the exhortations of Hebrews. It is within the exhortations that we find the author's pastoral concerns and inner passions expressed through ardent encouragement, fierce warnings, fervent admonishment, and inspired reminders. These are the parts of the epistle that teem with raw feeling, passion, and fervor from a pastor's pen. Unlike the static expositions, the exhortations flow with emotions and movement, pleadings and threats, and coaxing and persuasion. The exhortations are the most popular parts of the epistle and are frequently used as proof texts in sermons today, and yet their role in the overall context of the epistle is least understood. The author of Hebrews called his letter a "word of exhortation" (Heb 13:22), a phrase that is also used in Acts 13:15 to describe homilies in Jewish synagogues. Like all good sermons, the exhortations serve to stir, awaken, spur and move the congregation on to deeper things in Christ.

It is of no useful purpose to debate whether it is the expositions or the exhortations of Hebrews that have priority, for as noted earlier, the two are closely interwoven and dependent on each other. The epistle is not a treatise or essay of doctrinal teachings but a sermon that encourages its hearers not to stand still in their faith or retrogress but rather to move forward in spiritual growth and persevere toward the goal of entering God's promise. These exhortations, on the other hand, draw their meaning and force from the expositions that serve as their foundational bases. Hence, they both depend on each other. Before we start, however, a brief discussion on the overall strategies of exhortations is in order.

The Pastoral Strategies of Exhortations

As an exhortation, Hebrews belongs to the broad literary genre of antiquity called paranaesis. According to Perdue, paranaesis on the whole seeks to provide "guidance for the moral life" by employing combinations of one or more of four possible strategies: to convert the audience to a new way of life (socialization), affirm a particular way of life (legitimization), or subvert an existing social structure in order to overthrow and replace it (polemicization and conflict).[1] Attridge, in his close examination of the paranaetic aspects of Hebrews, concludes that the author uses a strategy that, though it is not legitimization or conflict, has features of both and should therefore be characterized separately as a homily (or paraclesis). The purpose of the paranaesis of Hebrews, he notes, is "not to socialize new members of a group, to legitimize a structure of authority, or to polemicize against an external social unit and its symbol system, but to reinforce the identity of a social sub-group in such a way as not to isolate it from its environment."[2]

In order to address the pastoral difficulties of his congregation, the author of the epistle to the Hebrews therefore uses a strategy made up of three prongs. First, through his typological interpretation of the Old Testament, he creates a specific *identity* for his congregation, which he then reinforces. Our examination of the exposition has demonstrated that this identity consisted of linking the members of the congregation to the camp of Israel in the wilderness surrounding the tabernacle with Jesus as their eternal high priest. His congregation was part and parcel of the migrant people of God, gathered around the tabernacle where Christ, their "Moses" and "Aaron," leads and ministers. In the exhortations, we shall find that Hebrews buttresses this identity further by demonstrating that the camp was a migrating camp, a mobile camp that is made of all God's people throughout salvation history. Believers are depicted as migrants and sojourners who are heading toward God's salvation (Heb 2:1–4), God's rest (Heb 4:1), God's perfection (Heb 6:1), and God's promise (Heb 10:36).

The second prong of our author's strategy was that he drew from the *collective memories* of this camp in order to underline the necessary behavior and moral life that accompanies the migrant people of God. The Old Testament counterparts of the people of God had a distinctive history that his congregation needed to share in order to be confirmed in their identity. Hebrews therefore cites the negative examples of infidelity,

---

1. Perdue, "The Social Character of Paranaesis," 5–39.
2. Attridge, "Paranaesis in a Homily," 211–26.

unfaithfulness, and spiritual failure of the Exodus generation, as well as the positive examples of faith and perseverance of members of this camp to reinforce this teaching. The supreme example in Hebrews, however, is Jesus, who throughout the epistle is portrayed as kinsman-redeemer (Hebrews 2), leader or pioneer (Hebrews 2), great high priest (Hebrews 3), apostle (Hebrews 3), path-breaker (Hebrews 2), and finisher (Hebrews 12) of our faith. He is accordingly the camp's Moses and Aaron, and he leads them "to Mount Zion, to the heavenly Jerusalem, the city of the living God" (Heb 12:22). The author thus encourages the migrant camp to "fix our eyes on Jesus, the author and perfecter of our faith, who for the joy set before him endured the cross, scorning its shame, and sat down at the right hand of the throne of God" (Heb 12:2).

In the third prong of his strategy, the author provides his audience with the *spiritual resources* for completing the migrant's journey to the "homeland." The major resource may be subsumed under the title of "faith" as broadly understood, for our author perceived "faith" as multifaceted. This faith is based on the finished work of Christ in the Holy of Holies and is grounded in the hope anchored there. Faith is faithfulness to the end, the faith that feeds patient endurance and perseverance in suffering, the faith that is the certainty "of what we do not see" (Heb 11:1). Along with faith, the other resources are hope in the fulfillment of God's promises and love within the fellowship of believers.

In summary, the main objective of the exhortations of Hebrews is to reinforce the identity of the believers as a migrant camp of the people of God who are migrating to the promise. By making references to their collective memory and elucidating the spiritual resources necessary for the journey, the author encourages believers to move forward toward the promise that God has prepared for his people.

The Exhortations of the Epistle to the Hebrews

A cursory reading of the exhortations of Hebrews shows that they are constructed around several metaphors of movement. Believers are warned not to "drift away" (Hebrews 2) from the great salvation or they would not "escape" God's punishment; they are to "enter" or "go in" to God's rest (Hebrews 4); they are to "leave" the basic doctrines behind and "go on" to perfection (Hebrews 6); and they are again to "enter" and "draw near" and not to "shrink back" from the promise (Hebrews 10). *Movement* is therefore the dominant motif that characterizes the exhortations of Hebrews and we will find that application of the metaphor of migration will greatly enhance our understanding of it.

In chapter three, we examined the cognitive aspects of human spatial movement and noted that the movement of a person is defined as his or her change of location relative to other places over time through the use of spatial direction and orientation. We defined spatial orientation as the process of alignment in relation to a specific direction of movement that involves the mental integration of sensory perception from the environment. We also emphasized that in human beings, input from the major organs of sensory perception, especially sight and hearing, are integrated in the brain to provide this spatial orientation, and these serve as rich sources of biblical metaphors related to the orientation of the believer as a person on the move. Memory also plays an important role in fine-tuning the perception required for orientation.

In addition, we learned that migration is a liminal situation, fraught with dangers that require effective functional *communitas* for completion. Like all movements, migration has three phases: separation, liminality, and entrance into the destination. We will now employ these concepts to explain the exhortations of Hebrews. The first part of the chapter will examine the exhortations of Hebrews by employing the concepts from migration as a heuristic grid. The second part will bring together the features of Hebrews, which demonstrate that it parallels the book of Numbers.

The Literary Structure of the Exhortations of Hebrews

According to George Guthrie, the exhortations of Hebrews are found in Heb 2:1–4, 3:1–4:13, 4:14–16, 5:11–6:20, and 10:19–13:17. Hebrews 3:1–6, 4:14–16, 6:18–20, and perhaps certain parts of Hebrews 11 combine both expositions and exhortations, hence demonstrating how difficult it is to separate these two elements.[3] As shown in table 5.1, each block of exhortation is made up of five specific elements that are treated by the author in varying lengths and depths:

1. Reference is made to paying attention to God's word
2. Warning against the consequences of retrogression or failure to progress
3. Encouragement to hold fast, persevere, move forward, and enter
4. Reminder of the community's past experiences

---

3. Vanhoye categorizes Hebrews 11 as an exposition, whereas Guthrie regards it as an exhortation.

5. Negative and positive examples of God's people from the Old Testament

Of these five elements, the central purpose of the exhortations is in the encouragement to hold fast to the confession, move forward in the spiritual journey, and enter. In a sense, therefore, Heb 4:1–16, 6:1–3, 12–20, 10:19–23, 35–39, and 12:1–3 are the main emphases of the exhortations. Indeed, Harold Attridge has suggested that the whole of the exhortations are adequately summarized by Heb 4:14 and 16. He notes, "The fidelity (*pistis*) which is of so much concern to Hebrews can readily be understood as a combination of both the 'static' and the 'dynamic' qualities suggested by these two exhortations."[4] The references to attention to God's word (perception), the negative and positive examples from the Old Testament people of God (collective memory), the harsh warnings about the consequences of retrogression and failure to persevere (dangers in liminality), and the reminders of the past experiences of the community (memory) are all supportive elements that the author uses to provide orientation in this movement.

In the background of each block of exhortation are not just a movement motif, but also allusions and echoes to the wilderness experiences of Israel. Thus each section is presented in such a fashion that it contains a stated or implied origin, destination, and dangers that could cause disorientation and encouragement to faith, hope, and love to enable orientation during the migration. As a result, the exhortations are best studied by employing the three phases of the migration metaphor: separation, liminality, and entrance into destination. We will now discuss each block of exhortation using these phases of migration as our grid.

Don't Drift from Your Salvation: Pay Attention to God's Word (Heb 2:1–4)

Brief Comments on the Passage

Hebrews 2:1 flows naturally from Heb 1:14. The author picks up the subject of salvation that the saints would inherit and warns that inattention to God's word and gradual unthinking drift in the journey of migration could lead to forfeiture of this salvation. In comparing his congregation with the redeemed people of Israel, Hebrews suggests discontinuity between the old dispensation and the new when he states that whereas the

---

4. Attridge, "Paranaesis," 221.

Table 5.1: The Five Elements of the Exhortations of Hebrews

	Heb 2:1–4	*Heb 3:7–4:16*	*Heb 5:12–6:20*	*Heb 10:19–13:17*
God's Word (Perception)	Heb 2:1	Heb 3:7–4:11	Heb 5:12–14	Heb 10:24–25
Warning (Dangers in Liminality)	Heb 2:1, 3	Heb 3:12–19	Heb 6:4–8	Heb 10:26–31, 12:25–29
Encouragement (Movement)	None	Heb 4:1–16	Heb 6:1–3, 12–20	Heb 10:19–23, 35–39, 12:1–3
Reminder (Memory)	Heb 2:4	None	Heb 6:9–11	Heb 10:32–34
Old Testament Examples (Memory and Communitas)	Punishment in Old Testament (Heb 2:2)	Wilderness Generation (Hebrews 3)	Wilderness Gen. and Abraham (Heb 6:12–15)	Positive and Negative Examples (Hebrews 11 & Esau 12:16)

angels gave the law through Moses to the people of old, it is Christ who preached salvation to the new generation. On the other hand, he also suggests continuity of the people of God since these same angels minister unto all those who would inherit God's salvation, old and new.

The passage also contains one of the important features of all the exhortations that highlight the fierce consequences of drifting away or "slipping." It would simply lead to a worse state of affairs than what happened to the Exodus generation. The author of Hebrews will return again and again to emphasize the grave consequences of backsliding. His aim, as we shall later emphasize, was to instill a godly fear that does not presume upon God or take his costly salvation for granted. Passionate, effective pastoral warning of God's judgment on the disobedient was an integral part of this author's discipleship ministry.

Separation, Liminality, and Entrance into the Destination

The first exhortation provides us with a powerful picture of the inauguration of the community behind Hebrews. Their separation from the world was instigated by the "pull" factor of the "great salvation." This is the salvation for which angels have been sent to minister to the saints (Heb 1:14) and which was first proclaimed by the Lord Jesus Christ and "was confirmed to us by those who heard him. God also testified to it by signs, wonders and various miracles" (Heb 2:3–4). The congregation was therefore made up of second-generation Christians who received the gospel from the apostolic fathers. As in other parts of the New Testament, the ministry of the apostles among them was accompanied by, in Paul's words, the "demonstration of the Spirit's power" (1 Cor 2:4). Our author will later refer to this experience of God's power among them as the tasting of "the powers of the coming age" (Heb 6:5). The separation phase of this group of believers was thus characterized by God's mighty intervention in human life that transformed them into new people, and their new life was signified by the expression of various "gifts of the Holy Spirit distributed according to his will" (Heb 2:4).

The references to signs, wonders, and various miracles accompanying their redemption parallels the Old Testament's formula for depicting the deliverance of Israel from the slavery of Egypt. Deut 26:8 describes how "the LORD brought us out of Egypt with a mighty hand and an outstretched arm, with great terror and with miraculous signs and wonders."[5] Similarly Psalm 135:8–9 describes how the Lord "struck down the firstborn of Egypt, the firstborn of men and animals. He sent his signs and wonders into your midst, O Egypt, against Pharaoh and all his servants." Rengstorf is therefore right in stating, "When the OT speaks of God's signs and wonders the reference is almost always to the leading of the people out of Egypt by Moses and to the special circumstances under which the people stood up to the passage of the Red Sea and in all of which God proved Himself to be the Almighty and showed Israel to be His chosen people."[6]

Though the miracles, signs, and wonders no doubt occurred at the inauguration of the Hebrews congregation, our author describes them in such a way that it parallels the deliverance of the people of Israel from Egypt. The author's reference to the giving of the law at Mount Sinai through the angels in Heb 2:2 supports such an interpretation. Indeed, the whole of Heb 2:1–4 echoes a similar statement by Jehovah to the failing Exodus generation in Num 14:22: "The people who have seen my glory and the signs that I did in Egypt and in the wilderness, and yet have tested

---

5. See also Exod 3:20, 7:3, 15:11; Deut 4:34, 6:22, 7:19.
6. Rengstorf, "Semeion," 216.

me these ten times and have not obeyed my voice" (NRSV). Deliverance in both cases of the Old Testament people of Israel and the New Testament congregation of Hebrews involved seeing God's glory and wonders. As opposed to their wilderness counterpart, Hebrews calls upon his congregation to pay attention to God's voice so that they do not also fall away.

The author expresses his concern that after a glorious separation phase, his congregation was succumbing to the dangers of laziness, neglect, and inattention during the liminal phase of the migration. The liminal phase is always dangerous. In Douglas's words, "Danger lies in transitional states, simply because transition is neither one state nor the next. The person who must pass from one to another is himself in danger and emanates danger to others."[7] Similarly, the liminal phase of the believer's journey is filled with dangers that threaten his or her fall. Here in Heb 2:1–4, our author thus expresses anxiety over the precarious state of the congregation's faith and warns them not to "neglect" their salvation, "drift away," or "slip back" from their position in Christ. Each of these words expresses a negative movement. As put by Koester, "'neglect' suggests a gradual, unthinking movement away from the faith."[8] Similarly "drift away" is a nautical metaphor depicting an unanchored ship that is drifting carelessly from the harbor into the sea. A constant danger of the liminal phase of any human movement is inattention, lack of focus or concentration, disorientation, and carelessness. The result of distraction is a precarious slide into a way of life that is worse than the former.

Throughout the exhortations, our author regarded the situation whereby one does not focus on Christ but drifts or shrinks back as tantamount to rebellion and rejection of Christ himself. Hence at each point, he issues harsh warnings about the terrible results of continual drift. These warnings also depict movement: "How shall we *escape* if we ignore such a great salvation" (Heb 2:3; emphasis added). The particular Greek word, *ekphensometha* ("escape") is used seven times in the New Testament; on four occasions it refers to escaping the apocalyptic judgment of God (Luke 21:36; Rom 2:3; 1 Thess 5:3; Heb 2:3.). The other three refer to escaping from other dangers such as imprisonment (Acts 16:27), physical harm (Acts 19:16), and persecution (2 Cor 11:33). Hebrews 12:25 will echo a similar sentiment to Heb 2:3, warning that those of the old dispensation "did not *escape* when they refused him who warned them on earth, how much less will we, if we turn away from him who warns us from heaven?"

---

7. Douglas, *Purity and Danger*, 119–20.
8. Koester, *Hebrews ABC*, 206.

(emphasis added). The author compares the divine judgment of Israel during the wilderness journey (i.e., "every violation and disobedience received its just punishment") with the judgment that could come on those who received the gospel, not from angels but from the superior Christ.

It has been debated throughout church history whether the envisaged consequences of drifting away, or falling away in Hebrews, amount to eternal damnation or some sort of temporary punishment or even lack of rewards. Important though this debate is, the intention of the author was aimed more at re-orienting drifting Christians on the move. The response he was looking for was not one that asks whether eternal damnation was at all possible for the Christian, but a response of constructive fear that is instilled by the knowledge of potential disaster if one is careless during liminality. Noah's fear (Heb 11:7) is one such example that reflected his faith and believers are therefore encouraged to cultivate a similar kind of fear (Heb 12:28–29).

The warning passages of Hebrews are, for that matter, integral to the author's argument, and interpretations that reduce their full force are similar to dismissing as exaggerations the warnings by a driving instructor about the dangers of driving while disoriented, at least in sociological terms. Since our author's dire warnings echo the warnings by the Lord (Matt 12:31–32), Paul (1 Cor 10; 1 Tim 1:20), and John (1 John 5:16–17) and yet equally emphasize the completeness of the salvation for which we are redeemed, the focus of interpretation should be on how they contribute to orienting the migrant and not whether they are exaggerations by the author. The knowledge of potential disaster during the journey should instill godly fear and careful concentration needed for orientation. After all our debates, what we need is this godly fear that produces concentration of the mind and careful attention to God's word. In this respect, our author's warnings parallel Paul's in 1 Cor 10:12, "If you think you are standing firm, be careful that you don't fall."

The primary encouragement and antidote to drifting away from the faith during the liminal phase is careful attention to God's word. The word of God, both written in the scriptures and spoken in the context of preaching, plays a central role in relation to the faith of the believer in Hebrews. In Hebrews 3–4, the wilderness generation hardened their hearts to God's word, resulting in their rebellion and departure from the living God. The "message they heard was of no value to them, because those who heard did not combine it with faith" (Heb 4:2). In Hebrews 5–6, Christians are described as people who "have tasted the goodness of the Word of God" (Heb 6:5). Like the manna in the desert, God's word, to quote Brown, is "the essential sustenance for the journey, the only satisfying food of life."[9] In Heb 13:7, the faith of the community's leaders "who spoke the word of God to you" is depicted as an example to be imitated. This parallels the author's earlier reference to Abraham's faith in God's promises, which he also enjoins the believers to emulate (Heb 6:12–13). Here in Hebrews 2, inattention to God's word results in drifting away from the faith.

In setting the great salvation in opposition to punitive punishment, the author of Hebrews conveys the notion of salvation as the *destination* of the migration of God's people. He had previously indicated in Heb 1:14 that believers will inherit this salvation; now he conveys some of its features. This salvation was first preached by the Lord (Heb 2:3), for he is the author (Heb 2:10) and the source (Heb 5:9) of it. It is a great salvation, because he provides it from within the Holy of Holies, "completely," "to the uttermost" (MKJV) to those who come to him (Heb 7:25). Though this salvation is in the future, since it will be inherited (Heb 1:14) and fully experienced at the second coming of Christ (Heb 9:28), its experience by the believers has already begun, for the angels have been sent to minister to them in this regard. Present entrance into it occurs now as we come to him (Heb 7:25), taste of its powers (Heb 6:5), and indeed escape "to take hold of the hope" before us (Heb 6:18).

It is therefore an "already and not yet" salvation. In Ladd's words, "Hebrews recognizes the present as the time of eschatological fulfillment (realized eschatology), while the consummation awaits the second coming of Christ."[10] Salvation in Hebrews is "the eschatological possession of a forward-looking faith,"[11] to borrow from Osborne. Here in Heb 2:1–4, our author's concern is that by sheer neglect, carelessness, and laziness, we could ignore this great salvation, leading to a severe punishment that would be far greater than what happened to the Israelites in the wilderness. The full benefit of this salvation, for that matter, requires all of our full attention, steadfastness, and commitment. Colijn is right when she posits, "For the author of Hebrews, salvation is a pilgrimage toward a promise, a journey toward God. It is grounded in relationship. Worship is both its means and its end."[12]

---

9. Brown, *The Message of Hebrews*, 109.
10. Ladd, *Theology*, 575.
11. Osborne, *Soteriology*, 145.
12. Colijn, "Let Us Approach," 572.

The Relationship between Heb 2:1–4 and the Expositions

How does this section of the exhortations of Hebrews fit with the expositions? In referring to the "the message spoken by the angels," our author links and compares the Hebrews community with the wilderness camp of Israel on their way to the promised land gathered at the foot of Mount Sinai to receive the commands through the agency of angels. Whereas the surrounding expositions depict a static camp of God's people with their heavenly high priest providing divine access and help, the exhortations depict the same camp on the move, in the liminal state, facing dangers and needing to persevere as it migrates to the promise. Hebrews 2:1–4 highlights the danger of carelessness and inattention to the word of God. This word of God is required for feeding the life of faith, and it is this faith that links the two sub-genres of the epistle. Whereas the expositions teach how faith has been secured through the ministry of the great high priest, the exhortations teach how faith is nurtured and maintained in the believer's life. Careful attention to God's word is what would maintain faith as the camp travels through the liminal phase.

Don't Depart from the Living God: Enter into His Rest (Heb 3:1–4:16)

Brief Comments on the Passage

Hebrews 3–4 constitute a long Midrash on the necessity of faith and faithfulness in order to enter into the presence of God. It is of major interest, for not only does it present features of the nature of liminality, it also unveils a very clear link between the theologies of Hebrews and the book of Numbers.[13] In addition, its complex teaching on God's rest is another indication in the epistle of the nature of the destination of the migrant's journey.

Hebrews 3:1–6 is an exposition sandwiched by two brief exhortations. Hebrews 3:7–4:13 is the main exhortation that employs Ps 95 to comment on the failure of the wilderness generation to enter into the promised land. It warns the Hebrews congregation not to commit the same sin of hardening of the heart as that generation did. Hebrews 4:14–16 is a transitional passage that summarizes the author's teaching and then encourages the believers to "approach the throne of grace" for help and strength for the journey. Based on this passage, Käsemann suggested that the theology of

---

13. Isaiah 66 may also have furnished important themes to this Midrash on the heavenly assembly, God's house, God's rest, disobedience, etc.

Hebrews might be considered under the title of the "Wandering People of God."[14] However, Käsemann "exaggerated Gnostic influence on the author of Hebrews"[15] and the emphasis of the passage is more on a journey to a specific destination rather than wandering in the spiritual wilderness. The whole passage indeed contains the full elements of the migration of the people of God from their separation, through liminality, to entrance into the destination.

Separation, Liminality, and Entrance into the Destination

As it was with the first exhortation, the separation phase of this group of believers is described in brief but dramatic terms. The author calls the believers "holy brothers, who share in the heavenly calling" (Heb 3:1). This way of identifying the believers demonstrates a number of themes that typify their separation. First, they are holy (i.e., they have been purified and set apart from the world unto God). This description looks back to the portrayal of believers in Hebrews 2 as people who have been freed from slavery and sanctified by the Son who declares God's name to them to praise him in the assembly (Heb 2:10–15). Second, the group's identity is one of collegiality, kinship, and partnership together in God's service—they had *communitas*. They "share" the same heavenly calling as Moses and the Son. The writer would later depict them as the "house of God" (Heb 3:6) that were separated from the world and "built" by the Son. Third, they have been called from and toward heaven. They are indeed children who are being brought to glory (Heb 2:10). The word "calling" is used throughout the New Testament to describe the Christian way of life[16] and denotes having to tread a specific direction and lifestyle that is heavenward.

In describing the believers as holy brothers sharing the same heavenly calling, our author is echoing a common Old Testament language for the liberated Exodus generation. At that time, God's word to Pharaoh through Moses was, "Israel is my firstborn son, and I told you, 'Let my son go, so he may worship me'" (Exod 4:22–23). Three months into Israel's migration journey, God told them at Mount Sinai, "You will be my treasured possession. Although the whole earth is mine, you will be for me a kingdom of priests and a holy nation" (Exod 19:5–6). God also spoke through Hosea,

---

14. Käsemann, *The Wandering People of God*, 1984.

15. Ellingworth, *Hebrews*, 43.

16. Rom 11:29; 1 Cor 1:26, 7:20; Eph 1:18, 4:4; Phil 3:14; 2 Thess 1:11; 2 Tim 1:9; 2 Pet 1:10.

no doubt with double meanings, "When Israel was a child, I loved him, and out of Egypt I called my son" (Hos 11:1). Sonship and priestly worship hence describe the calling of Israel from Egypt, just as they describe the "holy brothers" of Hebrews who are called to heaven. Consequently, in characterizing the believers of Hebrews in such terms, and linking it with a comparison of Jesus with Moses in Hebrews 3, the author of Hebrews depicts the separation phase of the believers in terms that echo the redemption of Israel from Egypt (Heb 3:16). Unlike Israel, however, the eventual destination of their journey is heaven, and not Canaan, though the author teaches that the promised land was figurative of heaven.

Hebrews 3–4 portrays the nature of the dangers that believers face in their condition of liminality as they travel to their heavenly destination. Using Ps 95's commentary on the failure of the Exodus generation to enter the promised land (Numbers 14), the author admonishes them about the necessity of faithfulness in persevering to the end and of faith to enter into God's rest. This may be summarized using Heb 3:12, "See to it, brothers, that none of you has a sinful, unbelieving heart that turns away from the living God." In the liminal state of the journey, carelessness leads to unbelief, which then leads to disobedience and departure from the living God. As in the first exhortation, carelessness emanates from inattention to God's word, so that "hearing God's voice" (i.e., paying attention to the word of God in faith) is its primary antidote.

The author of Hebrews teaches over and over again that God continues to speak today. To him, the God who spoke to the rebellious Exodus generation also spoke through David calling his day "today." The "today" of God's word is still present, even though a time will come when the opportunity for response is lost (Heb 4:7–9). The word of God, to Hebrews, is indeed "living and active," and it is only through careful attention to it that we will be kept from departing from the living God. The author moves further than the earlier exhortation by encouraging the sharing of God's word in the context of the fellowship as the antidote to carelessness. "Encourage one another daily, as long as it is called Today, so that none of you may be hardened by sin's deceitfulness" (Heb 3:13). They are to take opportunity of the *communitas* offered by their liminal state to strengthen and bolster one another's faith so that none of them slips into a life of faithlessness and disobedience.

Careful attention to God's word will also make believers "know God's ways," whereas inattention results in "their hearts always going astray" (Heb 3:10). "God's ways" is a movement metaphor that depicts both his powerful and gracious manner of dealing with his people and the instructions that he lays before them to follow (Deut 26:17). So Moses prayed to Jehovah, "Teach me your ways so I may know you and continue to find favor with you. Remember that this nation is your people" (Exod 33:13).

Underneath the depiction of the Christian life as "God's way(s)" is the imagery of a widely open wilderness, with several confusing paths, only one of which is God's way (i.e., God's direction). Only those who pay careful attention to his word will know his ways and remain in them. Hence, during the establishment of God's covenant with Israel in the wilderness, he charged them, "See, I am sending an angel ahead of you to guard you along the way and to bring you to the place I have prepared. Pay attention to him and listen to what he says . . . If you listen carefully to what he says and do all that I say, I will be an enemy to your enemies and will oppose those who oppose you" (Exod 23:20–22). Indeed, Coats has suggested that based on Exod 13:17–22, which explains the reason for Israel's rather long trek through the wilderness instead of the shorter route through the land of the Philistines, "the uniting motif in the wilderness theme is God's leadership."[17] Knowing God's ways, in the context of the wilderness motif of Ps 95 therefore evokes the imagery of the pillar of cloud and fire and the tabernacle that led God's people (Num 14:14).[18] Other parts of the Old Testament, especially the Wisdom Literature, similarly reflect this emphasis on God's way as a correct path in the wilderness.[19] Equally, the New Testament describes the first Christians as followers of "the Way" (Acts 9:2, 19:9, 23, 24:14, 22).

Inattention to God's word also results in unbelief, a menace that befell the Exodus generation in the wilderness. The wilderness motif in scripture symbolizes the hardships that may result in one questioning and doubting one's faith and mission in life (e.g., Deut 8:2–3) and testing of one's covenantal loyalty and faithfulness to God.[20] On the other hand, in the words of Dozeman, it is also a "location where God is encountered, where personal transformation takes place and where community

17. Coats, "Exposition of the Wilderness Traditions," 292.

18. Harrelson has also suggested that the whole of the theology of Numbers can be summarized under the notion of guidance in the wilderness. "The census (chap 1), the order of match and encampment (chap. 2–4), the legal prescriptions (chap. 3–10), though given at Sinai are clearly intended as preparatory acts for the coming journey. It is safe to say therefore that a single theme is dominant in the material found in Numbers: Yahweh's guidance and Testing of Israel in the wilderness" (Harrelson, "Guidance in the Wilderness," 27).

19. See Bricker, "The Doctrine of the 'Two Ways' in Proverbs," 501–17.

20. See Funk, "The Wilderness," 206–14.

The Migration of the Camp of God's People to the Promise

is formed,"[21] a place of preparation and of "judgment and renewal."[22] The wilderness motif therefore has positive and negative aspects. Everyone who passes through it is subjected to one test or another. Those who humble themselves and persevere in faith come out of it transformed, whereas those who succumb to the test and give up their faith and calling end up "departing from the living God."

From the narratives of the wilderness wanderings of Israel in the Pentateuch, their unbelief consisted of a continual questioning of God's love and intentions for his people (Exod 17:1–7), lack of will to believe God's promises of giving them the land (Numbers 13–14), and repeated rejection of the authority of God through his servant Moses (Deut 1). On all counts, unbelief is directly related to the rejection of the word of God and results in the hardening of the heart. In Lane's words, "Unbelief is not a lack of faith or trust. It is the refusal to believe God. It leads inevitably to a turning away from God in a deliberate act of rejection."[23]

The dire consequence of unbelief is "departure" or "turning away" from "the living God" (Heb 3:12). This is another means of describing apostasy. The characterization of Jehovah as "the living God" in the Old Testament (e.g., Deut 5:26; Josh 3:10; 2 Kgs 19:16) was a distinctive way of differentiating him from his Canaanite Baal rivals. Departing from the living God is hence a choice of the will not to yield to him or follow his ways; it is apostasy. The Exodus generation fell through their unbelief and rebellion and God therefore barred them from his rest (Heb 3:18). This was the exact danger that faced the Hebrews congregation if they continued in their spiritual malaise and inattention to God's word.

According to Hebrews 3–4, the destination of the Christian's migration is God's rest. Its exposition in Hebrews 3–4 is complex and the text indicates several shades of its meaning. The problem is that though the author repeatedly mentions God's rest and brings together the Old Testament dimensions of the doctrine, he does not define exactly what it was. It may have been that his congregation was already familiar with the concept. He uses three Greek words to express the concept: *katapausin* (Heb 3:11, 18, 4:1, 3, 5:10, 11; noun: reposing down, abode, rest); *katepausen* (Heb 4:4, 8; verb: settle down, colonize, desist, or cease); and *sabbatismos* (Heb 4:10; Sabbath rest, unique to Hebrews). In the Old Testament, it was a term used for the land of Canaan as the place of Israel's rest from their

---

21. Dozeman, "The Wilderness and Salvation History in the Hagar Story," 43.
22. Gibson, "Jesus' Wilderness Temptation according to Mark," 15.
23. Lane, *Hebrews 1–8*, 86.

enemies (Deut 3:20, 12:10), as the place where the Ark of the Covenant resides (i.e., the Holy of Holies; Ps 132:8, 13–14), and for the Sabbath Day Celebrations (Exod 35:2). The author of Hebrews combines all three in the exposition of rest in Hebrews 4.

Toussaint has correctly pointed out, "The writer of Hebrews is looking at several facets of rest. First, there is the seventh day rest of God when He ceased from His creative work (4:4, 10). There is a second aspect of rest, the rest which involved Israel's taking of the promised land (3:11, 18–19) . . . The third facet of rest is the promised rest."[24] The debate has been over the meaning of the third facet: is it a future eschatological condition that is part of life in heaven, the summary of the whole condition of heaven, or a spiritual state which though extending into the future heaven may be foretasted in this life?[25]

Oberholtzer, in subscribing to the first interpretation, has argued that rest represents the "eschatological rewards" in God's paradise and not the totality of life in heaven.[26] In his view, therefore, the warning was against losing rewards in heaven and not the loss of entry into heaven. Gleason, suggesting that rest is more easily summarized by the nature of the life of Adam and Eve in the Garden of Eden before the fall (thus subscribing to the second), has similarly suggested that the warning about forfeiting rest in Ps 95:11 "is best understood as a warning against forfeiting the right to worship before the presence of the Lord in His Holy sanctuary and to enjoy the covenantal blessings."[27] Isaacs, on the other hand, sees it as a purely future eschatological salvation "in the presence of God in heaven itself."[28] Thus it is an experience that awaits its fulfilment in the future.

I do subscribe to the view that rest, as a condition of spiritual communion in God's presence, may be experienced now as a foretaste of life in heaven and in the world to come. The language of Hebrews 4 suggests that rest is entered into only by faith (Heb 4:2–3), and available only to those who have professed this faith (Heb 3:16–19). As a condition or

---

24. Toussaint, "Eschatology of the Warning Passages," 71.

25. Generally, the promised rest has been interpreted either as "the condition of paradise in heaven" (e.g., Bruce, *Hebrews*, 77–79; Hewitt, *Hebrews*, 89; Hughes, *Hebrews*, 161–62; and Kent, *Hebrews*, 86–87) or the coming millennial kingdom (i.e., the world to come; e.g. Buchanan, *To the Hebrews*, 64–74; Lang, *Hebrews*, 75–80; Kaiser, "The Promise Theme," 138–50).

26. Oberholtzer, "The Kingdom Rest," 185–96.

27. Gleason, "The Old Testament Background of Rest," 296.

28. Isaacs, *Reading*, 63.

state, it was in the future of the congregation of Hebrews (Heb 4:11), but the author expressed the conviction that an assurance or foretaste of this condition may be experienced even as they were reading his letter: "Now we who have believed enter [literarily: in the process of entering into] that rest" (Heb 4:3). Rest is hence entered into not after death but "now," by faith, and its experience does not have to wait till a future time but "Today." That is the nature of the faith that our author would explain more fully in Heb 11:1–2. Bruce's words are right on the mark: rest "is evidently an experience which they [the audience] do not enjoy in their mortal life, although it belongs to them as a heritage, and by faith they may live in the good of it here and now."[29] The full nature of God's Sabbath's rest will certainly be experienced in the future when all the people of God "together with us" are made perfect (Heb 11:40). In eschatological terms, rest is in the future, whereas in soteriological terms, it represents realized salvation, a taste of what is in the future.

The Relationship Between Hebrews 3–4 and the Expositions

The expositions of Hebrews also help us to understand the nature of God's rest in this block of exhortation, for just as the Holy of Holies is symbolic of God's throne room (Heb 4:14–16), it is also symbolic of his rest (Ps 132:8, 13–14). And just as even now believers have the confidence to enter this throne room for help in time of need, they may also now experience a foretaste of the rest that God gives as they enter by faith. The complete experience of rest will, however, only be fully theirs in the "heavenly Jerusalem" (Heb 12:22) that is to come.

Inattention to God's word, disobedience, unbelief, and lack of perseverance are the obstacles that prevent believers from enjoying the aspects of God's rest in this life and the life to come. It is now clear that the cultic themes that our author develops in the expositions provide the solutions to the problems that he highlights and presses home in the exhortations. Whereas the expositions teach how the death and ministry of the exalted Christ procures and make available God's rest, the exhortations teach how to enjoy this rest by faith. This is exactly the nature of the theology of the book of Numbers. The problem of unbelief that plagued the Exodus generation was deeply spiritual. The institution of the tabernacle and its cultic worship was therefore meant to provide them with the access to God who helps them in their time of need. The failure of the Exodus generation to believe and persevere was a failure to draw from the spiritual resources

---

29. Bruce, *Hebrews*, 110.

from the throne room (Num 14:44). This was the same danger that faced the congregation of Hebrews.

Don't Delay Your Spiritual Growth: Go on to Perfection (Heb 5:11–6:20)

Brief Comments on the Passage

In this exhortation, our author decries the lack of spiritual progress among his congregation, expresses his deep anxiety that this made them prone to fall away, warns them of the dire consequences of such a result, conveys his confidence that they will persevere and not fall away, and encourages them to imitate the faith of God's people who in the past have relied on the sure and unfailing promises of God to persevere to the end.

The passage is the most challenging of the exhortations of Hebrews for a number of reasons. The warning is pretty severe, and Heb 6:4–8 in particular, which relates to the security of the believer, has been one of the most hotly debated passages in scripture. Unlike the other exhortations, no explicit reference to an Old Testament example is made, even though attention to the scriptural allusions and echoes will direct us again to the Exodus generation in Numbers. Abraham is briefly mentioned as a positive example to be imitated, but the author does not dwell on him, choosing rather to focus on the faithfulness of God and the eternal endurance of his promises. In addition, though the primary Old Testament example in the background of the passage is the migration of Israel, the metaphors he develops are not just those of movement, but also those of biological growth. Even then, the goal of spiritual growth is expressed as a movement involving "leaving" elementary issues and going on to "perfection." Like its earlier counterparts ("salvation" and "rest"), "perfection" is also a complex concept that combines features that may be experienced now, but its fullness will only be in the future eschatological age.

The passage is also of benefit in two other respects. It provides us with a list of some of the basic catechetical subjects that new believers were taught in the first century and furnishes us with an idea of how we may assess spiritual growth among our fellowship members. It also provides some detailed information about the past history of this congregation. Hebrews 6:10–11 suggests they were indeed people who had in the past been committed to the faith in sharing with the work of the gospel and associating with its missionaries. Somehow they became held up in the past, perhaps living on it and refusing to move on. They had become frozen to their past experiences and consequently stunted in their spiritual growth. The sobering warning to all of us is this: the believer who lives on his or her past is in as much danger of falling away as the one flirting with the enemy, being unfaithful, unbelieving, rebelling, and disobeying.

Hebrews 5:11–6:20 may be subdivided into four parts. Hebrews 5:11–6:3 reflects on the need to grow and move further in the knowledge of Christ. Heb 6:4–8 warns of the severe consequence that result from falling away. Heb 6:9–12 uses reminders of the previous experience and zeal of the congregation to encourage them to imitate the life of faith, and Heb 6:13–20 functions as a transitional passage which combines exposition on the certainty of God's promise with an exhortation and encouragement to hold firmly to the hope offered through Christ's ministry in the Holy of Holies.

Commentators disagree on the Old Testament background of the passage. R. T. France insisted that Ps 110 lies in the background of the whole of Heb 5:5–7:28 but this does not satisfactorily explain the allusions in Hebrews 6.[30] Attridge has, on the other hand, suggested Deut 11 as the background text, and indeed Heb 6:7 clearly echoes the covenantal blessings and curses on the land related to Israel's faithfulness to God as recorded in Deut 11:11–12.[31] Though this extends the wilderness theme of Hebrews, the other references in the passage are not sufficiently accounted for by allusion to Deut 11 alone. Ellingworth has therefore suggested that the passage "is not based on any Old Testament passage either: the writer is appealing to his readers in his own words."[32] It is very much unlike our author to develop ideas that are not directly or indirectly echoing the Old Testament, even though he presents them through allusions and uses his Greco-Roman rhetorical training to enrich the presentation. An Old Testament background is therefore very likely. I share the views of Gleason[33] and Mathewson[34] that the migration of Israel and the whole wilderness motif, Numbers 11–14 and Neh 9 (in addition to Deut 11) in particular, provide the Old Testament background to this exhortation.

---

30. France, "The Writer of Hebrews as a Biblical Expositor," 245–76.
31. Attridge, *Hebrews*, 169; Also, DeSilva, "Perseverance," 231–34.
32. Ellingworth, *Hebrews*, 42.
33. Gleason, "Old Testament Background of Hebrews 6," 62–91.
34. Mathewson, "Reading Heb 6:4–6 in light of the Old Testament," 209–25.

Separation, Liminality, and Entrance into the Destination

Two metaphors are used to represent the separation phase of the believer's journey in this passage: the metaphors of "birth" and of "flight." At the time the author wrote the homily, he felt the believers were "still an infant, is not acquainted with the teaching about righteousness," though they ought to have been mature by now (Heb 5:13–14). As babies they could only digest "milk," for "solid food is for the mature." Their redemption was regarded as new birth and our author expresses his disappointment that they remained infants after some period of time. In Heb 6:18, the author describes believers as people who have "fled to take hold of the hope" anchored in the Holy of Holies. Hebrews had earlier noted how salvation is an escape from severe punishment (Heb 2:2–3) and how before they were redeemed, believers were held as slaves by the devil to the fear of death (Heb 2:15). Here in Heb 6:18, "flight" conveys both notions: flight from severe danger and into a place of refuge.

Interestingly, both metaphors of birth and flight were associated with the deliverance of Israel from Egypt. God told Moses, "I have come down to rescue them from the hand of the Egyptians and to bring them up out of that land into a good and spacious land, a land flowing with milk and honey" (Exod 3:8). That day of deliverance became their birthday, the first day of their calendar year (Exod 12:2) and according to Bergant, the first day "primordially . . . [for] . . . it established the order of the created world and brought the people into existence in this world."[35] Paul also described the crossing of the Red Sea as a symbol of new birth and baptism (1 Cor 10:2). Though the primary allusion in Heb 6:18 is the altar in the priestly courtyard as the place of refuge (1 Kgs 1:50, 2:28), the depiction of the redemption of the Hebrews congregation also echoes the flight of Israel from Egypt (Exod 14:5) for refuge.

That our author should appropriate the Exodus narrative in this depiction of Christian migration should not be a surprise to us, for throughout history, this event has indeed inspired all peoples, not the least the black slaves of America. According to the African American religious historian Albert Raboteau, "The appropriation of the Exodus story was for the slaves a way of articulating their sense of historical identity as a people. That identity was also based, of course, upon their common heritage of enslavement . . . In identifying with the Exodus story; they created meaning and purpose out of the chaotic and senseless experience of slavery."[36]

---

35. Bergant, "An Anthropological Approach to Biblical Interpretation," 57.
36. Raboteau, *Slave Religion*, 311.

It is therefore unsurprising that a first-century Jewish congregation in Diaspora could see its experience in Christ as corresponding to that of the liberation, flight, and birth of the new Israel out of Egypt.

In addition, the depictions of the earlier experience of salvation of the Hebrews congregation in Heb 6:4–5 are full of allusions to the life of redeemed Israel in the wilderness. The believers "have once been enlightened, who have tasted the heavenly gift, who have shared in the Holy Spirit, who have tasted the goodness of the word of God and the powers of the coming age" (Heb 6:4–5). Salvation as spiritual enlightenment not only portrays a movement from ignorance to the knowledge of the truth (Heb 10:26), but also alludes to the pillar that gave Israel light on their journey (Exod 13:20–22, Num 14:14, and Neh 9:12, 9). Sharing in the Holy Spirit also alludes to the experience in the wilderness where, according to Neh 9:20, God "gave [His] good Spirit to instruct them." The book of Numbers describes the corporate ecstatic experience in the wilderness, where the Lord "took of the Spirit that was on him [Moses] and put the Spirit on the seventy elders. When the Spirit rested on them, they prophesied, but they did not do so again" (Num 11:25). The word of God as a "heavenly gift" to be tasted has no parallel anywhere else in the New Testament but is a clear allusion to the manna by which God fed his people in the wilderness (Exod 16, Num 11:7–9, Deut 8:3, 16, Neh 9:15). Thus the language that influences the author of Hebrews' depiction of the experience of salvation is largely drawn from the wilderness experience of the Exodus generation.

The liminal phase of the congregation may simply be put as a state of retrogression. They had become "slow to learn" or "dull of hearing" (MKJV). Hearing and understanding God's word is necessary for progress through faith, and inability to grasp the word of God is a sign of stagnation in spiritual growth. On the other hand, maturing believers are distinguished by their ability to teach the word to others, by virtue of the fact that they have understood it (Heb 5:12) and are able to apply it to judge between what is right from wrong (Heb 5:14). The role of the knowledge of God's word in Christian maturity cannot be overemphasized. In the words of Fortosis, "Though spiritual development is often reflected in behavior, its roots and rationale begin in the mind and emotion."[37] Here our author singles out the poor development of the biblical understanding of the Hebrews as symptomatic of stagnation in spiritual growth.

The depiction of lack of growth or progress is characteristic of persons in a liminal state. In Turner's conceptualization, liminas do not fit the

---

37. Fortosis, "A Developmental Model," 283.

categories that are available for the society's classifications but are rather "between and betwixt." Consequently, one of the main objectives for the separation of liminas is to instruct them to the point that they are capable of fulfilling the higher functions that will be required of them after incorporation. Similarly, in the reckoning of the author of Hebrews, the members of the congregation should have become teachers of God's word by now and accustomed to more complex doctrines. Instead, "You need someone to teach you the elementary truths of God's word all over again" (Heb 5:12). His objective, therefore, was to rouse them from their sloppy dependence to a life of deeper spirituality.

For many readers of Hebrews, what is unnerving about this passage is the relationship the author saw between lack of spiritual growth and possible apostasy. If the believers failed to leave the elementary issues of the faith and move on to perfection, he argues, the end result could be a wavering faith that leads to falling away. Thus once again, inattention to God's word and lack of serious progress in it lies at the root of difficulties in the believer's migration to the promise.

It is therefore not uncommon for interpreters to suggest that "falling away" is the author's way of expressing transitory lapse into sin and that it is not as serious as it sounds. This is not the complete picture, however, for to quote McKnight, "Falling away is not a momentary (however real) lapse into sin from which one repents. Rather . . . the writer has a particular sin in mind: apostasy."[38] It is a very serious situation of separation from God's presence and fear of it happening should therefore refocus and spur believers on to perfection. The author uses the most intense apocalyptic language of warning to instill this fear, for as noted by Nongbri, the actual words of apocalyptic language are not as important as "the specific kind of fear" that such language is designed to instill.[39] Hebrews explains that "falling away" amounted to recrucifying Jesus and subjecting him to so much public shame that it would be "impossible" to be brought back to repentance. The consequence of this state of "impossibility" is severe punishment. Such an end result, according to the author, is not unexpected in agricultural terms and not irrational when we take the covenantal blessings and curses in Deut 11 into consideration (Heb 6:7–8).

---

38. McKnight, "The Warning Passages," 26.
39. Nongbri, "A Touch of Condemnation," 265–79.

It is beyond the scope of this study to discuss the various scholarly views on the interpretation of the "impossibility" passage in Hebrews 6.[40] Whereas some scholars suggest that the "impossibility" is on the part of the church fellowship not being able to restore the fallen person, others assert that the "impossibility" is on God's part, since falling away is equivalent to the "sin against the Holy Spirit." My view is that since the hypothetical condition the author deals with here is apostasy, the "impossibility" is on the part of the person who has fallen away and not on God's part. And if such a person cannot repent, he or she cannot be renewed and restored. The author was convinced that this was not the lot of his audience, however, for the faithfulness of God, as well as theirs, was at stake in the matter. God was not unjust to forget their past zeal and commitment and would sustain them, if they would also remain faithful. Thankfully, the harsh warnings therefore serve another purpose. They are designed to instill fear that would spur the believer on from a life of immature dependence to go on to perfection.

Perfection is consequently the destination of the Christian's journey as expounded by our author in this part of the exhortations. The term perfection is used in Hebrews in a complex manner and plays the same roles that salvation and rest play in the previous exhortations. Throughout the epistle, our author uses four forms of the Greek word *teleiotēs* on sixteen occasions, three of which are directly applicable to the perfection of Jesus himself (Heb 2:10, 5:8–9, and 7:28). He uses the word in such a way that each occurrence has more than one semantic meaning. Ellingworth[41] has noted that in Hebrews, the meaning of perfection could span from the telic (i.e., to bring something to its goal or completion), to the cultic (i.e., qualify for participation in worship), ethical (i.e., remove imperfections), organic (i.e., make mature), and temporal (i.e., complete). In Heb 11:40, for example, perfection of all believers occurs in the future eschatological age, whereas in Heb 9:9–14, Jesus has attained cultic perfection already for us in the Holy of Holies by cleansing our consciences from dead works. Jesus was himself made perfect (Heb 2:10) through his death in order to make us perfect, so we may draw near to God (Heb 7:19).

Evidently, an aspect of perfection is now obtainable and experienced by believers but its fullness lies in the future. Bruce therefore defines perfec-

---

40. For discussion of views on this passage, see Koester, *Hebrews ABC*, 311–35.

41. Ellingworth, *Hebrews*, 162.

tion as "unimpeded access to God and unbroken communion with Him,"[42] whereas Silva[43] suggests an additional eschatological dimension. Lindars notes that perfection in the end is "the completion of God's Plan,"[44] the summation of the whole intention of God for humanity. Like salvation in Hebrews 2 and rest in Hebrews 4, perfection is also God's perfection. Perfection for that reason has a close association with rest and salvation, and indeed Heb 4:10 comes close to defining rest in terms of perfection: "those who enter God's rest also cease from their labors" (NRSV; i.e., they have completed, perfected their labors). Undoubtedly, when applied to Jesus, perfection has no ethical component but expresses his death that made him "complete" as our savior and so became the "perfecter of our faith" (Heb 12:2). He is the one who leads us to complete the process of our salvation.

With this background in mind, it is plainly insufficient for *teleiotēs* in Heb 6:1 to be translated purely as "maturity" as the NIV, for example, does. What our author had in mind is not only a mature stage in the Christian life when the person is able to teach and discern good from evil (Heb 5:12–14), but also one reaching forward to God's goal of the completion of the journey of migration that is marked out for us, characterized by an unbroken fellowship with him in his eternal presence. Perfection starts now and continues to end in the future eschatological age. This is why for our author, not leaving the elementary issues to go on to perfection, will certainly result in "falling away."

Going on to perfection, like going on to salvation and rest, requires faith and faithfulness. Many Christians are very familiar with our author's definition of faith in Heb 11:1, but Heb 6:12 is another powerful characterization of faith: "We do not want you to become lazy, but to imitate those who through faith and patience inherit what has been promised." Faith requires the rejection of laziness toward God's word, the imitation of the spiritual giants, the perseverance of patience, the inheritance of God's promises, and the continuous hope focused on what God has prepared ahead of his people (i.e., the promise that is the sum total of salvation, rest, perfection, heavenly city, heavenly kingdom, etc.). Typical of our author, he announces these five components of faith in advance but will deal with them in the subsequent exhortation. For now Hebrews cites Abraham

---

42. Bruce, *Hebrews*, 80.

43. Silva, "Perfection and Eschatology in Hebrews," 60–71.

44. Lindars, *Theology*, 44–45.

as an example of a hardworking and faithful spiritual giant who inherits God's promise.

The Relationship Between Heb 5:11–6:20 and the Expositions

The link between the exhortation and exposition is once again demonstrated here at the end of this exhortation. God's promise, according to the author, guarantees the hope of salvation, of rest, and of perfection. It is because God's promise is sure and secure that the hope that is anchored within the Holy of Holies (Heb 6:19) is also a sure and secure lifeline. It is anchored there because Christ our perfecter "has entered on our behalf" (Heb 6:20). Thus the promise of God takes hold of our faith and drives it toward the hope within the veil. Faith in the promise of God is the ability to hold firm and focus on the lifeline of hope before us, while we go on to perfection with patience and without laziness.

The camp of the migrant people of God had the tabernacle with its Holy of Holies as a symbol of their heavenly home where eternal perfection in God's presence would be theirs. The people of God needed perseverance fed by reliance on God's promises and faith based on God's word as they migrated to the promise. The Holy of Holies had multiple meanings for our author and all the work that Christ has accomplished there guarantees that the journey will be completed and made perfect.

Don't Despair in Suffering: Persevere to Inherit the Promise (Heb 10:19–13:17)

Brief Comments on the Passage

The final major section of Hebrews is a long cyclical exhortation extending from Heb 10:19–13:17. Guthrie rightly identifies the whole section as an exhortation, with Heb 10:19–25 serving as an introduction, and Heb 13:1–17 as a concluding paranaesis.[45] The tone of this block of exhortation is generally more positive than the previous three, even though it contains two sections of warnings that are designed to concentrate the minds and

---

45. Even though Vanhoye isolated Heb 11:1–40 as a doctrinal exposition on faith, it is clearly not in the didactic format as the other blocks of expositions in the epistle but rather uses wide-ranging examples to clarify the nature of the faith required for the Christian's orientation during their migration toward the promise. In that sense, Hebrews 11 plays the same role in the final block of exhortation as Heb 6:13–18 that expounds the certainty of God's promise as part of the third exhortation and hence should be considered as part of the whole exhortation.

efforts of the believers to persevere toward the goal of their migration to the heavenly city. Our author's focus in this closing exhortation is more on the finishing line—spurring, exhorting, and encouraging the congregation to "look for and see" the promise just ahead of them. In this respect, this block of exhortations parallels the more positive narratives that are reflected in the second half of the book of Numbers, which also contains narratives of pitfalls and implicit warnings to the new generation who had replaced the Exodus generation.

The format of the present exhortation also differs from the previous ones, even though it has the usual contents of reference to paying attention to God's word, warning against apostasy, encouragement to persevere and enter by faith, reminder of the past experience of the congregation, and Old Testament examples to emulate or eschew. This final exhortation may be structured in the following chiastic manner:

1. Summary Exhortation (Heb 10:19–25)
2. Warning against Rejection of God's Word (Heb 10:26–31)
3. Encouragement to Persevere in Suffering (Heb 10:32–39)
4. Nature and Examples of Faith for the Journey (Heb 11:1–12:3)
5. Encouragement to Persevere in Suffering (Heb 12:4–13)
6. Warning against Rejection of God's Word (Heb 12:14–29)
7. Summary Exhortation (Heb 13:1–17)

Hebrews 10:19–25 is a succinct summary of the whole epistle, which improves upon the summaries of Heb 4:14–16 and Heb 8:1–2. Whereas Heb 4:14–16 summarizes the two main points of the expositions—that we have the great high priest in heaven ministering on our behalf and so we have confidence to hold firmly to the faith and approach and enter the throne of grace in the Holy of Holies to receive mercy and help in time of need—Heb 10:19–25 improves upon this, adding that based on the same ministry we can, not only "draw near" with faith and hold firmly with hope, but also "spur one another on toward love and good deeds" (Heb 10:24). Faith, hope, and love, these three, constitute the internal dynamics of the exhortations in Hebrews 11–13. They play crucial functions in orienting the believer in his or her journey to the promise.

The Old Testament Background of the Exhortations of Hebrews 10–13

There is no single explicit Old Testament narrative in the background of the series of exhortations in the section. There are sufficient reasons to suggest, however, that the motif of the wilderness migration journey to the promised land continues to echo in the background of this long exhortation. This background also serves as a heuristic grid for explicating the three final chapters of Hebrews.

This judgment is based on the following reasons. First, following from the summary in Heb 10:19–25, the warning against the rejection of God's word in Heb 10:26–31 is heavily influenced by the Mosaic law against deliberate or willful sin promulgated in Lev 4–5 and Numbers 9 and 15 during the wilderness journey of Israel. Oberholtzer has suggested that the metaphor of fire in this warning is related to the prophecy of Isaiah 9:18–19 and 10:17 where God's anger is depicted as fire that scorches the land.[46] Yet, the explicit reference to Moses in Heb 10:28 lends some weight to the likelihood that the Old Testament background to the warning concerning God's judgment by fire is more appropriately related to Deut 4:24, 17:2–6, and 32:35–36.

Second, the ensuing encouragement in Heb 10:32–39 to live by faith is clearly influenced by the quotation from Hab 2:3–4 and illustrates the author's nuanced difference in interpretation of this Old Testament passage from Paul's in Rom 1:17 and Gal 3:11. Whereas Paul quotes only the second part of Hab 2:4, Hebrews quotes both Hab 2:3 and the second and third parts of 2:4 from the LXX. Moreover, Paul uses this verse to emphasize how it is by faith that we come into the right relationship with God (righteousness). Hebrews, on the other hand, emphasizes the importance of persisting in faith, faithfulness, and patience as we continue in this relationship with God. Paul and the author of Hebrews emphasize the two aspects of Habakkuk's statement concerning faith. As aptly put by Robertson, "Paul stressed that *by faith* a person is justified, and the writer to the Hebrews stressed that *by faith* a person who has been justified shall live."[47] Faith in Hebrews, as we shall find, is necessary for the beginning of the migration, the continual survival in the liminal phase of the journey, and the final entry into the heavenly kingdom.

Third, the theme of life in the wilderness of liminality holds the variety of imageries depicted in the exhortations of Hebrews 11–13 together. The sustained exposition of faith in Hebrews 11 is a rhetorical goldmine and merits a separate study on its own[48] but as demonstrated by Rhee,[49]

---

46. Oberholtzer, "The Warning Passages in Hebrews 10:26–39," 410–19.

47. Robertson, *The Books of Nahum, Habakkuk and Zephaniah*, 183.

48. For discussion of the rhetorical nature of this Hebrews 11, see Cosby, "Rhetorical Composition of Hebrews 11," 257–73.

49. Rhee, "Chiasm and the concept of faith in Hebrews 11," 327–45.

the chapter's chiastic structure locates Heb 11:13–16 in its central core. Since in principle the core of a chiastic literary structure points to the primary rhetorical intentions of its author, Heb 11:13–16 holds the clue to understanding the message of Hebrews 11. To put it simply, therefore, faith is the attitude that the wilderness migrant camp of Israel on their way to the promised land ought to have had. Faith, according to Heb 11:13–16, amounts to living the Christian life as if one is a diasporic migrant in a liminal wilderness state while oriented toward the inheritance of the promise. This understanding adequately summarizes the whole of Hebrews 11.

Fourth, the athletic imagery in Heb 12:1–3 to run the race toward the promise also has in its background the wilderness journey motif due to its indirect relationship with Isa 35. Similarly, the encouragement to persevere in suffering in Heb 12:4–11 is influenced by the paranaetic instructions of Proverbs 3–4, which in itself, is based on a journey motif. The instruction not to despise the Lord's discipline (Prov 3:11 cf. Heb 12:5) is set in the context of allowing God to "make your paths straight" (Prov 3:6). Hence Habel has noted that the root metaphor that controls the paranaesis in the whole of Prov 1–9 is that of "the route, the Way, the road."[50] The exhortation to endure hardship in Heb 12:4–11 therefore plays the same role as it does in Prov 3 (i.e., to encourage the believer not to despair of God's discipline as he directs him or her on the way to inherit his promise).

Finally, some of the imageries in the rest of the epistle from Heb 12:12–13:17 echo several parts of Isaiah's vision of the redeemed people in Isaiah 35, which is also placed in a wilderness journey setting. The exhortation to "strengthen your feeble arms and weak knees [and] make level paths for your feet" in Heb 12:12–13 not only quotes Prov 4:26, but also Isa 35:3, to "Strengthen the feeble hands; steady the knees that give way." The exhortation to "Make every effort to live in peace with all men and to be holy; without holiness no one will see the Lord" in Heb 12:14 echoes Prov 4:25–27 and Isa 35:5 and 8: "Then will the eyes of the blind be opened . . . And a highway will be there; it will be called the Way of Holiness." The reference to arrival at Mount Zion as the migrant's destination instead of Sinai in Heb 12:18–24 is very interesting, and though it is clearly our author's own construction, it has strong echoes of Isa 35:4, 10: "Your God will come; he will come with vengeance; with divine retribution he will come to save you . . . and the ransomed of the LORD will

---

50. Habel, "The Symbolism of Wisdom in Proverbs 1–9," 131–33.

return. They will enter Zion with singing; everlasting joy will crown their heads. Gladness and joy will overtake them." The virtual worshipping assembly of living believers with the angels and departed believers in God's presence in the heavenly kingdom that our author depicts here in Hebrews 12 contrasts sharply with the experience of the Israelites in the desert of Sinai, but in so doing, it again portrays the potent wilderness journey motif that it shares with Isa 35.

Within the concluding paranaesis of Heb 13:1–17 is another reference to the migrant camp of the people of God in Heb 13:9–14. Believers are depicted as priests who minister with Christ in the priestly courtyard of the camp-tabernacle complex. And just as Jesus suffered "outside the city gate," we are also exhorted to "go to him outside the camp, bearing the disgrace he bore" (Heb 13:13). Thompson has expertly examined the passage in detail and noted that there are mixtures of imageries in it. In addition to the imagery of the burning of the carcasses of sacrificial animals outside of the camp, the passage also has an element of Moses pitching his tent outside the camp to avoid defilement (Exod 33:7). Thompson consequently proposes, "For both Philo and Hebrews, 'outside the camp' means outside the earthly sphere . . . to give up earthly securities (11:8) and to accept the lifestyle of the pilgrim people."[51]

Like all the major points made by our author throughout the exhortations, the migration of Israel from Egypt toward the promised land is the background narrative that served as the master parable, controlling and directing his message. Hebrews 10–13 may therefore be conveniently studied using the phases of separation, liminality, and entry into the destination as a heuristic grid.

Separation, Liminality, and Entrance into Destination

The separation phase of the believer's migration is briefly described within Hebrews 10–13. The redemption of the Hebrews congregation is depicted as a movement from falsehood to truth (Heb 10:26) and from darkness into light (Heb 10:32). That salvation is equivalent to moving into the knowledge of the truth is also presented by Paul in 1 Tim 2:4 and 2 Tim 3:7 and sharply contrasts with the ignorance of living in sin (Acts 17:30; 1 Cor 15:34; Eph 4:18; 1 Pet 1:14, 2:15). The knowledge of the truth comes through the experience of the word of God and of God's Holy Spirit who is the Spirit of truth (John 14:17, 15:26, 16:13; 1 John 4:6, 5:6).

---

51. Thompson, "Outside the Camp," 62.

Our author's argument in Heb 10:26 therefore makes good sense, for the Mosaic law sharply separated willful or deliberate sin from sin committed out of ignorance (Leviticus 4–5; Numbers 15). As the believer has passed from ignorance into the knowledge of the truth, he or she should not continue in the life of ignorance any longer. In Josh 24:14, Joshua depicted life in Egypt as one of falsehood and idol worship and so challenged his people to give that life up and follow Jehovah. Similarly, and as already discussed in the previous exhortation of Heb 6:4, salvation as a movement from darkness into the light (Heb 10:32) also echoes the deliverance of Israel out of Egypt. Later on in Heb 12:18, our author would refer to the palpable "darkness and gloom" of Egypt that contrasts sharply to the joyful assembly at Mount Zion, the city of the living God, which is full of light. Two other indirect references are made to the separation phase: the separation of Abraham from Ur of the Chaldees is described as a "call" (Heb 11:8) and of Moses as "leaving" Egypt (Heb 11:27). Both utilize movement to depict the life of faith. Faith therefore is the primary means of separating from the origins to begin the journey of migration.

The way of life of the believer is described by our author as a "new and living way" through the torn "curtain" of the body of Christ (Heb 10:20). This new and living way is the liminal Christian experience, characterized by a diasporic migrant lifestyle in the wilderness. Here, the believer is faced with several dangers and therefore needs an effective and functional *communitas*, faith, faithfulness, and perseverance to survive to the destination. As noted in chapter three, a migrant often experiences a peculiar sense of place and consciousness that is described as diasporic. The migrant may feel "in place" but not at "home." This is how the author of Hebrews also describes the Christian experience. According to him, the Christian "pitches his tent" in this world, "like a stranger in a foreign country . . . aliens and strangers on earth . . . the world was not worthy of them. They wandered in deserts and mountains and in caves and holes in the ground" (Heb 11:9, 38). This peculiar sense of place orients the Christian psychologically, socially, and culturally so that he or she has a completely different identity—he or she belongs to "a better country—a heavenly one" (Heb 11:16).

Accordingly, as a migrant, the Christian is not actually intending to return to his or her origins: "If they had been thinking of the country they had left, they would have had opportunity to return" (Heb 11:15). Instead, the believer should have an "imaginative geography" of a heavenly homeland and long for a better country, a heavenly country, the heavenly Jerusalem, a city with foundations whose architect and builder is God

(Heb 11:10). Unlike Said's description, this "imaginative geography" is not one of "fantasy and the play of desire"[52] but is anchored in the certain and unchangeable promise of God (Heb 6:18).

The author's repeated references to looking, seeing, and longing (Heb 9:28, 11:26, 12:2, 11:10, 11:13) all point to the important role of having the correct perception that sustains the migrant's orientation in the journey to the promised land. The failure of the wilderness generation, as we pointed out in our analysis on Numbers 13 in chapter three, was a failure of this imagination. Their fear and unbelief stemmed from their lack of correct perception, the accurate "spiritual imagination" of the land, and condition that God had promised them. The positive exemplars of Hebrews 11, on the other hand, had this spiritual imagination that was anchored in God's promise. We shall revisit the role of vision in faith as expounded by our author shortly.

The journey of migration through the wilderness has a number of dangers that threaten to trip the Christian and Hebrews 10–13 highlights several of these. There is the danger of deliberate or willful sin (Heb 10:26–30), of withdrawing or shrinking back (Heb 10:38–39), of hardships and persecutions (Heb 11:32–38), of the weight and sin that would weigh the Christian migrant down into distraction and destruction (Heb 12:1–2), of weariness and faint heartedness, of fatigue, despair and giving up under suffering (Heb 12:3–13), and of internal spiritual decay and defilement that is caused by bitterness toward God and his people (Heb 12:14–17). Some of these dangers are of the believer's own making. Others are not but are part of the normal experience of spiritual growth and discipleship (Heb 12:4–11). All of them, however, have the potential to eat at and destroy the faith of the migrant on his or her journey to the promise. If they were not dealt with ruthlessly and quickly, the end result could be apostasy.

Like the previous exhortations, our author paints the worst-case scenario for any Christian who does not pay careful attention to God's word and instead allows him or herself to drift and fall away. The apostate situation, he points out, is equivalent to trampling the Son of God underfoot, treating his covenantal blood as an unholy thing and insulting the Spirit of grace (Heb 10:29). It amounts to refusing him who speaks and warns us from heaven (Heb 12:25). Hebrews was in no doubt that the consequences of apostasy are horrifying—it is one of experiencing God's fiery judgment (Heb 10:27), destruction (Heb 10:39), and loss of his blessings (Heb 12:17). The negative example of Esau is indeed sobering, for accord-

---

52. Said, *Orientalism*, 55.

ing to the author, "when [Esau] wanted to inherit this blessing, he was rejected. He could bring about no change of mind, though he sought the blessing with tears" (Heb 12:17).

Such a state of affairs is indeed "dreadful" and "terrifying" (Heb 10:27, 12:21), but our response will be completely inappropriate if we were to begin asking whether it is at all possible for a "true" believer to ever fall into such a state. The response that Hebrews clearly expected was not a complacent intellectual discussion as to whether it was possible for a "truly" saved person to fall into such a state of apostasy, as has been our response in evangelical circles. The correct response he aimed to elicit from his readers with these warnings was one of *fear, fellowship, faith,* and *faithfulness.*

The pivotal role of instilling godly fear through apocalyptic discourse has already been discussed. Our author cites Noah's fear as one such example: "By faith Noah, when warned about things not yet seen, in holy fear built an ark to save his family" (Heb 11:7). Noah took God's warnings seriously and so proceeded to build the ark, which led to the salvation of his household. In other words, Noah's holy fear led to his effective faith shown by his appropriate action. Noah's fear bolstered his faith, which modified his behavior. Hebrews consequently wished his audience to cultivate a similar fear as the response to God's word. He wanted them to "worship God acceptably with reverence and awe, for our 'God is a consuming fire'" (Heb 12:28–29). Not enough of this behavior-modifying role of godly fear is being emphasized in contemporary Christian circles.

In addition to godly fear, what the congregation also needed was an effective fellowship. Functional *communitas* is another answer to wilderness liminality. Hebrews encourages them to "consider how we may spur one another on toward love and good deeds. Let us not give up meeting together, as some are in the habit of doing, but let us encourage one another—and all the more as you see the Day approaching" (Heb 10:24–25). This *communitas* is not only with the individual members of the Hebrews congregation, but also with the faithful saints who were persecuted and with whom they "stood side by side" (Heb 10:33), with the Old Testament and inter-testamental believers who faithfully held to the promise and together with whom they are now being perfected (Heb 11:40) and who now serve as "a great cloud of witnesses" cheering them on to persevere to the end (Heb 12:1–2). They, together with the angels and the spirits of righteous men made perfect "have come to Mount Zion, to the heavenly Jerusalem, the city of the living God . . . to thousands upon thousands of angels in joyful assembly, to the church of the firstborn, whose names are written in heaven" (Heb 12:22–23). The believer is always in great company of glorious victors.

The fellowship of God's migrant camp has a long and large *collective memory* that should serve as a spiritual resource for his people. The solution to spiritual liminality is a rigorous discipleship that locks believers into identifying with this collective memory of God's people, past and present. This is why Hebrews therefore encourages them to "keep on loving each other as brothers" (Heb 13:1) for that was what was needed in the journey to the promise.

Faith and faithfulness are also needed for orientation during the migration. The term "faith" occurs some thirty-two times in this epistle, and even though two-thirds of these are in the special chapter eleven that is devoted to the subject, the rest are scattered throughout the epistle. Evidently, Hebrews saw faith and faithfulness as playing a crucial part in the migrant's journey to the promise. Bultmann was right when he described the earliest Christian "understanding of faith as the relationship people have with God. Faith can be belief, obedience or trust. It can be future-oriented as a hope for something yet to come."[53] This is very much reflected in our author's deliberations on this most important of Christian virtues.

Faith in Hebrews is not just a single act of belief, but also a continuous attitude required for the separation throughout the journey and then entry into the promise. This faith has two main aspects. On the one hand, it has an immediate certainty about it that is necessary for the separation from the world and entry into the promise. This type of faith is boldness (Heb 4:16), assurance (Heb 4:2, 6:11, 10:22), and confidence (Heb 10:23, 35). It is what our author defines in Heb 11:1: "Now faith is *being sure* of what we hope for and *certain* of what we do not see" (emphasis added). In MacRae's words, this faith "is *insight* into true reality. Faith sees into heaven and views Jesus as the pioneer and Perfecter of faith."[54] In other words, this aspect of faith is vertical and spatial. It is a faith that immediately rises up to our great high priest in heaven's throne room and gets his response.

This vertical aspect of faith has Christ as its object, for it is only because Christ has entered the Holy of Holies as our eternal high priest to make atonement for his brothers that the believer can come to him in faith (Heb 2:17–18, 4:14–16). Here again we see the link between the

---

53. Bultmann and Weiser, "Pisteou," 208.
54. MacRae, "Heavenly Temple," 185.

expositions and the exhortations of Hebrews. There has been the incorrect suggestion that faith in Hebrews does not have Christ as its object[55] and is therefore sharply distinguishable from Paul's teaching on faith, demonstrated by the differing utilization of Hab 2:3–4 by the two authors. This misunderstanding results from not taking Hebrews' elaborate exposition on the ministry of Christ in the Holy of Holies seriously, for our author's main point of the exposition was to demonstrate this "object of faith" in the heavenly tabernacle (Heb 8:1–2). To Hebrews, we can be "sure" and "certain" in our faith only because Christ is on the throne of grace in the Holy of Holies.

On the other hand, Hebrews presents the other aspect of faith as continuous trust, patience, perseverance, and endurance throughout the liminal journey while holding firm to the hope and promise. This faith, or better put, faithfulness, is constancy, loyalty, and fidelity. It is holding "fast the confidence and the rejoicing of the hope firm to the end" (Heb 3:6; MKJV). It is therefore a horizontal and temporal faith that holds on to enter into the promise, sees it afar off but lives now in view of it, and benefits from it in some respects but waits, endures, strives, and perseveres to inherit it at the end. This type of faith is hard work (Heb 6:12) and continuously needs reinforcing by reference to the camp's collective memory, both positive and negative examples (Heb 4:2–3). This is the faith exemplified by Abraham when "he made his home in the promised land like a stranger in a foreign country" (Heb 11:9). It is also the faith Moses had when he "refused to be known as the son of Pharaoh's daughter . . . [but] chose to be mistreated along with the people of God rather than to enjoy the pleasures of sin for a short time" (Heb 11:24–25).

This temporal and horizontal type of faith has Christ as its object, all right, for according to our author, Moses suffered "disgrace for the sake of Christ" (Heb 11:26). Much more than that, Christ is the exemplar, enabler, and perfecter of this second aspect of faith. He "for the joy set before him, endured the cross, scorning its shame, and sat down at the right hand of the throne of God" (Heb 12:2).

These two aspects of faith in Hebrews are not in opposition but are complementary to each other, for both depend on the word of God and the sure and certain promises of God. As Barrett puts it, "There is only one faith in Hebrews, with both spatial and temporal categories, vertical and at the same time horizontal, with both heaven/earth dualism and

---

55. For a review of this see Hamm, "Faith in the Epistle to the Hebrews," 270–91 and Rhee, "Christology," 83–96.

already/not yet interpretation."⁵⁶ Whereas the first aspect is necessary to begin the journey (Heb 6:1, 11:6–8), continue to receive grace and help during the journey (Heb 4:14–16), and end to the journey (Heb 4:2–3), the second aspect of faith is necessary to maintain the migrant on the journey during his or her wilderness liminality (Heb 6:12, 10:23). Faith in Hebrews is trust, belief, obedience, submission, endurance, patience, perseverance, assurance, and confidence in God's eternal word. The epistle to the Hebrews therefore presents the widest possible spectrum of faith in the New Testament.

The *orientation* of the Christian as a migrant on the way to the promise is provided by faith and hope. These two concepts are linked through a very interesting orientational scheme in the epistle to the Hebrews. MacRae has pointed out that the author's use of faith and hope in the epistle is related to his typological interpretation of the tabernacle. According to this interpretation, "Hope is the goal and faith is a means toward its full realization."⁵⁷ Hope, according to Hebrews, is anchored behind the veil (Heb 6:19) and faith is the way of life within the liminal priestly courtyard, which is aiming forward to this hope.

Because Christ's body, which is the veil, has been torn to make a new and living way (Heb 10:20), we can now "look" toward hope within the veil. This is why the concept of "seeing" or "looking for" as related to faith and hope is so important to the author of Hebrews. In the author's definition in Heb 11:1, faith is "the certainty of what is *not seen*" (emphasis added). What faith does for the believer is to emphasize a specific way of "seeing" that makes the unseen but heard promise of God a reality. In other words, and to borrow another metaphor, faith is a telescope that makes the unseen but heard promise visible to the spiritual imagination. Hence God's faith (Heb 11:3), Noah's faith (Heb 11:7), Abraham's faith (Heb 11: 10), Moses' faith (Heb 11:25), and Jesus' faith (Heb 12:2–3) all had a type of vision that made the unseen become a reality. This vision is not fantasy but a tenacious spiritual imagination that is constructed based on hearing God's word.

What is this specific way of seeing by faith? Our author sets the tone with regard to the role of vision in relation to faith in the programmatic Heb 2:8–9: "At present we do not see everything subject to him. But we see Jesus . . ." What *we do not yet see,* as highlighted in Hebrews 2, is the fulfillment of the full potential of humanity, the fulfillment of the promise

---

56. Barrett, "Eschatology," 385.
57. MacRae, "Heavenly Temple," 192.

that God has made through the death and resurrection of Christ. We do not yet see humanity's full salvation, we do not yet see humanity's enjoyment of God's rest, we do not yet see humanity's perfection, we do not yet see humanity inheriting the promise, even though the righteous exemplars of Hebrews 11 saw it at a distance and welcomed it (Heb 11:13).

On the other hand, what *we can see* with the telescope of faith is the Lord Jesus exalted and seated at God's right hand as our eternal and great high priest. It is he, the "apostle and high priest of our confession" (Heb 3:1), whom we should "consider" (Heb 3:1) and it is on him, "the pioneer and perfecter of our faith," that we should "fix our eyes" (Heb 12:2) as we journey to the promise in faith, and "look" for his second coming (Heb 9:28). Because we can, through this spiritually constructed vision based on God's word, see Jesus exalted on high in the Holy of Holies, faith is certain that all his promises will be fulfilled.

The promise is consequently the destination of the believer's journey in the last exhortation of Hebrews. Like salvation, rest, and perfection, the promise is again a complex concept in Hebrews, which has several facets. It may generally be experienced in part in this world, though its fullness will only be inherited in the future world. To start with, our author uses the singular *a* promise (Heb 4:1, 6:3) or *the* promise (Heb 6:15, 10:36, 11:39) interchangeably with the plural promises (Heb 6:12, 7:6, 8:6, 11:13, 17, 33) in a fashion that suggests there is no considerable difference.

The promise in Hebrews is an umbrella term that brings together all the promises of God. Craig Koester has rightly noted, "In Jewish and early Christian sources the term was often used for God's promise that Abraham would become the father of a great nation and would inherit the land and for the return of the land after exile (2 Macc 2:18; Deut 30:3)."[58] Lindars clarifies this by noting that the promise is "the completion of God's plan. The people of Old all contributed to the working out of God's plan in so far as they acted in faith, but they never saw the ultimate goal . . . once the plan is complete, i.e. in the general resurrection which is soon to take place at the parousia, these people's time of waiting in paradise will come to an end and they will receive their due reward."[59] Ellingworth hence surmises, "Men and women of the OT were given promises which received at that time a limited fulfillment, but the completion of God's plan is found in Jesus."[60]

58. Koester, *Hebrews ABC*, 268.
59. Lindars, *Theology*, 112.
60. Ellingworth, *Hebrews*, 239.

The promise is God's promise and consists of the promise of eternal salvation that believers will inherit (Heb 1:14, 9:28), the promise of the "world to come" in which humanity will fulfill its full potential (Heb 2:5), the promise of sharing in God's Sabbath rest (Heb 4:1), the promise of perfection for all believers (Heb 11:39–40), the promise of a better resurrection (Heb 11:35), the promise of righteousness that comes by faith (Heb 11:7), the promise of a better country (Heb 11:16), and the promise of entering the heavenly Jerusalem (Heb 12:22). It is the promise of a kingdom that cannot be shaken (Heb 12:28), the promise of "an enduring substance" (Heb 10:22), an eternal city that endures (Heb 13:14), and whose architect and builder is God (Heb 11:10). The promise is the sum total of all that God has promised the Christian as a migrant on his or her way to the inheritance. It is, in effect, the "pull factor" of the Christian's migration. Like salvation, rest, and perfection, an aspect of the promise is experienced now but its fullness will be in the future (Heb 12:22–24).

In chapter three, we pointed out how the concept of belonging to a mother city was a strong mark of the citizenship of the migrant Jew. This attachment toward a home city stimulates the migrant's vision or ideal and represents his or her dreams and aspirations. Christians look for and look to the heavenly eternal city of God and so live in this world as strangers whose citizenship is from heaven (Phil 3:20). In this city, according to Hebrews, there is eternal salvation, eternal divine rest, and perfection for all who enter. It was this promise that the disoriented Hebrews congregation was in danger of forfeiting.

Summary of the Exhortations of Hebrews

We have shown that, like the expositions, the exhortations also have a scheme that governs our author's choice of concepts and teachings. This movement scheme is best analyzed using sociological models from human migration that involves the phases of separation, liminality, and entry into a destination (see table 5.2). We have also shown that the master narrative that controlled this scheme is the migration of the Camp of Israel from Egypt to the promised land. The author of Hebrews saw a typological correspondence between his congregation and the camp of Israel. Through the lens of the death, resurrection, ascension, and exaltation of Jesus he interprets the experiences of that camp and applies the lessons to deal with the pastoral problems of his congregation. In chapter four, we demonstrated that each block of exposition focuses on each of the spaces of the camp and its spatiality. The exhortations, on the other hand, focus on the movement of the same camp of God's people migrating to its God-ordained destination. The theme of the migration of the camp of God's people therefore fittingly summarizes the whole of the epistle to the Hebrews.

Table 5.2: The Migration Scheme in the Exhortations of Hebrews

	Heb 2:1–4	*Heb 3:1–4:13*	*Heb 5:11–6:20*	*Heb 10:19–13:17*
Separation	Signs and Wonders	Holy and Called to Heaven	Birth and Flight	Falsehood to Truth Darkness to Light
Disorienting Dangers	Neglect and Drift	Unbelief and Disobedience	Immaturity and Falling Away	Deliberate Sin, Fatigue, and Bitterness
Orienting Praxis	Pay Heed to God's Word	Faith and Perseverance	Know God's Word and Faith	Faith, Hope, and Love
Destination	Salvation	Rest	Perfection	The Promise

The Theology and Literary Structures of Numbers and Hebrews

We are not yet through to a satisfactory explanation of the nature of the presentation of the whole book of Hebrews, for a nagging but crucial question remains to be answered. If the movement and migration of the camp of God's people is the uniting theme of Hebrews, why does our author choose to present it in this circular manner? Why does he use an alternating exposition/exhortation literary structure, which does not make such a theme immediately obvious to us today?

The answer to this all-important question, and which we shall now devote ourselves to explain, is this: the author of Hebrews aimed his homily to match not only the theology but also the literary structure of the book of Numbers. Since he perceived a typological correspondence between his congregation and the Exodus generation of Numbers, the author of Hebrews has produced a sermon whose theological themes, allusions, and to some extent literary style mirror the book of Numbers.

The social history and location of the community behind Hebrews have already been discussed in chapter two. Like the Exodus generation, the community of Hebrews had been delivered from the bondage of sin and had passed from death to life, from darkness to light, and from ignorance to truth (Heb 2:3–4). Like the Exodus generation, they had experienced the "signs and wonders" of God's power and presence and were now in the liminal stage as they moved toward the promised land. It is hence of no surprise that there is almost complete unanimity among biblical scholars that the recipients of this epistle were converted Christians. In both Numbers and Hebrews, the focus was more on re-orienting, persevering, and reaching forward to the promise rather than persuading the reader to come to faith in the first place. Though Hebrews discusses the redemption of the congregation, the author's efforts were more directed toward their spiritual growth and progress and not their conversion.

The dangers that confronted the Hebrews congregation, though materially different from the Exodus generation, were of similar spiritual and social nature. The danger of inattention to God's word, unbelief, and disobedience that led the Exodus generation into destruction were equally real to the Hebrews generation. The danger of spiritual and emotional fatigue, resulting in disorientation and lack of focus on the promise ahead and a desire to return to and fulfill the carnal desires of "Egypt" were similarly plaguing the Hebrews congregation. The rebellious attitude to Moses in the wilderness (Numbers 11–16) was perhaps of a higher order than what appears to have been happening in the Hebrews congregation (Heb 13:17, 24), but the "separatist tendencies"[61] of the Hebrews congregation would underline a possible dissenting attitude akin to that of the Exodus generation (Numbers 11). The "waning commitment"[62] and drift into spiritual malaise and lethargy of the Hebrews congregation also parallels the increasing carnality and internal corruption of the Exodus generation in Numbers

Though urbanized, and most likely based in Rome,[63] the Hebrews congregation, as Jewish Christians in Diaspora, may well have been experiencing the "exilic wilderness" mentality. This made their migrant and diasporic consciousness as Christians even more acutely real to them. Some of them, and perhaps most of the members, would have frequented

---

61. Guthrie, *New Testament Introduction*, 684.

62. Attridge, *Hebrews*, 13.

63. Though the geographical location of the congregation remains a matter of conjecture, most recent commentaries have tended to agree on this destination.

Jerusalem on pilgrimage on several occasions, since they may have been well to do (they lost their goods in the earlier persecution and were well able to provide hospitality—Heb 10:33–34, 13:2–5, 14–16). Talking about the necessity for spiritual orientation to the promise therefore very much suited the social identity of the congregation and matches the liminal status of the Exodus generation in the wilderness who were "between and betwixt" and never at home in the wilderness. Their disastrous failure to enter the land and rather dying in the wilderness was uppermost on the author of Hebrews' mind as he considered the pastoral difficulties of his congregation. He evidently perceived strong parallels between his congregation and the congregation in Numbers and therefore penned a sermon that would deal with such an imminent and ominous spiritual disaster.

Hebrews accordingly approached his sermon by paralleling some of the theological themes and to a lesser extent the literary structure of the book of Numbers. The traditional Hebrew title of the book of Numbers was *Waydabber*, which means "And He Spoke" and comes from its very first words. In fact, the phrase "the LORD spoke" occurs more than fifty times in Numbers and reflects one of the dominant themes of the book of Numbers (i.e., the revelation and guidance of God for his people as they approached the promised land).

This emphasis on the speech or word of God is paralleled by the generous nature of Hebrews' references to God's speech and his word (e.g., Heb 1:1, 3:10, 4:4, 5:5, 7:21, 8:8, 10:15). The author of Hebrews may indeed have been deliberately paralleling the title and first verse of Numbers when he also begins his epistle with God's speech through his exalted Son ministering in the heavenly tabernacle in these last days (just as God spoke to Moses in the tabernacle in Num 1:1). Another Hebrew title that was used for the book of Numbers was the fourth word of the book, *Bemidbar*, meaning "In the Wilderness." These Hebrew titles of Numbers more appropriately mirror the theological themes of that fourth book of Moses than the present English title, which is derived from the LXX.

The life of Israel in the wilderness was characterized by liminality[64] and disorientation, themes that also characterize the theology of Hebrews. Indeed, Timothy Ashley has suggested that the book of Numbers may be structured into three parts: orientation (Numbers 1–10), disorientation (Numbers 11–21), and new orientation (Numbers 22–36).[65] This corresponds to the dominance of the orientation/disorientation theme in

---

64. Dunnill, *Covenant and Sacrifice*, 1992.
65. Ashley, *Numbers*, 8.

the epistle to the Hebrews. Harrelson has also pointed out that the major theme of the book of Numbers is "Yahweh's guidance and testing of Israel in the Wilderness."[66] This guidance theme fits very well with the emphasis on orientation in both Numbers and Hebrews. God provided his word, the angelic presence, the pillar of fire and cloud, and his constant presence in the tabernacle to guide and lead Israel to the promised land. Similarly, the author of Hebrews highlights the primary role of the word of God in guiding and orienting the faith of the Christian on his or her way to the promise. The expositions of Hebrews, as we have seen in the previous chapter, are centered on the ministry of the tabernacle and teach the doctrine of the accessibility of the presence of God through Christ to enable the orientation of the believer.

The theme of the fulfillment of God's promise is another parallel between the two books. The book of Numbers systematically presents how the promise God gave to Abraham was being fulfilled one after another, even though it stops short of its full inheritance by Israel. The Balaam cycle in Numbers 22–25 serves to highlight this fulfillment theology, for in that story, we see how nothing visible or invisible, human or spiritual, would frustrate the fulfillment of God's intention for his people. Likewise, the victorious partitioning of the land in Numbers 31 is an indication of the coming inheritance of which God's people were to take hold. Correspondingly, Hebrews declares in Heb 2:16 that Jesus shared in the humanity of the descendants of Abraham to make their inheritance possible. At the close of the epistle, our author declares how through faith the promise is being possessed, not only by the previous generation of God's people, but also by the Hebrews congregation, if they persevered to the end.

God's promise of salvation will be fulfilled, for he has sent his angels to minister to the saints who will inherit it. God's promise of rest "remains" (Heb 4:9) and so the author encourages believers to "combine" (Heb 4:2) the hearing of God's word with the "sight" of faith in order to enter it. God's promise of perfection is even now being fulfilled by the work of the "God of peace" (Heb 13:20–21) in us, and we shall soon join the other perfected saints in worship at Mount Zion, the city of God (Heb 12:23). The theology of the fulfillment of God's promise to Abraham, through the work of Christ on our behalf permeates the whole of the epistle to the Hebrews, just as it does in Numbers.

---

66. Harrelson, "Guidance in the Wilderness," 27.

The journey motif, as we have already demonstrated, strongly characterizes the epistle to the Hebrews, just as it does in the book of Numbers. The whole book of Numbers lends itself to geographical structuring, so that Numbers 1–10 occurred at Mount Sinai, Numbers 11–19 occurs between Sinai and Kadesh-Barnea, and Numbers 20–36 between Kadesh-Barnea and the Plains of Moab. On three occasions (Numbers 9–11, 20–21, 33) the writer of Numbers takes pains to detail the itinerary of the congregation of Israel. Though beset by internal and external troubles, and despite the forty years that it took, Israel made progress toward the promised land. MaCrae has summed up this journey motif of Numbers by noting, "No other book of the Old Testament contains so much that is exactly parallel to the pilgrim journey of the Christian in the present age."[67] It is right to say also that no other book in the New Testament presents the Christian experience on this side of heaven as a movement, pilgrimage, or, more appropriately, migration to heaven than Hebrews. These correspondences and parallels between Numbers and Hebrews are unlikely to have been mere coincidences.

The tabernacle and its cultic rituals literally and metaphorically played a central role in the Exodus generation in preserving its relationship with God during its migration. Numbers places the tabernacle at the center of the life and activities of the people of God, making reference to it on more than a hundred occasions. The whole camp was arranged in a concentric manner around the tabernacle (Fig 5.1, next page), and in Gordon Wenham's words, "Both at rest and on the move, the camp was organized to express symbolically the presence and kingship of the Lord."[68]

The tabernacle played multiple functions in wilderness Israel, ranging from the cultic (Num 1:53, 4:15), military (Num 10:35–36, 31:6), social (Num 7:8–9), and judicial (Numbers 11) functions. It acted as both a symbol of God's mercy (Num 1:53, 18:5) and also of the burning fire of God's wrath (Numbers 16). It provided access for the spiritual well being and preparation of the people of God as they migrated to inherit the promise. Similarly, the author of Hebrews took great pains to stress that the new covenant provided an ever-present and better ministry of Jesus for the people of God. Repeatedly, our author exhorts the congregation to draw near, approach, and enter into God's presence for grace, mercy, and help.

67. MaCrae, "The book called 'Numbers,'" 52.
68. Wenham, *Numbers*, 56.

Fig 5.1: Concentric Arrangement of the Camp of Israel in the Wilderness (Numbers 1–10)

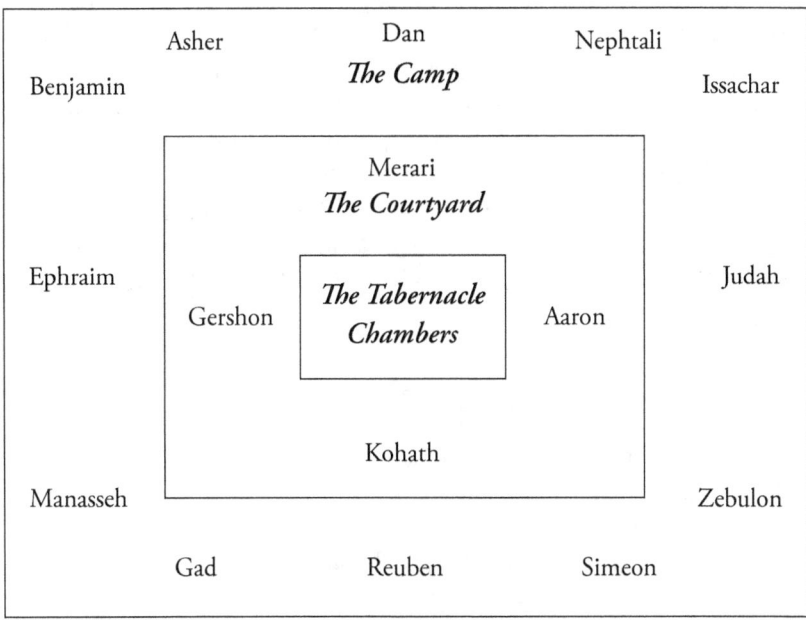

The two books also share similar reputations as among the most difficult books to structure in terms of their literary designs. Like Hebrews, Numbers is structured in such a way that narratives of rebellion and disorientation on the part of the Israelite congregation alternate with laws, many of which are of cultic and ritual nature designed to re-orient them. This superficially haphazard nature of Numbers earned the book the unfortunate reputation as one with "confusion and lack of order in its contents,"[69] to cite just one of Noth's extreme comments. This "confusion," however, is in the mind of the modern exegete who goes to the scriptures with preconceived ideas of what "it should be like." For the author of Numbers, however, his deliberate design perfectly fit his theological intentions. The alternating narrative/laws structure of Numbers is not just a way of producing a polyphony that compares idealism (the six laws) with real human experience (the seven narratives), as suggested by Leveen,[70] but more than that, it reflects the theology of the guidance and presence of God among his redeemed migrant people.

69. Noth, *Numbers*, 4.
70. Leveen, "Variations on a Theme," 201–21.

There have been difficulties with delineating the literary structure of Numbers until recently when Mary Douglas, using the spatial and orientational indexes in Numbers, noted that the book is made up of a chiastic concentric ring structure "formed of alternating stories and laws set in parallel with each other, twelve in all."[71] This structure (Fig 5.2) mirrors very much the spatial structure of the camp arranged around the tabernacle as described in Numbers 1–10. The chiasmic structure has also been noted by Milgrom, who argues, "The main structural device, to judge by its attestation in nearly every chapter of Numbers, is chiasm and introversion."[72] This statement would have been equally true if it were made of Hebrews.

Fig 5.2: The Chiastic Structure of the Book of Numbers (Adapted from Douglas)

1. Story (Numbers 1–4) *God's Order*
  2. Law (Numbers 5–6) *Keeping the Faith*
    3. Story (Numbers 7–9) *Offerings*
      4. Law (Num 10:1–10) *Holy Times*
        5. Story (Num 10:11–14:45) *Revolts*
          6. Law (Numbers 15) *Offerings and Purification*
            7. Story (Numbers 16–17) Core: *Triple Threat to God's Order*
          6' Law (Numbers 18–19) *Offerings and Purification*
        5' Story (Numbers 20–27) *Revolts*
      4' Law (Numbers 28–30) *Holy Times*
    3' Story (Num 31:1–33:49) *Offerings*
  2' Law (Num 33:50–35:34) *Keeping the Faith*
1' Story (Numbers 36) *God's Order*

If, for argument's sake, we were to reject the centrality of chiasms in both Numbers and Hebrews, two alternative proposals for their literary structures also have parallels between them. Ashley's tripartite proposal for the structure of Numbers which was mentioned earlier parallels closely Nauck's proposal, that Hebrews may similarly be divided into three parts separated by Heb 4:13 and Heb 10:18.[73] In Nauck's contention, each block of the three sections is opened and closed by an exhortation related to God's word. This orientation that is provided by God's word

---

71. Douglas, *In the Wilderness*, xxiii.
72. Milgrom, *The JPS Torah Commentary: Numbers*, xxii.
73. See Lane, *Hebrews 1–8*, lxxxviii.

The Migration of the Camp of God's People to the Promise

in Hebrews also parallels the theme of orientation in the three blocks of Ashley's proposed structure.

On the other hand, the parallel structuring of Hebrews into expositions and exhortations as noted by Guthrie matches the book of Numbers' narratives and laws. Thus Noth has suggested that one may study Numbers by separating the two genres, even though as rightly noted by Wenham, the mixture of the two genres of Numbers, just as in Hebrews, is not "incomprehensible."[74] Equally, by separating the expositions from exhortations in Hebrews, we have been able to highlight the migrant camp motif, which lies in the background of this great epistle.

It may legitimately be asked that if the book of Numbers so influenced the author of Hebrews, why does he not quote it as profusely as he does the other parts of scriptures? As we noted in chapter two, it is not clear if our author ever quoted from the book of Numbers. Even though there are several word similarities that could suggest direct citations of Numbers,[75] it is the allusions to and echoes of Numbers scattered throughout the epistle that are more significant.

It must be appreciated that allusions can sometimes be more vital in identifying an author's intentions in a piece of literature than direct, explicit quotations. Frequently, and this is very true of our author, explicit quotations are employed to buttress arguments that have been made based on allusions. The background narrative that heavily influences the presentation may be a more important indicator of the concepts that shape the arguments rather than the explicit quotations that he uses in supporting the allusions. For our author, this background narrative is the migration of the camp of God's people on their way to inherit the promise as presented in the Pentateuch and in Numbers in particular (see Table 5.3 on next page).

Clearly, the author of Hebrews has greatly transformed the theology of Numbers through his reading, using the death, resurrection, ascension, and exaltation of Jesus as his lens. The differences between Numbers and Hebrews are many. The congregation of Hebrews had not yet apostatized as the older Exodus generation did. Whereas the Exodus generation had Moses and Aaron as their leaders, the Hebrews congregation had Jesus as their apostle and high priest. The tabernacle and Ark of the Covenant in

---

74. Wenham, *Numbers*, 196.

75. E.g., Heb 1:1 (Num 1:1); Heb 9:6 (Num 3:7, 4:19, 8:15); Heb 10:5–10 (Num 7:8–9); Heb 3:1–6 (Num 12:1–8); Heb 2:1–4 (Num 14:22); Hebrews 3 (Numbers 14); Heb 10:26 (Num 15:24–25); Heb 9:4 (Num 17:10); Heb 9:13 (Num 18:17); Heb 7:5 (Num 18:24); Heb 9:13 (Numbers 19).

Table 5.3: Similarities between the Books of Numbers and Hebrews

Parameter	Numbers	Hebrews
Social History of Congregation	Already delivered from the bondage of Egypt, have experienced signs and wonders, heading toward the promise.	Already believers who have experienced "signs and wonders" and heading toward their salvation, God's rest, perfection and the promise.
Social Location	Migrant community in Diaspora.	Migrant Jews in Diaspora, perhaps in Rome.
Dangers	Unbelief, disobedience, rebellion, and strife (Numbers 11–14).	Separatist predisposition (Heb 10:25, 13:17, 24), spiritual malaise, and strife.
Literary Structure	Cocentric chiastic form.	Cocentric chiastic form.
God's Speaking	Emphasized more than fifty times. Begins with speech of God.	Emphasized more than forty-five times. Begins with speech of God.
Devotion	Increasing carnality.	Waning commitment to the faith.
Orientation Theme	May be structures according to theme of orientation.	Themes of orientation related to faith, hope, and love.
Guidance Theme	Guidance in wilderness by pillar of fire and the tabernacle.	Guidance by the apostle and high priest of our confession who ministers in heavenly tabernacle.
Fulfillment	The promise of rest in Land of Canaan.	Sabbath rest for God's People.
Journey Motif	Structured by the journey of the camp of God's people.	Structured by the journey of God's people to the promise.

Numbers were physical objects that were symbolic of the tabernacle of heaven where the superior and exalted Christ is seated on the right hand of God Almighty. The new covenant he has inaugurated is far superior to the "faulty" and "disappearing" old covenant that operated in Numbers. The Hebrews congregation was therefore in a better position than the Numbers congregation to attain the promised salvation, rest, perfection, and promise.

Nevertheless, the experiences of the Exodus generation were "examples" (as Paul also described it in 1 Cor 10:6) for the Hebrews congregation and also for us. The epistle to the Hebrews is evidently a Christian interpretation of the book of Numbers. In the next and concluding chapter, we shall explore how this understanding of Hebrews should transform our interpretation and application of the various parts of this glorious epistle.

6

Hebrews, the Metaphor of Migration, and Discipleship

THE MEMBERS of the congregation to whom the epistle to the Hebrews was written were in an imminently disastrous spiritual condition. This situation emanated from a combination of factors, from public harassment and persecution by the government to an internal spiritual malaise and loss of inner confidence in the faith. The condition threatened to disorient the believers and shift them from their focus on Christ. The author of Hebrews rightly perceived a typological correspondence between the situation of his congregation and the wilderness camp of Israel who were migrating from Egypt to the promised land. Through his Christological reading of the Old Testament, Hebrews constructed a sermon that essentially represents the Christian as a redeemed person in the spiritual wilderness migrating toward the promise of God in heaven. He depicted the condition of heaven as salvation, rest, perfection, the city, the kingdom of God, and the promise.

Like all movements, there are dangers in this journey of migration that could cause the believer to become disoriented, to carelessly drift, to stubbornly disbelieve and disobey, and to disloyally shrink back from entering God's promise. The author therefore used his sermon to warn the believers about their unstable and perilous situation and encouraged them to realign themselves to the faith. He points out that faith, faithfulness, focus on God's word, and hope will enable the immigrant to maintain his or her orientation toward the promise. In addition, the close fellowship of believers, past and present, provides a much-needed *communitas* during the liminal stage to strengthen and encourage the believer in his or her fatigue and despair in the spiritual wilderness.

During the migration, the Hebrews Christians, more than their counterparts in the book of Numbers, have continual unimpeded access to approach and draw near to the Holy of Holies where our eternal high priest, the superior and exalted Christ, ministers and intercedes on our behalf. His ministry and the access he provides are superlatively effective because of who he is and the work he has done through his death. He is the Son of God, equal in stature to his Father, though for a brief moment in his eternal existence he became human like us and tasted our death. Through this death, he defeated the devil, and he has atoned for our sins by his blood. He now ministers in the heavenly Holy of Holies, where he has anchored the hope that sustains our faith and so provides for us all the grace, mercy, and help that we need for the journey. He himself continues to lead us during the migration, beckoning us not only to follow him and his example of perseverance, but also to fix our eyes on him to maintain our orientation. If we do that, our faith will be sustained, we will be able to shake off our spiritual malaise, and we will be re-invigorated to persevere to the end.

The above is in effect is the summary of the book of Hebrews. Armed with this summary, how do we go about applying Hebrews in spiritual formation and discipleship in our churches? How does the author's application of the story of the Exodus generation of Numbers as a background metaphor or parable influence our devotional reading, group Bible study, and public preaching from the various parts of the epistle to the Hebrews? This is the subject to which we now turn our attention. We proceed by highlighting some important guidelines that we must share with the author of Hebrews in order to apply his marvelous sermon in our personal devotions, Bible studies, and preaching. We will then synthesize the theological doctrines of the epistle and summarize some devotional and homiletic themes that may be gathered using the Old Testament background that this book has explored.

A Guideline for Interpreting Hebrews

It is important to state again that Hebrews was written for people who were already born-again Christians. Though there is much in this epistle that may serve as very powerful evangelistic messages (e.g., the emphasis on the atonement, the new covenant, warnings of apocalyptic judgment), the author did not craft the sermon with the intention of converting people who were unconvinced about the salvific merits of the death and resurrection of Jesus. Instead, the whole sermon was aimed at people the author knew had already put their trust in Jesus and who rather needed a rigorous discipleship to continue in the journey and not to slip or shrink back. As a result, the epistle is most powerfully effective today when employed for stabilizing, confirming, and reinforcing the spiritual development and discipleship of believers.

A second basic assumption is the author of Hebrews' style of multiple interpretation of the tabernacle-camp complex. He believed that the tabernacle was a sign and parable of divine truths (Heb 8:5) and therefore he adopts at least seven interpretations of the tabernacle in his teaching. It is our ability to understand these multiple interpretations that will help us follow his argument. As shown in table 6.1 (next page), Hebrews categorizes many of the theological themes and schemes in such a way that they follow this multiple typological interpretation of the camp-tabernacle complex. He interprets the Holy of Holies as symbolic of heaven, the new covenant, and the eschatological world to come. It is also symbolic of hope, rest, perfection, and the promise. The important thing to remember is that the author does not overtly mention these interpretive schemes but rather assumes them.

Accordingly, in Heb 6:18–19, for example, the author states that believers have fled to take hold of "the hope set before us" (MKJV) and this hope is an anchor that "enters the inner sanctuary behind the curtain." Whereas hope is within the Holy of Holies, faith is defined as the present assurance of hope (Heb 11:1). In other words, and in the spatial scheme of Hebrews, the believer has fled from unbelief in the camp to faith within the priestly courtyard and Holy Place and is now looking forward toward hope. Of course the believer can "see" hope ahead because the curtain, which is the body of Christ, has been torn to make a "new and living way" (Heb 10:20). And so the believer can, through faith, "see Jesus" (Heb 2:9) exalted at God's right hand and can fix his or her eyes on him (Heb 12:2) as he or she perseveres toward the promise. This example illustrates how we need to keep the multiple interpretations of the tabernacle-camp complex in mind as we navigate this glorious epistle.

What this also means is that, like all books of the Bible but Hebrews in particular, the whole epistle must be used to interpret its constituent parts. No single verse of Hebrews stands on its own and atomistic interpretations of the verses of the epistle, though popular, do not fully unveil their meaning. For a good understanding of the individual verses of Hebrews, it is better to have an initial panoramic view of the whole epistle, its structure, its central message, and its style of interpretation. Then may the individual passages be interpreted in the light of the panoramic view of the epistle.

This study's aim has been to provide this panoramic view that will enable explication of the individual passages and verses. Thus if we are

Table 6.1 The Multiple Interpretations of the Tabernacle in Hebrews

	The Camp	*Priestly Courtyard and Holy Place*	*Holy of Holies*
Cosmological	This world (Heb 6:19–20, 8:1–4)	The house of God (Heb 3:1–6)	Heaven (Heb 9:24)
Eschatological	The present time (9:8–10)		The eschatological world to come (Heb 9:10, 6:5)
Covenantal	Old covenant (9:15–22)		New covenant (9:15–22)
Anthropological	Time of the flesh (9:8–10)	Time of the conscience (9:8–10)	
Soteriological	Enslaved by the devil (Heb 2:5–15)	Partakers of the heavenly calling (Heb 3:1)	Uttermost salvation (Heb 7:25) **Divine rest** (Heb 3–4) **Perfection** (Heb 7:19, 10:1) The promise (Heb 8:6)
Believer's Orientation	Unbelief (Heb 3:12)	Faith (Hebrews 11) and **Love** (Heb 3:13, 10:24–25)	Hope (Heb 6:18–20)
Christological	Christ, lower than the angels in solidarity with humanity (Heb 2:5–18)	The veil as the body or flesh of Christ (Heb 10:19–20). He is seated at God's right hand (Heb 8:1–2). Some scholars[1] also understand Heb 9:11–12 as referring to the whole body of Christ as the "building," the tabernacle	

to have a study of Heb 1:5–14, for example, it is important to note that the author's focus is on what is ongoing in the heavenly assembly and the nature of the "conversation" between God the Father and his Son in the presence of the angels. We may, if we choose, go into minute details to explore the Old Testament contexts and meanings of the seven quotations that the author makes in that passage, but in the end, all the understanding we acquire must be brought to bear on what the author aimed to portray in the whole passage. If we do not approach the epistle this way, our understanding of it may easily become fragmented.

It is for this reason that the best way to study Hebrews in a Bible study setting is in three stages. In the first stage, a generalized approach, which takes the various chapters as wholes to understand the general flow of the argument, should be done. One may choose, as we have done in this book, to separate out the expositions from exhortations for this purpose. Though this makes the study easier, a generalized study that follows the chapter divisions will equally suffice. The second stage goes into the various details of the passages and verses to understand how they contribute to the overall message and their applications. The third stage resynthesizes the theological themes and messages of the epistle.

This leads us to another point that needs to be borne in mind when approaching the epistle. Unlike Romans or even the Corinthian letters, Hebrews is not an intentional theological treatise. It is more of a religious sermon, designed to stimulate the heart and address a particular pastoral situation. The author therefore assumes knowledge of many of the theological doctrines that he uses to construct the homily. He weaves together a wide range of theological doctrines, from the doctrine of revelation, of scripture, of angels, of sin and its results, of humanity's fall, of salvation, of redemption, of atonement, of the last things, etc., in a very stimulating way to serve the exhortational purpose of the sermon. In many cases the author presupposes that his hearers have some background knowledge of these doctrines and so he does not attempt to go into detail but rather employs their significance to construct his argument.

Take the exploration of the concept of "the conscience" as an example. We have no clear-cut explanation of this doctrine in the epistle, which is referred to on five occasions at crucial parts of the epistle (Heb 9:9, 14, 10:2, 22, 13:18). The author assumes that his audience knew that human nature is made up of "flesh" and "conscience" and that what sin and evil does is to infect both. In his argument in Hebrews 9–10, he explains that the old covenantal cultic practices cleansed the "flesh" part of humanity without affecting the "conscience." It is in the new covenant that Christ has inaugurated that the cleansing of "our consciences from acts that lead to death" (Heb 9:14) occurs. In order for us to grasp his argument, we need to approach the sermon, sharing the author and first readers' prior knowledge about human nature. This is another reason why the study of the epistle is most appreciated by Christians who have been in the faith for some time. Indeed, E. F. Scott had advocated that Hebrews may have been a sermon written "from a teacher to teachers." Although this may slightly exaggerate the degree of maturity of the first readers, as Heb 5:11–14 indicates, there is little doubt that these Christians had been around for some time, even if their spiritual growth had not been matched by their months or years of Christian faith. The crucial point here is that prior systematic knowledge of some of the basic doctrines of the faith will greatly enhance our study of this epistle.

The one doctrine that the author of Hebrews does not assume and so deliberately pursues and develops is the doctrine of Christ as our great high priest seated at God's right hand. The doctrine is not unique to Hebrews, but it is only in this epistle that it is explored in depth to make plain its benefits. Even then, and as we have stressed throughout, the author's elaboration of this doctrine was to serve the exhortational purpose of his sermon. Christ is seated at God's right hand and provides for us unimpeded access into God's presence to receive grace and mercy for the journey. He is also there as our apostle, pioneer, and perfecter, and so we are to follow him and his example of perseverance.

Since an applicable understanding of the various parts of Hebrews must proceed from a prior appreciation and synthesis of its general motifs and doctrines, we shall now summarize some of these doctrines.

The Theological Motifs of Hebrews

By understanding the theological themes that Hebrews weaves into the sermon, we will be able to explain the parts in terms of the whole. Table 6.2 (next page) is a summary of the common theological themes of the epistle, many of which have already been discussed at some stage in this study. We will now synthesize the top six of these theological themes: Christology, scripture, sin, salvation, eschatology, and ecclesiology.

The Christology of Hebrews

The Christology of Hebrews is so sustained and prominent in its emphasis that until the middle of the twentieth century, it was assumed by many scholars that this was the author's main purpose for the homily. Smalley described the doctrine of the high priesthood of Christ as the "central category . . . which draws together the theology of the Epistle and gives it its distinctive character."[1] Similarly, Hughes has argued that the "comprehensive theme" of the epistle is "the absolute supremacy of Christ."[2]

Table 6.2: Common Theological Themes of Hebrews

1.	Doctrine of Christ
2.	Doctrine of Scripture
3.	Doctrine of Sin
4.	Doctrine of Salvation
5.	Eschatology of Hebrews
6.	Ecclesiology of Hebrews
7.	The Conscience in Hebrews
8.	Doctrine of Angels
9.	Faith in Hebrews
10.	Worship in Hebrews

This view, though highlighting what is clearly a major component of the author's argument, does not adequately account for the whole epistle, as noted in chapter one. Whereas most of the first-century Christian discourses featured prominent Christological emphases,[3] these prominent elaborations were almost always employed not for their own sakes but for other purposes, whether apologetic, evangelistic, or discipleship. The popular high Christological hymn in Phil 2:5–11, for example, was employed by Paul not so much for its praise and adoration of the glorious and exalted Christ, but for exhorting and challenging the Philippian believers, "Your attitude should be the same as that of Christ Jesus" (Phil 2:5). Even when some indication of the nature of the person of Jesus is made in the New Testament, the purpose is often to stress the doctrine's relationship to his work. When the author of Hebrews, for instance, stresses the divinity of Jesus, it is in relation to his work at creation, and when his humanity is emphasized, it is in relation to his redemptive and high priestly activity.

1. Smalley, "Atonement in the Epistle to the Hebrews," 36.

2. Hughes, *Hebrews*, 2.

3. Cullman has, for example, noted, "Early Christian theology is in reality almost exclusively Christology," *Christology*, 2–3.

Therefore, the high Christology of Hebrews is employed by its author to serve the exhortational purpose of the epistle.

It is nevertheless vital to map out the Christology of Hebrews, for it is in Hebrews that our author brings together the two natures of Christ in their fullness. While we are left in no doubt about the deity of Christ in Hebrews, we cannot equally escape taking note of his full humanity. So, according to Hebrews, the Son, who as God, "laid the foundations of the earth, and the heavens are the work of your hands" (Heb 1:10) "had to be made like his brothers in every way, in order that he might become a merciful and faithful high priest in service to God" (Heb 2:17). The two natures are stressed so that we understand that it is indivisible natures, operating always at the same time. That is the particular strength of the Christology of Hebrews.

The prominent Christological emphases of Hebrews are:

1. Divine Son Christology (Hebrews 1), in which Jesus is depicted as God's enthroned Son in heaven, by whom and through whom God operates and reveals himself. Jesus is called Son of God four times (Heb 4:14, 6:6, 7:3, 10:29) and Son eight times in Hebrews. He is also addressed as God by God the Father in Heb 1:8 and called "Lord" six times (Heb 1:10, 2:3, 7:14, 8:2, 12:14, 13:20).
2. Redeemer Christology (Hebrews 2), in which Jesus shares our human nature and through his death defeats the devil to liberate and redeem enslaved humanity. Hebrews' theology of redemption is one of the richest in the Bible and this is so because it places Jesus rather than the believer at its center.
3. Apostle Christology (Hebrews 3) depicts Jesus as the sent one, God's representative and ambassador, who, like Moses, leads his redeemed people into glory. In addition to stating that Jesus is God's final prophetic word (Heb 1:1–2), the author also emphasizes that he came in obedience to do God's will (Hebrews 10). This teaches the pre-existence of Christ.
4. High Priestly Christology (Hebrews 5–10) is the most prominent of all. The single passage that summarizes this Christology is Heb 8:1–2: "We do have such a high priest, who sat down at the right hand of the throne of the Majesty in heaven, and who serves in the sanctuary, the true tabernacle set up by the Lord, not by man."
5. Pioneer, Perfecter, and Example Christology (Hebrews 2 and 12) presents Jesus as the believer's senior brother, helper, leader, and example to be followed.

It is clear from the above summary of the Christology of Hebrews that the full "career" of Jesus, from his pre-existence, his earthly life, death, resurrection, ascension and exaltation, and his future return, are all presented in full in Hebrews. In Hebrews, "Jesus Christ is the same yesterday and today and forever" (Heb 13:8). This is why it has sometimes been assumed that Hebrews contains a "late" Christology. This assumption is, however, incorrect, for the same scholars agree that the Christological hymn of Phil 2:5–11 is "early" and contains a similar stress on the pre-existence, earthly life, and eternal ministry of Jesus.

In addition to the above emphases by Hebrews, the author makes references to other Christological motifs, which he does not explore but assumes that his first readers had knowledge of.

1. Logos Christology: In describing Jesus as the Son through whom God has spoken in these last days (Heb 1:1–4), the author of Hebrews shares with John's Gospel the portrayal of Jesus as the word, *the logos*. Like John, Hebrews does not continue to pursue this teaching, even though references to God's word are prominent throughout the epistle. Hebrews 4:13 may also have a reference to Christ as *the logos*, for the living and active word of God, we are told, is a person from whose sight nothing is hidden. It is, however, disputed among scholars whether the "he" in Heb 4:13 refers to God (so the NIV) or Christ (as in the KJV).[4]

2. Wisdom Christology: The portrayal of Jesus within the prologue of Hebrews as "the radiance of God's glory and the exact representation" (Heb 1:3) of God's being and by whom creation is sustained was a common expression of first-century Jewish Wisdom teachings.[5] Unlike Paul's 1 Corinthians 1–2, however, this doctrine of Wisdom Christology is again assumed within Hebrews and not pursued.

3. Adam Christology: In Rom 5 and 1 Cor 15, Paul depicts Jesus as the last Adam and typologically compares and contrasts Jesus to the first human being. In Heb 2:5–9, the author describes the failure of humanity (what Adam represents) to fulfill its full potential as steward of God's creation. This is followed in Heb 2:9–18 with a description of how Christ, in identifying with humanity, reverses this failure. Thus

---

4. See Smillie, "The Other Logos," 19–25.

5. E.g., Ps 33:6, 58:10, 107:20, 42; Prov 3:19–20; 8:22–36; Job 11:14; Isa 55:11; Jer 23:29; 2 Esd 6:38; Wis 9:1.

the author's depiction has an element of the Adam Christology. Again, however, the teaching is not pursued as much as Paul does.

All these Christological emphases of Hebrews are designed to encourage and exhort the believers. In the migration theme of Hebrews, Jesus' past work has enabled the liberation of God's people from slavery, death, despair, and darkness and to become God's children who are moving on into his glory (Heb 2:10). He is their pioneer and example who leads them through their present migration. He also ministers in the heavenly sanctuary and so provides them access into God's presence for grace, mercy, and help in their journey. In the not so distant future, he will come again to judge and reward his people. Hence the believer should persevere and keep looking forward to his return. Plainly, the author has applied his Christological emphasis for the practical purpose of building discipleship.

The Doctrine of Scripture in Hebrews

As already noted in chapter one, the author of Hebrews was so steeped in the Old Testament that almost every sentence has a direct or indirect intertextual reference to the scriptures. To him, the source of scripture is God himself (Heb 1:5, 12:19), who has spoken through the prophets of old (Heb 1:1–2), through the angels (Heb 2:2), the apostles (Heb 2:3), the leaders of the congregation (Heb 13:7), and through his Son Jesus (Heb 1-2) and his Holy Spirit (Heb 3:7). God's word is the final authoritative and powerful basis by which doctrine and life is judged (Heb 4:11–13). It gives direction and guidance for the journey (Heb 4:6), it sustains us during the journey (Heb 5:12, 6:5), and it judges our motives and actions (Heb 4:12). It also assures and comforts us since it is in God's word that we have the promises (Heb 4:1–2, 6, 8). God's word therefore provides the perception and direction necessary for orientation in our migration to the heavenly kingdom.

The author particularly stresses the *hearing* of God's word in the context of preaching as of paramount importance. Of course, during his time, there were fewer copies of the scriptures to go around for all members of the congregation to read as we now have. On the other hand, the author also believed in the powerful and transforming function of the preached word (Heb 3:15, 4:2, 6–8, 12:19). Without saying it explicitly, but implying it all along, he believed like Paul that "faith comes from *hearing* the message, and the message is heard through the word of Christ" (Rom 10:17;

emphasis added). Certainly, hearing the preached word is not enough, for it has to be "combined" with faith (Heb 4:2). Nevertheless, a good study of Hebrews should crush any doubts we may have about the transformative power of the faithful preaching of God's word. The hearing of God's word activates the imagination and vision that feed the life of faith, which orients us in the journey into the eternal presence of God.

The primary expected response to the hearing of God's word is faith, although, as we have noted in chapter five, the author of Hebrews had the broadest definition of faith in the Christian's journey to the promise. Responding to God's word by faith means paying earnest heed to it so it doesn't slip (Heb 2:1), taking what it says as evidence and assured substance of what it proclaims (Heb 11:1), obeying it (Heb 2:2, 5:9), and not hardening the heart in stubborn refusal (Heb 3:16, 4:7). This is the exact response that is required of us when reading this epistle.

The Doctrine of Sin in Hebrews

Though the word "sin" and its cognates occur in Hebrews at an average of more than two per chapter, the author, unlike Paul in Romans, assumes that his audience had thorough knowledge of the causes and effects of sin. The doctrine Hebrews develops is how Christ has once and for all dealt with sin and how believers should therefore appropriate the benefits of his work and reject sin's pleasures and pursue holiness. In Hebrews, sin is also called transgression (2:2, 9:15), iniquity (1:9, 8:12, 10:17), disobedience (2:2), dead works (6:1, 9:14), and unrighteousness (8:12). In Heb 2:8, the author deems the failure of humanity's stewardship of God's creation as a reflection of sin's devastating consequences. It is because Adam sinned that in the theology of Hebrews the stewardship of this created order was handed over to the angels. Humanity's failure is epitomized by the problem of death—another result of sin (Heb 2:9, 15, 3:17). And it is the fear of death that the devil has exploited to enslave them "all their lives" (Heb 2:15). It took God to become human in Jesus for our sorry state to be fully corrected in "the world to come" (Heb 2:5).

Another result of sin that Hebrews extensively evaluates is ritual defilement. In his prologue, the author was quick to state one of his main theses concerning the person and work of Jesus the Son: "After he had provided purification for sins, he sat down at the right hand of the Majesty in heaven" (Heb 1:3). Sin, in Hebrews' estimation, is a poisonous pollutant in the God-human relationship. It defiles the body as well as the conscience and separates humanity from God (Heb 9:13–14). To restore humanity to a meaningful relationship with God requires prior cleansing from this pollutant. This is the doctrine that our author painstakingly develops in the central part of the epistle and his thoroughness suggests that he felt it was very important that his first hearers grasp the manner in which sin is dealt with in the Christian dispensation.

Indeed, this emphasis in the epistle led Lindars to suggest that the main purpose of Hebrews was to teach its first readers how to deal with "post-baptismal sin."[6] Lindars reckoned that some members of the congregation were "oppressed by renewed consciousness of sin, and the gospel as they had received it appeared not to allow for it." He therefore proposed that the author of Hebrews used the explication of the ceremonies of the Day of Atonement to teach them that whereas sin may still come the way of the believer, the great high priest forever lives to make intercession for them and maintain the unimpeded access to God for help and mercy. Though this doctrine is a crucial part of Hebrews, it is perhaps an overstatement to regard it as the main purpose of the epistle. Nevertheless, the doctrine no doubt contributes to the whole theme of maintaining the orientation and movement of the migrating people of God to the promise, ensuring that the believer is conscious of the resources within Christ's ministry in the tabernacle of heaven.

Other presentations of the nature of sin in Hebrews include sin as unbelief (Heb 3:12) and as deceitful and tempting (Heb 3:13), which may admittedly give some temporary pleasures (Heb 11:25), but eventually results in the hardening of the heart and departing from the living God (Heb 3:12). Sin is willful disobedience of God's law (Heb 10:26), it is a weight or hindrance to the progress of the believer (Heb 12:1–2), and a debt that only the blood of Christ can wipe away (Heb 8:12, 10:17). Sin follows temptation (Heb 2:17, 4:15) and so the believer needs the grace and help of Christ the high priest to overcome it (Heb 2:17–18).

Overcoming sin is not always easy and requires perseverance and "striving" (Heb 12:4), in which, mercifully for the first readers of Hebrews, they had "not yet resisted to the point of shedding their blood" (Heb 12:4) in the process. "Striving" is a way of saying that one needs to persevere in one's focus toward holiness and live to please God regardless of harassment and persecution. On two occasions, our author describes sin as dead works (Heb 6:1, 9:14). Scholars have interpreted this phrase in one of three ways: as idolatry (as in 1 Thess 1:9, for example), as Jewish ritual acts that do get in the way of faith (as in Rom 3:28), or a general term for acts and

---

6. Lindars, *Theology*, 13.

attitudes of sin, since death is the main result of sin. Given that in Heb 6:1 dead works must be repented of, and in Heb 9:14 the conscience is defiled by dead works, it is best to interpret dead works as actions and attitudes of sins.

The death of Jesus provides the final answer to the problem of sin. In enumerating the qualifications of the high priest, the author of Hebrews in Heb 5:1–4 notes that Jesus's humanity and appointment by God at his exaltation (Ps 110:1–4) fully qualified him to deal with the problem of sin. His humanity enabled him to take on the devil, defeat him, and free humanity from slavery (Heb 2:9–15). Like any other human being, Jesus faced temptations, but he, unlike us, overcame and was without sin (Heb 4:15). Spotless and unblemished, he did not put a foot wrong in his obedience to the Father (Heb 10:9). By his obedience unto death, Jesus was "once made perfect" and so "became the source of eternal salvation for all who obey him" (Heb 5:9). As high priest, "He sacrificed for their sins once for all when he offered himself" (Heb 7:27) and did "away with sin by the sacrifice of himself" (Heb 9:26). The author stresses that this obedient sacrifice was a costly experience for Jesus, for it involved "prayers and petitions with loud cries and tears" (Heb 5:7) and the shedding of his blood (Heb 9:22–26, 12:4). Jesus is therefore at the same time the sacrifice and sacrificer, the "Lamb of God who was slain" (Rev 5:12), and the high priest who offers his blood in the Holy of Holies (Heb 9:12, 13:12). This is, in effect, the doctrine of atonement that is expounded by the author of Hebrews.

How then should the believer deal with sin? Sin must surely be repented of (Heb 6:1) and repudiated (Heb 6:6). We must seek help from our faithful and merciful high priest who ministers in the Holy of Holies in order to overcome sin (Heb 2:17–18), but this victory comes at the price of perseverance and striving (Heb 12:1–3, 10–14). Perseverance emanates from faith, which needs to be reinforced daily through effective and loving fellowship with other believers (Heb 3:12–14, 10:24–26). The surest way of persevering unto perfection is through constant fellowship with other believers who encourage, exhort, and "provoke" us "toward love and good deeds" (Heb 10:24).

By way of summary, and in the wilderness camp model of Hebrews (Fig 6.1), we may schematize the author's teaching about how the problem of sin is dealt with in three spheres. Within the camp itself, humanity experiences deliverance from the power of sin through the death of Christ. In the priestly courtyard and Holy Place, believers persevere in faith in

Fig 6.1: The Wilderness Camp Scheme and Doctrine of Sin in Hebrews

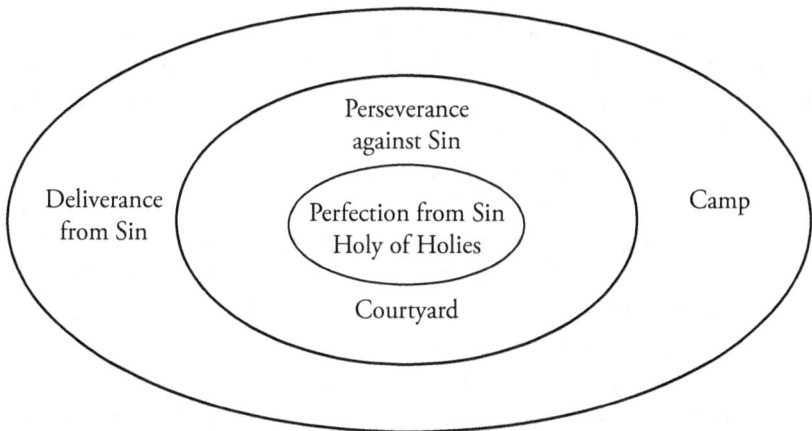

their struggle against sin by looking unto Jesus, and in the Holy of Holies, we are completely perfected from sin by the blood of Jesus our high priest.

The Doctrine of Salvation in Hebrews

As one would expect, in Hebrews the doctrine of salvation is closely linked with the doctrines of Christ and sin. It is what Christ has done in the tabernacle with regard to sin that shapes Hebrews' presentation of the doctrine of salvation. Since Jesus always lives to make intercession for his people, "He is able to save completely those who come to God through him" (Heb 7:25). Whereas Paul, especially in Romans, presents salvation in forensic and judicial language such as justification and adoption, Hebrews' method was to depict salvation as a journey of migration from the camp through the priestly courtyard and Holy Place into the Holy of Holies. Salvation is from the inhabited world through "the house of God" into the city that God has built for his people. This scheme correspondingly follows the typology of the migration of Israel from Egypt through the wilderness into the promised land.

By using the migration of Israel from Egypt to Canaan as the master parable, the author of Hebrews teaches that salvation is a movement from the inhabited world to heaven, from profanity to holiness (Heb 3:1), from ignominy to glory (Heb 2:10), and as birth that requires growth to perfection (Heb 5:11–14). Salvation in Hebrews is also a flight from danger and punitive punishment into the refuge of God's house (Heb 2:2–3, 6:18) full of hope before us (Heb 3:6, 6:18–20). It is a movement from falsehood to truth (Heb 10:26) and from darkness into light (Heb 10:32).

It is this interesting and dynamic way of portraying the believer's salvation—not as a static, once and for all event, but rather as a continuous process and journey—that makes Hebrews one of the most potent epistles for discipleship today. Clearly, believers need to know and appreciate the once and for all forensic event that has indeed occurred in their lives on becoming Christians. On the other hand, an over-emphasis or imbalance in understanding this "once and for all" aspect of salvation could (when confronted with difficulties in this world as was the case with the Hebrews congregation) lead to the state of affairs similar to the congregation's spiritual malaise, frustration, and despondency.

Many of the problems with postmodern Christianity may also be traced to this imbalance. When we fully appreciate that salvation is a process that culminates in the eternal presence of God, then will we be able to keep orienting ourselves on a daily basis toward the heavenly calling and so work out our salvation "with fear and trembling," (Phil 2:12 MKJV) as Paul describes it. This understanding of the Christian life as a journey of migration is one of the most important contributions of Hebrews to discipleship today.

Hebrews uses several different terminologies and adjectives to depict the nature of salvation. In Heb 2:3, the author describes it as "so great a salvation"—and so it is, considering that it took God becoming human to secure it for the saints. It is also an "eternal salvation" (Heb 5:9, 9:12) and one that is "uttermost" (Heb 7:25; MKJV). It is described as a deliverance from the power of devil (Heb 2:15), redemption from the debts and results of sin (Heb 9:12–15), entrance by faith into God's Sabbath's rest (Heb 3–4), perfection in the eternal presence of God (Heb 11:40, 9:9–14), and inheritance of God's promise (Heb 1:14, 9:28).

Hebrews particularly stresses the eschatological timescale of salvation by noting that whereas many of the benefits of salvation are experienced in this world, it is in the "world that is to come" (Heb 2:5) that the process of salvation will be completed (Heb 11:40, 12:28). We are saved by Christ, who by being "sacrificed once" (Heb 9:28) has delivered us from the tyranny of the devil (Heb 2:10–15). We are now being saved by him who as author of our salvation (Heb 2:10) leads us as "holy brothers" (Heb 3:1) on into glory (Heb 2:10). We will be saved in the future eschatological age when "he will appear a second time, not to bear sin, but to bring salvation to those who are waiting for him" (Heb 9:28). It is therefore an "already and not yet" salvation.

How does one enter salvation? It is only by faith (Heb 4:1–3, 11:8) in response to hearing God's word (Heb 3:7–8) and persisting in it (Heb 2:1–3) and by coming to Christ who ministers in the heavenly Holy of Holies (Heb 7:25) to be cleansed by his blood, which speaks better things than the blood of Abel (Heb 12:24).

The Eschatology of Hebrews

The author of Hebrews declares his eschatological scheme with his first few words: "In the past God spoke to our forefathers through the prophets at many times and in various ways, but in these last days he has spoken to us by his Son" (Hebrews 1–2). He accordingly divides "time" into what is essentially two periods: "the past" and "these last days." The "last days" began with the first coming of Christ, who by his death and resurrection has inaugurated the kingdom of God.

Hebrews expresses this eschatological design with his spatial typology of the wilderness camp and tabernacle. In this scheme, the space from the camp through the priestly courtyard to the Holy Place represents "the present time" (Heb 9:8–10), whereas the Holy of Holies represents the eschatological age, which is "the world that is to come" (Heb 2:5, 6:5, 13:14). The priestly courtyard and Holy Place are fused together as is usual in Hebrews and is regarded as a liminal period of time in which God is perfecting the saints as they taste the power of the world to come (Heb 6:5) while waiting for the second coming of Christ (Heb 9:28, 10:37).

This second coming is fast approaching (Heb 10:25) when Christ will judge all people (Heb 10:27–30). At his coming, heaven and earth will be shaken by his word (Heb 11:3, 12:26) and be replaced by his unshakeable kingdom, a city that God has built for his people (Heb 11:10) and the homeland that believers strive toward (Heb 11:14). Believers in Christ will experience a better resurrection on that day (Heb 11:35) and Christ himself will subjugate his enemies (Heb 10:13). This world to come is expressed variously in Hebrews as a hope behind the veil (Heb 6:18–20) and the fulfillment of God's purposes for humanity (8:8–10, 9:11, 10:1). It is salvation that will be inherited (Heb 1:14), God's Sabbath rest to be entered (Hebrews 3–4), perfection to be completed (Heb 6:1, 11:40), and the promise to be enjoyed (Heb 6:15). Though Hebrews does not present any visionary picture of the eschatological age, these characteristics portray a perfect world in the full presence of God where his will is done.

It is fair to say, therefore, that in the eschatological scheme of Hebrews, the author has used time and space interchangeably by employing the camp-tabernacle complex. There has been an academic debate as to whether the thought processes of the author of Hebrews are primarily spatial or temporal and whether it is cosmology or eschatology that structures the author's thought. Whereas Spicq has, for example, argued that the thought of the author of Hebrews is primarily shaped by a mid-Platonic dualistic cosmology,[7] Isaacs has countered that the cosmology is used as a "vehicle of eschatology."[8] MacRae, on the other hand, believes that Hebrews mixes Jewish apocalyptic eschatology with a Greco-Roman Platonic cosmology in his presentation.[9]

This debate, however, betrays a false dichotomy that is made between space and time in academic discussions of the theology of Hebrews. As we noted in chapter three, there is a very close interchangeable relationship between space and time, which the Greek philosophers appreciated and Einstein was later on to prove in his theories of relativity. Human thought and language about time is often expressed in spatial terms, so that 1:00 p.m., for instance, *"comes before"* 2:00 p.m. "Comes before" is a spatial phrase that is relating two measures of time. These measurements of time are in actual fact based on measurement of movement and space. Thus when we refer to hours and days, we are actually talking about the time it takes for the earth to revolve around its own axis. Similarly, when we talk of months and years, we are describing the time it takes for the moon to revolve around the earth, and years as the time it takes for the earth to revolve around the sun. Space and time are in a continuum, and hence there is no question about any clumsy mixture of apocalyptic eschatology with platonic cosmology in Hebrews. That the author would typologically interpret the camp-tabernacle spatial complex in terms of an eschatological time frame should therefore be of no surprise at all.

The Ecclesiology of Hebrews

In his assessment of the doctrine of the church in Hebrews, Lindars asserts: "Hebrews does not have a developed theology of the church,"[10] by which he meant that there were no clear-cut and direct instructions on church government and worship as Paul, for example, does in 1 and 2 Timothy or on baptism and the Lord's Supper as in 1 Corinthians. This assessment of Hebrews nonetheless belies a very attractive and yet simple

7. Spicq, *Hébreux*, 1952.
8. Isaacs, *Reading*, 12.
9. MacRae, "Heavenly Temple," 190.
10. Lindars, *Theology*, 127.

image of the nature, function, and position of the church that the epistle portrays throughout its chapters. The author's approach depicts the church as a migrant camp with the superior and exalted Christ in their midst, ministering in the heavenly tabernacle to provide access to God for them. Ellingworth is right when he points out, "Hebrews is a profoundly ecclesiological writing."[11] The paucity of references to church institutional orders and the sacraments only suggests that these were not of any primary concerns to the fellowship.

The image of the church that Hebrews proffers is one of collegiality, kinship, and partnership that believers share together in the gospel—the *communitas* of the migrant and liminal Church of God. Unlike many of Paul's epistles, the author does not single any person(s) out for praise or rebuke, but rather addresses the believers together as a unit. As Brown insightfully comments, "This epistle has little time for the spiritual individualist."[12] This collegiality of God's people is boldly linked with the Lord Jesus himself (Heb 2:14), so that the one who saves and "sanctifies and they who are sanctified are all of one, for which cause He is not ashamed to call them brothers" (Heb 2:11, cf. Heb 2:17 MKJV). As senior brother, not only does he lay down his life to redeem his brothers from the tyranny of the devil (Heb 2:15), but he also leads them into glory (Heb 2:10), in worship (Heb 2:12), and rescues them from temptation (Heb 2:18). In describing the believers as "holy brothers, who share in the heavenly calling" (Heb 3:1), the epistle advocates the doctrine of the "priesthood of all believers."

The believers in the congregation are all "brothers, having boldness to enter into the Holy of Holies by the blood of Jesus" (Heb 10:19 MKJV). They are hence exhorted to "consider one another to provoke to love and to good works . . . exhort one another daily, while it is called today, lest any of you be hardened through the deceitfulness of sin" (Heb 10:24 and 3:13 MKJV). This doctrine of the priesthood of all believers is made clearer in Heb 13:10–14, where believers are portrayed as priests who minister in the priestly courtyard and are exhorted to follow Christ to go outside the camp. Going outside the camp means leaving the world and its pleasures behind and following hard after Christ. It is equivalent to denying yourself, taking up the cross, and following Jesus (Luke 9:23). It is in this sense that the author encourages the believers to share the responsibilities

---

11. Ellingworth, *Hebrews*, 68.
12. Brown, *The Message of Hebrews*, 127.

of exhorting and encouraging each other daily so that they do not fall into unbelief, disobedience, and sin (Heb 3:12–14, 10:24–25).

It is this portrayal of the church as a closely knit and mutually respectful fellowship that led Bornhauser to suggest that the members of the Hebrews congregation were former Jewish priests or religious devotees similar to the members of the Qumran Essenes sect.[13] There is no sufficient evidence, however, for this suggestion, even though it is possible. It is generally agreed among commentators that the community of Hebrews was most likely a "house church" whose governing arrangement was largely rudimentary. They had leaders (Heb 13:7) whose ministry had been to teach and set an example of faith and conduct, but no one person is singled out as their "person in charge." It is fair to conclude that fellowship responsibilities were mutually shared among the believers of the congregation in Hebrews. The fellowship most probably had a program for discipling new converts. They were taught the "first principles" of the beginning of Christ, consisting of emphasis on repentance, faith, baptism, and other relevant doctrines, which to our author were relevant survival "milk" for the spiritual infant (Heb 5:12–6:2). It was the reluctance of some members to move further on to more solid doctrines and spiritual growth and perfection that bothered our author. There is much to learn from Hebrews on how the fellowship of believers should function.

The theme of worship runs throughout the epistle. The influence of the language of Hebrews on the liturgical worship of the early church is demonstrated by the use of it by Clement[14] and the second Vatican Council.[15] Its use in worship may have been influenced also by the frequent reference in the epistle to Psalm 95, which was a Jewish Psalm of call and guide to worship. Pfitzner has therefore pointed out that "every climactic point in the epistle is a statement about worship."[16] To the author, the central call of God's word is a call to live in fellowship in God's very presence.

In highlighting that Jesus is a faithful and merciful high priest (Heb 2:17) who rescues his brothers and sisters, the epistle to the Hebrews lays a strong foundation for its doctrine on the means of grace (i.e., the means by

---

13. Bruce, *Hebrews*, 7.

14. 1 Clement 40:2, 5 uses parallels between the Christology of Hebrews and the Levitical priesthood to set out the orders of ministry in the church.

15. Heb 5:1 is used to support the appointment of priests by Roman Catholics; Abbott, *Documents of Vatican II*, 536.

16. Pfitzner, *Hebrews*, 8.

which we acquire spiritual strength and favor from God in order to persevere as migrant saints). So, in addition to a strong and effective fellowship (Heb 3:13–14, 10:24–25), believers have been provided unimpeded access into God's very presence by the great high priest. Since Christ ministers at God's right hand, we can "come boldly to the throne of grace, that we may obtain mercy and find grace to help in time of need" (Heb 4:16, MKJV). Indeed, we are exhorted to "draw near to God with a sincere heart in full assurance of faith" (Heb 10:22). Worship in the form of prayer and fellowship with other believers sustains the faith of the migrant people of God.

Preaching from Hebrews

Using the migration of the people of Israel from Egypt to the promised land as his master parable and the death, resurrection, ascension, and exaltation as his interpretive key, the author of Hebrews produced a powerful and stimulating homily that for centuries has inspired and stirred generations of believers on to greater and deeper things in Christ. How may we in our generation also apply his stirring words to enthuse our congregations to move on toward the promise?

It was a common practice for a number of scholars of a generation ago to insist that the concepts and style of our author are so foreign to us that it is too difficult to understand and appreciate. Scott has described the approach of our author whereby "the ardent appeal which breaks out at intervals is weakened by the long-drawn out theological argument" and results in a method that is bound to "defeat its own ends."[17] He points out that when Paul wanted to stir his congregations, as he does in Corinthians and Galatians, he steered them away from theological speculations to the simplicity of the gospel. According to Scott, the author of Hebrews does the opposite and rather uses "difficult speculations" to attempt the same end of stirring his congregation.

This negative assessment of the rhetorical effects of our author's sermon is not uncommon among certain Christian groups today. As a result, several preachers today would frequently pick and choose one or two verses of Hebrews from here and there to preach on instead of presenting the whole message of the epistle for building up believers. The opportunity to harness the potent transformative power of expositional preaching from the epistle to the Hebrews has been missed with this haphazard approach.

---

17. Scott, *The Epistle to the Hebrews*, 42.

Our misconception of Hebrews emanates from not appreciating the way author is matching the book of Numbers, and how the "long-drawn out theological argument" focuses on the camp of God's people and what God, in becoming human, has done and continues to do on their behalf. The expository argument of Hebrews is necessary because this was the "solid food" (Heb 5:14), which was hard to understand and that our author needed to explain. In the end, what we need to see in the expositions is the ministry of Jesus in the tabernacle that enables our progress throughout all the phases of our migration to the promise. The answer to the problem of preaching from Hebrews today is to employ the background narrative of the migration of Israel as the parable that interprets the various parts of the epistle. Approached this way, Hebrews becomes a most powerful book for expositions aimed at spiritual formation and discipleship.

Based on the theme of migrant camp of the people of God, five categories of messages may be preached from Hebrews: sermons on the person and work of Christ in the heavenly tabernacle, those on the separation phase of the migration of the believer, those that highlight and give rigorous warnings on the dangers in liminality, those that encourage and stress the praxis necessary for realignment and orientation, and those that focus on the promise ahead of the migrant people of God (table 6.2). Doxological sermons inspire praise and worship, devotional sermons encourage listeners unto deeper love for and submission to Christ, ethical sermons stress the principles and practice of living in faithful trust and obedience to God, pastoral sermons grapple with the challenges, hardships, and difficulties that the migrant people of God face on their way to the promise, and evangelistic sermons explain the gospel of salvation and invite hearers to respond to it by faith. When Hebrews is therefore exposited by using the metaphor of migration and the underlying Old Testament story of the migration of Israel to the promised land, it provides opportunity for all the five general categories of sermons to be preached.

Admittedly, Hebrews is not very strong for preaching on practical ethical instructions. The writer stresses obedience, perseverance, love, avoiding financial greed, and honoring the marital bed. But he does not reel out lists of sins and bad attitudes and habits to rebuke. Neither does our author provide any messages on the ethical code of the family apart from a reference to marriage in Heb 13:4. If we are looking to preach on a "practical" list of ethical sins to rebuke or correct in the discipleship of our congregations, Hebrews is not where we may look. What the epistle lacks in "practical" lists, however, it makes up for in powerful motivational inspiration to ethical holiness. Believers are portrayed as holy saints

Table 6.3: Five Categories of Sermons from Hebrews

Sermon Category	Applications
The Person and Work of Christ	Doxological, Evangelistic, Devotional
The Separation Phase of Christian Migration	Evangelistic
Warning Against Dangers in Liminality	Ethical, Devotional, Evangelistic, Pastoral
Encouragement to Praxis for Orientation	Ethical, Devotional, Pastoral
The Promise Before the Migrant People of God	Evangelistic, Devotional, Ethical, Doxological

and priests of God in the priestly courtyard with access into the Holy of Holies, and it is through pursuing holiness that they may "see" God (Heb 12:14).

For the author of Hebrews, it is when his congregation have come to appreciate their *identity*, where they had come from as the migrant people of God—the identity which they share with all the saints of God from Abraham through the wilderness generation to the New Testament believers—that they will shake themselves out of the spiritual sluggishness they were in. It is when they come to know the immense *spiritual resources* of faith, faithfulness, hope, and love that they share with all the people of God that they would appropriate them to overcome their daily temptations to give up. And it is when they also come to know that they can have confidence and approach the merciful and great high priest in the Holy of Holies to receive all the help they need to keep their *orientation* and *move* in the direction toward the goal of salvation, rest, perfection, and the promise that they will persevere to the end. It is when all these aims are achieved that the practical difficulties in their lives as strangers and immigrants in this world will be adequately dealt with. This is the immense contribution of Hebrews to discipleship today.

Fig. 6.2: The Migrant Camp of the People of God: A Summary Diagram

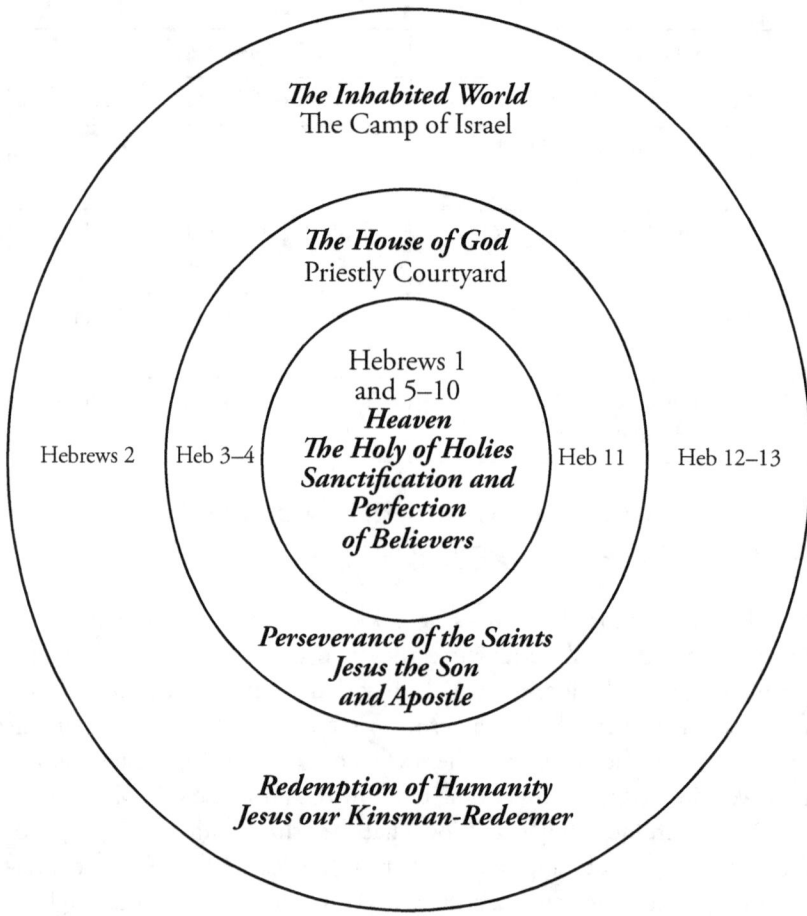

Bibliography

Aristotle, *Physica*, Bk. 4 Chp. 4 G3r, *The Works of Aristotle*. Translated by W.D. Ross. Volume 2, 1930. Accessed March 2, 2005. http://etext.lib.virginia.edu/etcbin/toccernew2?id=AriPhys.xml&images=images/modeng&data=/texts/english/modeng/parsed&tag=public&part=all.

Ashley, Timothy R. *The Book of Numbers*. In NICOT. Grand Rapids: Eerdmans, 1993.

Attridge, Harold. *The Epistle to the Hebrews: A Commentary on the Epistle to the Hebrews*. Philadelphia: Fortress Press, 1989.

———. "Paranaesis in a Homily (logos parakleseos): The Possible Location of, andSocialization in, the 'Epistle to the Hebrews.'" *Semeia* 50 (1990) 211–26.

Avishur, Yitshak. *Studies in Biblical Narrative: Style, Structure and the Ancient Near Eastern Literary Background*. Tel Aviv-Jaffa Archaeological Center, 1999.

Balch, David. "Rich Pompeiian Houses, Shops for Rent and the Huge Apartment Building in Herculaneum as Typical Spaces for Pauline House Churches." *JSNT* 27 1 S (2004) 27–46.

Barclay, William. *The Letter to the Hebrews* (The New Daily Study Bible). Louisville/London: Westminster John Knox Press, 1976.

Barrett, Charles K. "The Eschatology of the Epistle to the Hebrews." In *The Background of the New Testament and its Eschatology: Studies in Honor of C. H. Dodd*, edited by Davies, W. D. and D. Daube. Cambridge: University Press, 1954.

Baumann, Martin. "Diaspora: Genealogies of Semantics and Transcultural Comparison." *Numen* 47 (no 3) (2000) 313–37.

Beaudoin, Tom. "Foucault Teaching Theology." *Religious Education* 98 no 1 Wint (2003) 25–42.

Beck, John. "Geography and the Narrative Shape of Numbers 13." *BibSac* July–Sep (2000) 271–80.

Bergant, Diane. "An Anthropological Approach to Biblical Interpretation: The Passover Supper in Ex 12:1–20 as a Case Study." *Semeia* 67 (1994) 43–62.

Black, David A. "The Problem of the Literary Structure of Hebrews: An Evaluation and a Proposal." *Grace Theological Journal* 7.2 (1986) 163–77.

Bollnow, Otto F. *Mensch und Raum ("Man and Space,")*; Nold Egenter's online translation in the *Internet Journal of Architecture entry of 12/8/2002*, accessed on March 4, 2005. http://www.cetarchis.org/archi-journal/view_index.asp?id=26&flag=7.

Bricker, Daniel P. "The Doctrine of the 'Two Ways' in Proverbs." *JETS* 38 D (1995) 501–17.

Brown, Raymond. *The Message of Hebrews: Christ Above All*. In *The Bible Speaks Today*, edited by John W. Stott. Leicester, Downers Grove, IL: IVP, 1982.

Bruce, Frederick Fyvie. *The Epistle to the Hebrews (Revised)*. In NICNT. Grand Rapids, MI: W. B. Eerdmans Publishing Company, 1990.

———. "Kerygma of Hebrews," *Int* 23 Jan (1969) 3–19.

Bibliography

Brueggemann, Walter. *The Land*. Philadelphia: Fortress Press, 1977.
Buchanan, George Wesley. *To the Hebrews*. Hermeneia, NY: Doubleday, 1972.
Bultmann, Rudolf and Artur Weiser.. "Pisteow." In *TDNT* vol 1, edited by Gerhard Friedrich, translated by Geoffrey Bromiley. Grand Rapids, MI: W. B. Eerdmans, 1968.
Castelli, Elizabeth. *Imitating Paul: A Discourse of Power*. Louisville, Westminster: John Knox Press, 1991.
Charles, Daryl. "The Angels, Sonship and Birthright in the Letter to the Hebrews." *JETS* 33/2 (1990) 171–78.
Coats, George. "Exposition of the Wilderness Traditions." *Vetus Testamentum* 22 no 3 Jl (1972) 288–95.
Colijn, Brenda. "Let Us Approach: Soteriology in the Epistle to the Hebrews." *JETS* 39/4 (Dec 1996) 571–86.
Cook, Stephen and Ronald Simkins. "Introduction: Case Studies from the Second Wave of Research in the Social World of the Hebrew Bible." *Semeia* no 87 (1999) 1–14.
Cosby, Michael R. "The Rhetorical Composition of Heb 11." *JBL* 107/2 (1988) 257–73.
Cullmann, Oscar. *The Christology of the New Testament*. Study Ed. London: SCM Press Ltd., 1963.
Dahms, John V. "The First Readers of Hebrews." *JETS* 20.4 (1977) 365–75.
Davies, John H. *A Letter to the Hebrews: Cambridge Bible Commentary on the New English Bible*. Cambridge: University Press, 1967.
de Blij, Harm J. and A. B. Murphy. *Human Geography: Culture, Society, and Space*. 7th ed. Hoboken, NJ: John Wiley & Sons Inc., 2000.
DeSilva, David A. "Exchanging Favour for Wrath: Apostasy in Hebrews and Patron-Client Relationships." *JBL* 115/1 (1996) 91–116.
——. *Honor, Patronage, Kinship & Purity: Unlocking New Testament Culture*. Dowers Grove, IL: IVP, 2000.
——. *Perseverance in Gratitude: A Socio-Rhetorical Commentary on the Epistle to the Hebrews*. Grand Rapids, MI: W. B. Eerdmans, 2000.
Domeris, William R. "Sociological and Social Historical Investigations." In *Text and Interpretation: New Approaches in the Criticism of the New Testament*, edited by P. Hartin and K. Petzer. 215–34. Leiden: E. J. Brill, 1991.
Douglas, Mary. *In the Wilderness: The Doctrine of Defilement in the Book of Numbers*. Oxford: Oxford University Press, 2004.
——. *Purity and Danger: An Analysis of Concept of Pollution and Taboo*. London and New York: Routledge Classics, 2002.
Dozeman, Thomas. "Spatial Form in Ex 19:1–18a and in the Larger Sinai narrative." *Semeia* 46.1 (1989) 87–101.
——. "The Wilderness and Salvation History in the Hagar Story." *JBL* 117 Spring (1998) 23–43.
Dreyfus, Hubert L. and Paul Rabinow. *Michel Foucault: Beyond Structuralism and Hermeneutics*. 2nd ed. Chicago: University of Chicago Press, 1982.
Dunnill, John. *Covenant and Sacrifice in the Epistle to the Hebrews*. In SNTSMS 75. Cambridge: Cambridge University Press, 1992.
Eliade, Mircea. *The Sacred and the Profane: The Nature of Religion*. Translated by Willard R. Trask. San Diego: Harcourt, Brace, 1987.
Ellingworth, Paul. *The Epistle to the Hebrews*. In NIGNT. Grand Rapids, MI: W. B. Eerdmans, 1993.

Bibliography

Elliot, John. *A Home for the Homeless: A Sociological Exegesis of 1 Peter: Its Situation and Strategy.* Philadelphia: Fortress, 1981.

———. *1 Peter: A New Translation with Introduction and Commentary.* New York: Doubleday, 2000.

Filson, Floyd V. "The Journey Motif in Luke–Acts." In *Apostolic History and the Gospel: Biblical and Historical Essays Presented to F.F. Bruce,* edited by W. W. Gasque and R. P. Martin. Exeter: Paternoster Press, 1970.

Flanagan, James. "Ancient Perception of Space/Perceptions of Ancient Space." *Semeia* 87.1 (Issue 87) (1999) 15–43.

Fortosis, Stephen. "A Developmental Model for Stages of Growth in Christian Formation." *Religious Education* 87 Spring (1992) 283–98.

Foucault, Michel. "Of Other Spaces." *Diacratics* 16.1 (1986) 22–27.

———. *The Archaeology of Knowledge.* London: Routledge, 1969.

France, Richard T. "The Writer of Hebrews as a Biblical Expositor." *TynB* 47.2 (1996) 245–76.

Funk, Robert W. "The Wilderness." *JBL* 78, (1959) 206–14.

Gager, John G. *The Origins of Anti-Semitism: Attitudes toward Judaism in Pagan and Christian Antiquity.* New York: Oxford University Press, 1983.

Gibson, Jeffrey B. "Jesus' Wilderness Temptation according to Mark." *JSNT* no 53 March (1994) 3–34.

Gleason, Randall C. "Angels and the Eschatology of Hebrews 1–2." *NTS* 49, (2003) 90–107.

———. "The Old Testament Background of the Warning in Hebrews 6:4–8." *BibSac* 155 Jan–Mar (1998) 62–91.

———. "The Old Testament Background of Rest in Heb 3:7–4:11." *BibSac,* 157 no 627 Jl-S (2000) 281–303.

Gray, Patrick. *Godly Fear: The Epistle to the Hebrews and Greco-Roman Critiques of Superstition.* Academia Biblica 16. Atlanta: SBL, 2003.

Guthrie, Donald. *New Testament Introduction.* Revised Ed. Downers Grove, IL: IVP, 1990.

Guthrie, George. *The Structure of Hebrews: A Text Linguistic Analysis.* Grand Rapids, MI: Baker Book House, 1998.

Habel, Norman. "The Symbolism of Wisdom in Proverbs 1—9." *Int 26* (1972) 131–57.

Hamm, Dennis. "Faith in the Epistle to the Hebrews: The Jesus Factor." *CBQ* 52 April (1990) 270–91.

Harrelson, Walter. "Guidance in the Wilderness: The Theology of the Book of Numbers." *Int* 13 Jan (1959) 24–36.

Hays, Richard. *Echoes of Scripture in the Letters of Paul.* New Haven and London: Yale University Press, 1989.

Héring, Jean. *The Epistle to the Hebrews.* London: Epworth Press, 1970.

Hewitt, Thomas. *The Epistle to the Hebrews.* Grand Rapids, MI: W. B. Eerdmans, 1960.

Hughes, Philip E. *A Commentary on the Epistle to the Hebrews.* Grand Rapids, MI: W. B. Eerdmans, 1977.

Isaacs, Marie E. *Reading Hebrews & James: A Literary and Theological Commentary.* Macon, GA: Smyth & Helwys Publishing Company, 2002.

———. *Sacred Space: An Approach to the Theology of the Epistle to the Hebrews.* JSNTSup 73. Sheffield: JSOT Press, 1992.

Bibliography

Janicaud, Dominique. "Rationality, Force and Power: Foucault and Habermas's criticisms." In *Michel Foucault: Philosopher*, edited by Timothy J. Armstrong. London: Routledge, 1992.

Johnsson, William G. "The Pilgrimage Motif in the Book of Hebrews." *JBL* 97 (1978) 239–51.

Johnston, *Ron*, et al. *The Dictionary of Human Geography*. Oxford: Blackwell, 2000.

Jones, Peter R. "The Figure of Moses as a Heuristic Device for Understanding the Pastoral Intent of Hebrews." *RevExp* 76, Winter, (1979) 95–107.

Kaiser Jr., Walter C. "The Promise Theme and the Theology of Rest." *BibSac* 130, (1973) 138–50.

Kallai, Zecharia. "The Wandering–Traditions from Kadesh–Barnea to Canaan: A Study in Biblical Historiography." *Journal of Jewish Studies* 33 (1982) 175–84.

Kant, Immanuel. *Critique of Human Reason*. Translated by N. K. Smith. Accessed February 17, 2005 at http://www.hkbu.edu.hk/~ppp/cpr/toc.html.

Käsemann, Ernst. *The Wandering People of God: An Investigation of the Letter to the Hebrews*. Translated by Harrisville, R. A. and I. L. Sandberg. Minneapolis, MN: Augsburg Publishing House, 1984.

Kent, Harold A. *The Epistle to the Hebrews: A Commentary*. Grand Rapids, MI: Baker, 1972.

Koester, Craig. *The Dwelling of God: The Tabernacle in the Old Testament, Inter-testamental Jewish Literature, and the New Testament*. In CBQMS 22. Washington DC: Catholic Biblical Association, 1989.

———. *Hebrews: A New Translation with Introduction and Commentary*. In Anchor Bible Series, Vol 36. New York: Doubleday, 2001.

———. "Hebrews, Rhetoric and the Future of Humanity." *CBQ* 64 no 1 Jan (2002) 103–23.

Kummel, Werner G. *Introduction to the New Testament*. Translated by H. C. Kee. Nashville, TN: Abingdon, 1975.

Kunin, Seth D. *God's Place in the World: Sacred Space and Sacred Place in Judaism*. London and New York: Cassell, 1998.

Ladd, George E. *A Theology of the New Testament*. Grand Rapids, MI: Eerdmans, 1974.

Lakoff, G. and M. Johnson. *Metaphors We Live By*. Chicago, IL: University of Chicago Press, 1980.

Lane, William. *Hebrews 1–8*. In *World Bible Commentary*, Vol 47a. Nashville, TN: Thomas Nelson Publishers, 1991.

Lang, George H. *The Epistle to the Hebrews*. London: Paternoster, 1951.

Lee, Everest. "A Theory of Migration." *Demography* 1966 3 (11) 47–57.

Lefebvre, Henri. *The Production of Space*. Translated by D. Nicholson-Smith. Oxford: Blackwell, 1991.

Leveen, Adriane B. "Variations on a Theme: Differing Conceptions of Memory in the Book of Numbers." *JSOT* 27 no 2 D (2002) 201–21.

Levenson, Jon D. *Sinai and Zion: An Entry into the Jewish Bible*. Minneapolis/Chicago/New York: Winston, 1985.

Levine, Etan. "The Land of Milk and Honey." *JSOT* (2000) 43–57.

Lindars, Barnabas. *The Theology of the Letter to the Hebrews*. Cambridge: Cambridge University Press, 1991.

Long, Thomas. "Bold in the Presence of God: Atonement in Hebrews." *Int* 52 no. 1 Jan (1998) 53–69.

Bibliography

Longenecker, Richard. *Biblical Exegesis in the Apostolic Period.* Grand Rapids, MI: Eerdmans, 1975.

———. *The Christology of Early Jewish Christianity.* Vancouver: Regent College Publishing, 1970.

Lotman, Yuri. *The Structure of the Artistic Tex.* Translated from the Russian by Gail Lenhoff and Ronald Vroon; Michigan Slavic Contributions 7. Ann Arbor, MI: University of Michigan Press, 1977.

Lund, Nils W. *Chiasmus in the New Testament: A Study in the Form and Function of Chiastic Structures.* Chapel Hill, NC: University of North Carolina Press, 1942 (reprint, Peabody, MA: Hendrickson).

Luther, Martin. "Sermon for Fifth Sunday in Lent on Hebrews 9:11–15." In *The Sermons of Martin Luther* (163–8). Grand Rapids, MI: Baker Book House, 1909.

MaCrae, Alan A. "The Book called 'Numbers.'" *BibSac* 111 (441), Jan. (1954) 47–53.

MacRae, George W. "Heavenly Temple and Eschatology in the Letter to the Hebrews." *Semeia* 21.1 (1978) 179–99.

Malbon, Elizabeth S. "The Jesus of Mark and the Sea of Galilee." *JBL* 103 S (1984) 363–77.

Malina, Bruce. "Apocalyptic and Territoriality." In *Early Christianity in Context: Monuments and Documents.* Edited by F. Manns and E. Alliata, 369—80. Studium Biblicum Franciscanum Collectio Maior 38. Jerusalem: Franciscan, 1993.

———. *Christian Origins and Cultural Anthropology: Practical Models for Biblical Interpretation.* Atlanta, GA: John Knox Press, 1986.

———. Review of "Despising Shame: Honour Discourse and Community Maintenance in the Epistle to the Hebrews." *JBL* 116 Sum (1997) 378–9.

———. *The New Testament World: Insights from Cultural Anthropology,* Revised and Expanded. Louisville: Westminster John Knox Press, 2001.

———. *The New Jerusalem in the Revelation of John: The City as Symbol of Life with God.* Collegeville, MN: Liturgical Press, 2000.

Matera, Frank. *New Testament Christology.* Louisville: Westminster John Knox Press, 1999.

Matthews, Victor. "Physical Space, Imagined Space, and Lived Space in Ancient Israel." *BTB* Spring (2003) 12–20.

Mathewson, David. "Reading Heb 6:4–6 in Light of the Old Testament." *WTJ* 61 (1999) 209–25.

McCarter, Kyle P. "Exodus." In *Harper's Bible Commentary.* Edited by J. L. Mays. San Francisco: Harper and Row, 1988.

McKnight, Scot. "The Warning Passages of Hebrews: A Formal Analysis and Theological Conclusions." *TrinJ* 13 (1992) 21–59.

Meier, John P. "Symmetry and Theology in the Old Testament citations of Heb 1:5–14." *Bib* 66 (1985) 504–33.

Milgrom, Jacob. *The JPS Torah Commentary: Numbers.* Philadelphia: The Jewish Publication Society, 1990.

Montefoire, Hugh. *The Epistle to the Hebrews.* In *Black's New Testament Commentaries,* edited by H. Chadwick. London: A and C Black, 1964.

Moxnes, Halvor. *The Economy of the Kingdom: Social Conflict and Economic Relations in Luke's Gospel: Overtures to Biblical Theology.* Philadelphia: Fortress, 1988.

Moule, Charles Francis D. "Sanctuary and Sacrifice in the Church of the New Testament." *JTS New* Series 1 (1950) 29–41.

Moyise, Steve. "Intertextuality and Biblical Studies: A Review." *Verbum et Ecclesia* 23, (2002) 418–31.

Nelson, Richard D. "He Offered Himself: Sacrifice in Hebrews." *Int* 57 no3 (2003) 251–65.

Neyrey, Jerome. *Honor and Shame in the Gospel of Matthew.* Louisville: Westminster John Knox, 1998.

———. "Spaces and Places, Whence and Whither, Homes and Rooms: 'Territoriality' in the Fourth Gospel." *BTB* 32 (2002) 60–74.

———. "'Teaching You in Public and from House to House' (Acts 20:20): Unpacking a Cultural Stereotype." *JSNT* 26.1 (2003) 69–102.

———. "What's Wrong With This Picture? John 4, Cultural Stereotypes of Women, and Public and Private Space." *BTB* 24 (1994) 77–91.

———. "Without Beginning of Days or End of life (Hebrews 7:3): Topos for a True Deity." *CBQ* 53, (1991) 439–55.

Noiriel, Gérard. "Immigration: Amnesia and Memory." *French Historical Studies*, Vol. 19, No. 2 (Autumn, 1995) 367–80.

Nongbri, Brent. "A Touch of Condemnation in a Word of Exhortation: Apocalyptic Language and Greco-Roman in Hebrews 6:4—12." *NovT* XLV 3 (2003) 265–79.

Noth, Martin. *Numbers: A Commentary.* Translated by J. D. Martin. London: SCM, 1968.

———. *Exodus: A Commentary.* Translated by J. S. Bowden. London: SCM, 1962.

O'Neill, John C. "Who Is Comparable to Me in My Glory: $_4Q_{491}$ fragment 11 ($_4Q_{491C}$) and the New Testament." *NovT* 42 no 1 (2000) 24–38.

Oberholtzer Kim. "The Kingdom Rest in Hebrews 3:1–4:13." *BibSac* April–June (1988) 185–96.

———. "The Warning Passages in Hebrews: The Danger of Wilful Sin in Hebrews 10:26–39." *BibSac*, Oct–Dec (1988) 410–19.

———. "The Thorn-Infested Ground in Hebrews 6:4–12." *BibSac* 145 (1988) 319–328.

Oropeza, Brisio J. "Apostasy in the Wilderness: Paul's Message to the Corinthians in a State of Eschatological Liminality." *JSNT* no 75 S (1999) 69–86.

Osborne, Grant R. "The Christ of Hebrews and Other Religions." *JETS* 46/2 (June 2003) 249–67.

———. "Soteriology in the Epistle to the Hebrews." In *Grace Unlimited*, edited by C. H. Pinnock. Minneapolis: Bethany House, 1975.

Partin, Harry B. *The Muslim Pilgrimage: Journey to the Centre.* Ph.D. diss., University of Chicago, 1967.

Payne, Michael. "Voice, Metaphor and Narrative." In *Mappings of the Biblical Terrain: The Bible as Text*, edited by Vincent L. Tollers and John Maier. Lewisburg, PA: Bucknell University Press, 1990.

Perdue Leo G. "The Social Character of Paranaesis and Paranaetic Literature." *Semeia* 50 (1990) 5–39.

Pfitzner Victor. *Abingdon New Testament Commentary: Hebrews*. Nashville, TN: Abingdon Press, 1997.

Raboteau, Albert. *Slave Religion*. New York/Oxford: Oxford University Press, 1973.

Reed, Walter. *Dialogues of the Word: the Bible as Literature According to Bakhtin*. New York: Oxford University Press, 1993.

Rengstorf, Karl H. *"Semeion." TDNT*, Vol 7 (1939) 216.

Rhee, Victor. "Chiasm and the Concept of Faith in Hebrews 11." *BibSac* 155 July–Sept (1998) 327–45.

———. "Christology and the Concept of Faith in Heb 5:11–6:20." *JETS* 43 no 1 March (2000) 83–96.

Richardson, Cyril. *Early Christian Fathers,* Philadelphia: Westminster Press, 1953.

Robertson, Palmer O. *The Books of Nahum, Habakkuk and Zephaniah.* In NICOT. Grand Rapids: Eerdmans, 1990.

Sack, Robert. *Human Territoriality: Its Theory and History.* Cambridge: Cambridge University Press, 1986.

Safran, William. "Diasporas in Modern Societies: Myths of Homeland and Return." *Diaspora,* Vol 1 (1991) 83–93.

Said, Edward. *Orientalism: Western Conceptions of the Orient.* London: Penguin, 1995.

Santiago, Guijarro O. "Domestic Space, Family Relationship and the Social Location of the Q People." *JSNT* 27 no 1 S (2004) 69–81.

Schmidt, Thomas. "The Penetration of Barriers and The Revelation of Christ in the Gospels." *NovT* XXXIV, 3 (1992) 229–46.

Scott, Brett R. "Jesus' Superiority Over Moses in Hebrews 3:1–6." *BibSac* 155 (April–June 1998) 201–10.

Scott Jr., Julius J. "Archegos: The Salvation History of the Epistle to the Hebrews." *JETS,* 26/1 (1986) 47–54.

Scott, Ernest F. *The Epistle to the Hebrews: Its Doctrine and Significance.* Edinburgh: T & T Clark, 1922.

Silva, Moyise. "Perfection and Eschatology in Hebrews." *WTJ* 39 (1976) 60–71.

Smalley, Stephen S. "The Atonement in the Epistle to the Hebrews." *EvQ 33* (1961) 36–43.

Smillie, Gene R. "The Other Logos at the end of Heb. 4:13." *NovT* XLVII, 1 (2005) 19–25.

Smith, Jonathan. *To Take Place: Toward Theory in Ritual.* Chicago: University of Chicago Press, 1987.

Smitten, J. R. and A. Daghistany. *Spatial Form in Narrative.* Ithaca: Cornell University Press, 1981.

Soja, Edward W. *Thirdspace: Journeys to Los Angeles and Other Real-and-Imagined Places.* Oxford: Blackwell, 1996.

Spicq, Ceslas. *L'Epître aux Hébreux.* Paris: I Gabalda, 1952.

Stein, Philip D. "The Land Flowing with Milk and Honey." *Vetus Testamentus* XLII, 4 (1992) 554–7.

Stock, Augustine. "Chiastic Awareness and Education in Antiquity." *BTB 14* (Jan, 1984) 23–27.

Strenski, Ivan. "Religion, Power, and the Final Foucault." *JAAR* 66 Sum (1998) 345–67.

Synge, Francis C. *Hebrews and the Scriptures.* London: SPCK, 1959.

Thompson, James. "Outside the Camp: A Study of Hebrews 13:9—14." *CBQ* 40 (1978) 53–63.

———. "Structure and Purpose of the Catena in Heb 1:5–13." *CBQ* 38 (1976) 352–63.

Thornton, Timothy G. "Reviews." *JTS* New Series 15 (1964) 137–41.

Toulmin, Stephen. *Cosmopolis: The Hidden Agenda of Modernity.* Chicago: University of Chicago, 1990.

Toussaint, Stanley. "The Eschatology of the Warning Passages in the Book of Hebrews." *Grace Theological Journal* 3, Spring (1982) 67–80.

Tuan, Yi-Fu. *Space and Place: The Perspective of Experience.* Minneapolis: University of Minnesota Press, 1990.

Bibliography

Turner, Victor. *Dramas, Fields, and Metaphors: Symbolic Action in Human Society.* Ithaca: Cornell University Press, 1974.

van Gennep, Arnold. *Rites of Passage.* Translated by Monika Visedom and Gabrielle Caffee. Chicago: University of Chicago Press, 1961.

Vanhoye, Albert. *La structure littéraire de l'Epître aux Hébreux.* Paris/Buges: StudNeot, 1963.

Vine, William E. *Vine's Expository Dictionary of Old & New Testament Words.* Nashville: Thomas Nelson Publishers, 1997.

Wellhausen, Julius. *Prolegomena to the History of Ancient Israel.* Translated by Menzies and Black (1883 edition). New York: Meridian, 1957.

Wenham, Gordon. *Numbers: Tyndale's Old Testament Commentaries Series.* Downers Grove, IL: IVP, 1981.

Williamson, Ronald. "Platonism and Hebrews." *SJT* 16, (4) 1963 415–24.

Wright, Nicholas. *Hebrews for Everyone.* London: SPCK, 2003.

www.ingramcontent.com/pod-product-compliance
Lightning Source LLC
Chambersburg PA
CBHW060608230426
43670CB00011B/2018